Using the *Teach Yourself in 24 Hours* Series

Welcome to the *Teach Yourself in 24 Hours* series! You're probably thinking, "What, they want me to stay up all night and learn this stuff?" Well, no, not exactly. This series introduces a new way to teach you about exciting new products: 24 one-hour lessons, designed to keep your interest and keep you learning. Because the learning process is broken into small units, you will not be overwhelmed by the complexity of some of the new technologies that are emerging in today's market. Each hourly lesson has a number of special items, some old, some new, to help you along.

Minutes

The first 10 minutes of each hour lists the topics and skills that you will learn about by the time you finish the hour. You will know exactly what the hour will bring with no surprises.

Minutes

Twenty minutes into the lesson, you will have been introduced to one aspect of HTML. In the constantly evolving Web publishing arena, knowing as much as possible about each element will aid you enormously now and in the future.

Minutes

Before 30 minutes have passed, you will have learned at least one useful task. These tasks use a hands-on approach, telling you exactly which menus and commands you need to use to accomplish the goal. This approach is found in each lesson of the *24 Hours* series.

40 Minutes

You will see after 40 minutes that many of the tools you have come to expect from the *Teach Yourself* series are found in the *24 Hours* series as well. Notes and Tips offer special tricks of the trade to make your work faster and more productive. Warnings help you avoid those nasty time-consuming errors.

50 Minutes

By the time you're 50 minutes in, you'll probably run across terms you haven't seen before. Never before has technology thrown so many new words and acronyms into the language, and the New Terms elements found in this series will carefully explain each and every one of them.

60 Minutes

At the end of the hour, you may still have questions that need answered. You know the kind—questions on skills or tasks that come up every day for you, but that weren't directly addressed during the lesson. That's where the Q&A section can help. By answering the most frequently asked questions about the topics discussed in the hour, Q&A not only answers your specific question, it provides a succinct review of all that you have learned in the hour.

Teach
Yourself

HTML 3.2

in 24 Hours

Bruno Rangel
Carcassole

03·10·98

Teach Yourself
HTML 3.2
in 24 Hours

Dick Oliver

201 West 103rd Street
Indianapolis, Indiana 46290

Copyright © 1997 by Sams.net Publishing

FIRST EDITION

International Standard Book Number: 1-57521-235-8

Library of Congress Catalog Card Number: 96-71214

2000 99 98 97   4 3 2 1

Interpretation of the printing code: the rightmost double-digit number is the year of the book's printing; the rightmost single-digit, the number of the book's printing. For example, a printing code of 97-1 shows that the first printing of the book occurred in 1997.

Composed in AGaramond and MCPdigital by Macmillan Computer Publishing

Printed in the United States of America

Trademarks

Publisher and President Richard K. Swadley
Publishing Manager Mark Taber
Acquisitions Manager Beverly M. Eppink
Director of Editorial Services Cindy Morrow
Managing Editor Kitty Jarrett
Assistant Marketing Managers Kristina Perry, Rachel Wolfe

Acquisitions Editor
Beverly M. Eppink

Development Editor
Scott Meyers

Production Editor
Mary Ann Abramson

Indexer
Ben Slen

Technical Reviewer
Pam Sheppard

Editorial Coordinator
Katie Wise

Technical Edit Coordinator
Lorraine Schaffer

Editorial Assistants
Carol Ackerman
Andi Richter
Rhonda Tinch-Mize

Cover Designer
Tim Amrhein

Book Designer
Gary Adair

Copy Writer
Peter Fuller

Production Team Supervisors
Brad Chinn
Charlotte Clapp

Production
Jeanne Clark
Laura A. Delfeld
Svetlana Dominguez
Polly Lavrick

Overview

Contents

Acknowledgments

This book would almost certainly not exist today were it not for the author's loving family, who brought enough fresh carrot juice, tender popcorn, and buttery kisses to sustain him through the long hours of its creation.

Nor would you have ever had the enjoyment of reading these pages without the kind-hearted support (and insistent "nagging") of my beloved acquisitions editor, Beverly Eppink.

Special thanks must also go to the folks at the Buffalo Mountain Food Cooperative in Hardwick, Vermont, for providing the carrots, popcorn, and butter.

This book is dedicated to my mother, Darlene Hewins (`http://netletter.com/hewins/`), *who had to teach herself HTML without this book.*

About the Author

Dick Oliver (`dicko@netletter.com`) is the tall, dark, handsome author of lots of great books and software, including *Web Page Wizardry, Netscape Unleashed, Create Your Own Web Page Graphics*, and *Tricks of the Graphics Gurus*. He is also the president of Cedar Software and the warped mind behind the *Nonlinear Nonsense Netletter* at `http://netletter.com` (and several other Web sites). When he isn't banging on a keyboard, he's usually snowboarding, sledding, skiing, or warming up by the woodstove in his cozy Northern Vermont home (where they celebrate a day of summer each year, too). He likes writing HTML, eating killer-spicy Indian food, and waltzing wildly around the office with his daughters—not necessarily in that order. He also thinks it's pretty cool that authors get to write their own "About the Author" sections.

Tell Us What You Think!

As a reader, you are the most important critic and commentator of our books. We value your opinion and want to know what we're doing right, what we could do better, what areas you'd like to see us publish in, and any other words of wisdom you're willing to pass our way. You can help us make strong books that meet your needs and give you the computer guidance you require.

Do you have access to CompuServe or the World Wide Web? Then check out our CompuServe forum by typing **GO SAMS** at any prompt. If you prefer the World Wide Web, check out our site at http://www.mcp.com.

JUST A MINUTE

> If you have a technical question about this book, call the technical support line at (800) 571-5840, ext. 3668.

As the publishing manager of the group that created this book, I welcome your comments. You can fax, e-mail, or write me directly to let me know what you did or didn't like about this book—as well as what we can do to make our books stronger. Here's the information:

FAX: 317/581-4669

E-mail: newtech_mgr@sams.mcp.com

Mail: Mark Taber
          Sams.net Publishing
          201 W. 103rd Street
          Indianapolis, IN 46290

Introduction

In the next 24 hours, approximately 100,000 new Web pages will be posted in publicly accessible areas of the Internet. At least as many pages will be placed on private intranets to be seen by businesspeople connected to local networks. Every one of those pages—like over 100 million pages already online—will use the *Hypertext Markup Language*, or HTML.

If you read on, *your* Web pages will be among those that appear on the Internet in the next 24 hours. And this will be the day that you gained one of the most valuable skills in the world today: mastery of HTML.

Can you really learn to create top-quality Web pages yourself, without any specialized software, in less time than it takes to schedule and wait for an appointment with a highly-paid HTML wizard? Can this thin, easy-to-read book really enable you to teach yourself state-of-the-art Web page publishing?

Yes. In fact, within two hours of starting this book, someone with no previous HTML experience at all can have a Web page ready to place on the Internet's World Wide Web.

How can you learn the language of the Web so fast? By example. This book breaks HTML down into simple steps that anyone can learn quickly, and *shows* you exactly how to take each step. Every HTML example is pictured right above the Web page it will produce. You see it done, you read a brief plain-English explanation of how it works, and you immediately do the same thing with your own page. Ten minutes later, you're on to the next step.

The next day, you're marveling at your own impressive pages on the Internet.

JUST A MINUTE

Before you go any further, there's something you should know from the outset. Professional Web page authors talk about three kinds of HTML pages:

☐ *First-generation* pages use old-fashioned HTML 1.0, and are mostly text with a hokey picture or two stuck in the middle. They were the best you could do in 1989, but having a first-generation page today marks you as more technologically backward than having no Web page at all.

☐ *Second-generation* pages use a few HTML 2.0 tricks, such as putting a pretty (or garish) background behind a page, arranging text in tables, and offering an online order form. They can look nice, but rarely match the quality that people have come to expect from paper documents.

☐ *Third-generation* pages are what the world is talking about now that HTML 3.2 is the standard. They use creative layout, custom color, fast graphics, fonts, and interactive feedback to make your Web site more engaging than anything on paper.

The goal of this book is to help you skip past the first and second generations, straight into the exciting world of third-generation Web pages. So don't expect to learn obsolete HTML, or create boring pages with no visual interest. Fortunately, if you start with a "third-generation mindset," learning HTML can be faster, easier, and more rewarding than ever.

How to Use This Book

There are several ways to go through this book, and the best way for you depends on your situation. Here are five recommended options. Pick the one that matches your needs.

1. *"I need to get some text on the Internet today. Then I can worry about making it look pretty later."*

   ☐ Read Chapter 1, "Welcome to HTML."

   ☐ Read Chapter 2, "Creating a Web Page."

   ☐ Read Chapter 4, "Publishing Your HTML Pages."

   ☐ Put your first page on the Internet!

   (Total work time: 2–4 hours.)

   ☐ Start with Chapter 3, "Linking to Other Web Pages," and read the rest of the book.

   ☐ Update your pages as you learn more HTML.

2. *"I need a basic Web page with text and graphics on the Internet as soon as possible. Then I can work on improving it and adding more pages."*

   ☐ Read Chapter 1, "Welcome to HTML."

   ☐ Read Chapter 2, "Creating a Web Page."

   ☐ Read Chapter 9, "Putting Images on a Web Page."

   ☐ Read Chapter 10, "Creating Web Page Images."

   ☐ Read Chapter 4, "Publishing Your HTML Pages."

   ☐ Put your first page on the Internet!

   (Total work time: 4–8 hours.)

   ☐ Start with Chapter 3, and read the rest of the book.

   ☐ Update your pages as you learn more HTML.

3. *"I need a professional-looking business Web site with an order form right away. Then I can continue to improve and develop my site over time."*

☐ Read all four chapters in Part I, "Your First Web Page."

☐ Read Chapter 9, "Putting Images on a Web Page."

☐ Read Chapter 10, "Creating Web Page Images."

☐ Read Chapter 13, "Backgrounds and Color Control."

☐ Read Chapter 18, "Creating HTML Forms."

☐ Put your pages and order form on the Internet!

(Total work time: 6–12 hours.)

☐ Start with Chapter 5, "Text Formatting and Alignment," and read the rest of the book.

☐ Update your pages as you learn more HTML.

4. *"I need to develop a creative and attractive 'identity' Web site on a tight schedule. Then I will need to develop many pages for our corporate intranet as well."*

☐ Read all four chapters in Part I, "Your First Web Page."

☐ Read all four chapters in Part II, "Web Page Text."

☐ Read all four chapters in Part III, "Web Page Graphics."

☐ Read all four chapters in Part IV, "Web Page Design."

☐ Put your pages on the Internet and/or your intranet!

(Total work time: 8–16 hours.)

☐ Start with Chapter 17, "Interactive Layout with Frames," and read the rest of the book.

☐ Update your pages as you learn more HTML.

5. *"I need to build a cutting-edge interactive Web site or HTML-based multimedia presentation—fast!"*

☐ Read this whole book.

☐ Put your pages on the Internet and/or CD-ROM!

(Total work time: 12–24 hours.)

☐ Review and use the techniques you've learned to continue improving and developing your site.

JUST A MINUTE

It may take a day or two for an Internet service provider to set up a host computer for your pages, as discussed in Chapter 4, "Publishing Your HTML Pages." If you want to get your pages online immediately, read Chapter 4 now so you can have a place on the Internet all ready for your first page.

No matter which of the above approaches you take, you'll benefit from the unique presentation elements which make this book the fastest possible way to learn HTML.

Visual Examples

Like the "Instant HTML" reference card in the front of this book, every example is illustrated in two parts. The text you type in to make an HTML page is shown first, with all HTML commands highlighted. The resulting Web page is shown as it will appear to people who view it with the world's most popular Web browser, Netscape Navigator 3.0. You'll often be able to adapt the example to your own pages without reading any of the accompanying text at all.

Special Highlighted Elements

To Do:

As you go through each chapter, sections marked "To Do" guide you in applying what you just learned to your own Web pages at once.

NEW TERM Whenever a new term is used, it will be highlighted in a special box like this one. No flipping back and forth to the glossary!

TIME SAVER

Tips and tricks to save you precious time are set aside so you can spot them quickly.

JUST A MINUTE

Crucial information you should be sure not to miss is also highlighted.

Q&A, Quiz, and Activities

Every chapter ends with a short question-and-answer session that addresses the kind of "dumb questions" everyone wishes they dared to ask. A brief but complete quiz lets you test yourself to be sure you understand everything in the chapter. Finally, one or two optional activities give you a chance to practice your new skills before you move on.

Coffee Breaks

In every chapter, you'll find a "Coffee Break" section that takes you to an extensive Internet site called the *24-Hour HTML Café* (`http://www.mcp.com/sams/books/235-8/`). I built and opened the café especially to provide readers of this book with oodles more examples and reusable HTML pages than I could ever picture in a short book.

At the *24-Hour HTML Café*, you'll find every example in this book and many more complete Web pages designed to reinforce and expand your knowledge of HTML. In fact, you'll see how I developed the *24-Hour HTML Café* Web site itself, step-by-step, as you go through the book.

You'll also get to have some fun with whimsical "edutainment" pages and break-time surprises. You'll find links to a wide variety of Internet resources to help you produce your own Web pages even faster. See you there!

PART
I

Your First
Web Page

Hour

Hour 1

Welcome to HTML

Before you begin creating your own Web pages with HTML, you need some background knowledge about what Web pages are, how they work, and what you can expect to achieve with them. This chapter provides a quick summary of those basics and some practical tips to make the most of your time as a Web page author and publisher.

To Do:

This book assumes that you have spent some time exploring Web pages on the Internet. If you haven't, please take at least a couple of hours to do so now. Trying to produce your own Web pages without having "surfed" the World Wide Web would be like trying to become a famous author without ever having seen a piece of paper!

Here's a review of what you need to do before you're ready to use the rest of this book:

1. Get a computer. I used a Windows 95 computer to create the figures in this book, but you can use any Windows, Macintosh, or UNIX machine to create your Web pages. (You can look at Web pages with a TV nowadays, but you can't make them with one… yet!)

2. Get a connection to the Internet. You should be able to get one through either a modem or the local network of your school or business. An old UNIX "shell" account won't do the trick; it has to be a modern PPP (Point-to-Point Protocol) connection, which most Internet service providers (ISP) now offer for about $20 per month. Your access speed should be at least 14.4 Kbps, though faster is better. The ISP, school, or business that provides your connection can help you with the details of setting it up properly.

3. Get a copy of Netscape Navigator and/or Microsoft Internet Explorer (version 3.0 or higher). Together, these two Web browser programs are used by over 90 percent of the people who look at Web pages, so it's a good idea to get them both. You can buy them in software stores, or get them free through the Internet at http://home.netscape.com and http://www.microsoft.com.

4. Explore! Use Netscape Navigator or Microsoft Internet Explorer to look for pages that are similar in content or appearance to those you'd like to create. Make notes about what frustrates you about some pages, what attracts you and keeps you reading, and what makes you come back to some pages over and over again.

JUST A MINUTE

If you plan to put your HTML pages on the Internet (as opposed to publishing them on CD-ROM or a local intranet), you'll need to transfer them to a computer that is connected to the Internet 24 hours a day. The same company or school that provides you with Internet access may also let you put Web pages on its computer; if not, you may need to pay another company to "host" your pages.

You can start learning HTML with this book right away and wait to find an Internet host for your pages when they're done. However, if you want to have a place on the Internet ready for your very first page as soon it is finished, you may want to read Chapter 4, "Publishing Your HTML Pages," before you continue.

What Is a Web Page?

Once upon a time, back when there weren't any footprints on the moon, some far-sighted folks decided to see whether they could connect several major computer networks together. I'll spare you the names and stories (there are plenty of both), but the eventual result was the "mother of all networks," which we call the Internet.

1

Until 1990, accessing information through the Internet was a rather technical affair. It was so hard, in fact, that even Ph.D.-holding physicists were often frustrated when trying to swap data. One such physicist, the now famous Tim Berners-Lee, cooked up a way to easily cross-reference text on the Internet through "hypertext" links. This wasn't a new idea, but his simple *Hypertext Markup Language* (HTML) managed to thrive while more ambitious hypertext projects floundered.

 Hypertext means text stored in electronic form with cross-reference links between pages.

By 1993, almost 100 computers throughout the world were equipped to serve up HTML pages. Those interlinked pages were dubbed the *World Wide Web* (WWW), and several Web browser programs had been written to allow people to view Web pages. Because of the popularity of "the Web," a few programmers soon wrote Web browsers that could view graphics images along with the text on a Web page. One of these programmers was Marc Andreessen; he went on to become rich and famous selling the world's most popular Web browser, Netscape Navigator.

Today, HTML pages are the standard interface to the Internet. They may include animated graphics, sound and video, complete interactive programs, and good old-fashioned text. Millions of Web pages are retrieved each day from thousands of Web server computers around the world.

The Web is on the verge of becoming a mass-market medium, as high-speed Internet connections through TV cables, modernized phone lines, and direct satellite feeds become commonplace. You can already browse the Web using a $300 box attached to your television instead of using your computer, and the cost of such devices is likely to fall sharply over the next few years.

Yet the Internet is no longer the only place you'll find HTML. Most private corporate networks now use HTML to provide business information to employees and clients. HTML is now the interface of choice for publishing presentations on CD-ROM and the new high-capacity digital versatile disk (DVD) format. Microsoft is even integrating HTML directly into the Windows operating system, allowing every storage folder in your computer to be associated with an HTML page and hypertext links to other folders and pages.

In short, HTML is everywhere. Fortunately, you're in the right place to find out how HTML Web pages work and how to create them.

How Web Pages Work

When you are viewing Web pages, they look a lot like paper pages. At first glance, the process of displaying a Web page is simple: You tell your computer which page you want to see, and the page appears on your screen. If the page is stored on a disk inside your computer, it appears almost instantly. If it is located on some other computer, you might have to wait for it to be retrieved.

Of course, Web pages can do some very convenient things that paper pages can't. For example, you can't point to the words "continued on page 57" in a paper magazine and expect page 57 to automatically appear before your eyes. Nor can you tap your finger on the bottom of a paper order form and expect it to reach the company's order fulfillment department five seconds later. You're not likely to see animated pictures or hear voices talk to you from most paper pages either (newfangled greeting cards aside). All these things are commonplace on Web pages.

But there are some deeper differences between Web pages and paper pages that you'll need to be aware of as a Web page author. For one thing, what appears as a single "page" on your screen may actually be an assembly of elements located in many different computer files. In fact, it's possible (though uncommon) to create a page that combines text from a computer in Australia with pictures from a computer in Russia and sounds from a computer in Canada.

Figure 1.1 shows a typical page as seen by Netscape Navigator, the world's most popular software for viewing Web pages. A Web browser such as Netscape Navigator does much more than just retrieve a file and put it on the screen; it actually assembles the component parts of a page and arranges those parts according to commands hidden in the text by the author. Those commands are written in HTML.

 A *Web browser* is a computer program that interprets HTML commands to collect, arrange, and display the parts of a Web page.

Figure 1.2 shows the text, including the HTML commands I typed to create the page in Figure 1.1. This text file can be read and edited with any word processor or text editor. It looks a bit strange with all those odd symbols and code words, but the text file itself doesn't include any embedded images, boldface text, or other special formatting.

Figure 1.1.

A Web browser assembles separate text and image files to display them as an integrated page.

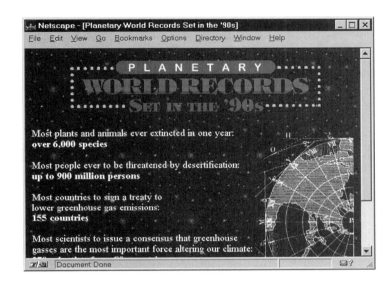

All the images and formatting you see in Figure 1.1 are added by Netscape Navigator. It reads the coded HTML commands in the text, which tell it to look for separate image files and display them along with the text itself. Other commands tell it which text to display in boldface and how to break up the lines of text on the page.

Figure 1.2.

This is the text I typed to create the page in Figure 1.1. The words between < and > are HTML tags.

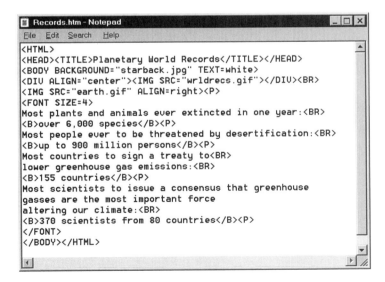

TIME SAVER

To see the HTML commands for any page on the Web, select View | Document Source in Netscape Navigator or View | Source in Microsoft Internet Explorer. This is a great way to get an intuitive idea how HTML works and learn by other's examples.

You'll learn how to understand and write HTML commands soon. The important point to note right now is that creating a Web page is just a matter of typing some text. You can type and save that text with any word processor or text editor you have on hand. You then open the text file with Netscape Navigator or Microsoft Internet Explorer to see it as a Web page.

When you want graphics, sound, animations, video, or interactive programming to appear on a Web page, you don't insert them into the text file directly, as you would if you were creating a document in most paper-oriented page layout programs. Instead, you type HTML text commands telling the Web browser where to find the media files. The media files themselves remain separate, even though the Web browser will make them *look* as if they're part of the same document when it displays the page.

For example, the HTML document in Figure 1.2 refers to three separate graphics images. Figure 1.3 shows these three image files being edited in the popular graphics program Paint Shop Pro.

Figure 1.3.

Though text and graphics appear integrated in Figure 1.1, the graphics files are actually stored, and can be edited, separately.

1

You could use any graphics program you like to modify or replace these images at any time. Changing the graphics might make a big difference in how the page looks, even if you don't make any changes to the HTML text file. You can also use the same image on any number of pages while storing only one copy of the graphics file.

You'll learn much more about incorporating graphics files into Web pages in Part III, "Web Page Graphics."

The Many Faces of HTML

A single Web page can take on many different appearances, depending on who views it and what they view it with. Figure 1.4 is the same Web page pictured earlier in Figure 1.1, as seen with the text-based Lynx Web browser. Lynx users can only see the images if they click on the [IMAGE] links at the top of the page.

Figure 1.4.

The page from Figure 1.1 looks very different in the DOS Lynx browser.

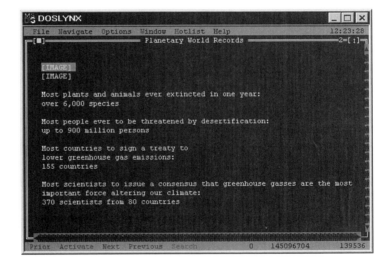

People who are using different versions of the same Web browser may also see significant differences in a page. Version 1.2 of Netscape Navigator was used to display the page in Figure 1.5. Notice that the title graphic placement is different than displayed by Netscape Navigator version 3.0 in Figure 1.1.

Even users of the same version of the same Web browser can alter how a page appears by choosing different display options. Both Netscape Navigator and Microsoft Internet Explorer allow users to override the background and fonts specified by the Web page author with those of their own choice. Screen resolution, window size, and optional toolbars can also change how much of a page someone sees when it first appears.

Figure 1.5.
Netscape Navigator version 1.2 may display some pages differently than other versions of the same browser.

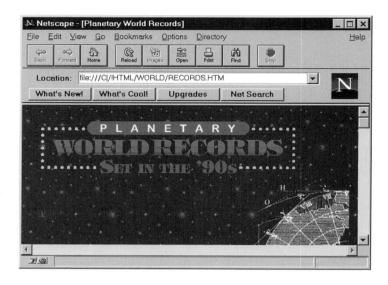

You can't even assume that people will be viewing your Web pages on a computer screen. The page in Figures 1.1, 1.4, and 1.5 might also be read on a low-resolution television screen (see Figure 1.6) or a high-resolution paper printout (see Figure 1.7).

Figure 1.6.
Television screens may blur images, and TV Web browsers usually use a larger font to make text readable from a distance.

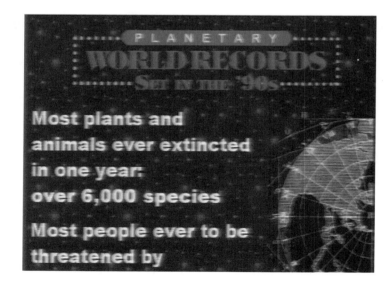

1

Figure 1.7.

Web browsers usually change the background to white when sending pages to a printer.

PLANETARY
WORLD RECORDS
SET IN THE '90s

Most plants and animals ever extinced in one year:
over 6,000 species

Most people ever to be threatened by desertification:
up to 900 million persons

Most countries to sign a treaty to
lower greenhouse gas emissions:
155 countries

Most scientists to issue a consensus that greenhouse
gasses are the most important force altering our climate:
370 scientists from 80 countries

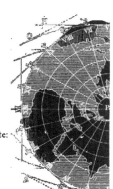

As you learn to make your own Web pages, remember how many different forms they may take when people view them. Some Web page authors fall into the trap of trying to make pages appear "perfect" on their computer and are sorely disappointed the first time they discover that it looks different on someone else's screen.

In Part IV, "Web Page Design," you'll find many tips and tricks for ensuring that your pages look great in the widest variety of situations.

Creating HTML with a Text Editor

There are two basic approaches to making an HTML page: you can type out the text and HTML commands yourself with a text editor, or you can use graphical software that generates the HTML commands for you.

Chapter 23, "Web Site Authoring Tools," introduces some of the HTML editing tools that are available and discusses when to use each type of tool. For now, however, I strongly recommend that you *do not* use a graphical, "what-you-see-is-what-you-get" Web page editor, such as Microsoft FrontPage or Netscape Navigator Gold (which is a different program than Netscape Navigator).

You will be able to follow along with this book and learn HTML much more easily if you work with an editor that shows the actual HTML text. Any word processor or text editor you already have—even the Windows Notepad or Macintosh SimpleText editor—will do nicely.

COFFEE BREAK

In this book, you'll encounter many sample Web pages. The accompanying *24-Hour HTML Café* Web site (http://www.mcp.com/sams/books/235-8/) has even more sample pages for you to explore.

In addition to all these examples, you can follow the development of a complete, sophisticated Web site from the ground up as you go through the book. You might like to preview this "construction site" now at

http://www.mcp.com/sams/books/235-8/cafe1.htm

Doing so will give you an overview of how this book presents HTML and help you plan the development of your own pages. It will also help you see which chapters cover the aspects of HTML you're most likely to use in the pages you plan to build.

Summary

This chapter introduced the basics of what Web pages are and how they work. You learned that coded HTML commands are included in the text of a Web page, but images and other media are stored in separate files. You also saw that a single Web page can look very different, depending on what software and hardware are used to display it. Finally, you learned why typing HTML text yourself is often better than using a graphical editor to create HTML commands for you.

1

Q&A

Q **I'm still not quite sure what the difference between a "Web page" and an "HTML page" is.**

A If you want to get technical, I suppose a "Web page" would have to be from the Internet instead of a disk on your own computer. But in practice, the terms "Web page" and "HTML page" are used interchangeably.

Q **I've looked at the HTML "source" of some Web pages on the Internet, and it looks frighteningly difficult to learn. Do I have to think like a computer programmer to learn this stuff?**

A Though complex HTML pages can indeed look daunting, learning HTML is several orders of magnitude easier than other computer languages like BASIC, C, or Java. You don't need any experience or skill as a computer programmer to be a very successful HTML author.

Q **Do you need to be connected to the Internet constantly while you create HTML pages?**

A No. In fact, you don't need any Internet connection at all if you only want to produce Web pages for publication on a CD-ROM, Zip or floppy disk, or local network.

Quiz

Questions

1. Define the terms *Internet*, *Web page*, and *World Wide Web*.
2. How many files would you need to store on your computer to make a Web page with some text and two images on it?
3. Can you create Web pages with Microsoft Word or WordPerfect?

Answers

1. The Internet is the "network of networks" that connects millions of computers around the globe.

   A Web page is a text document that uses commands in a special language called HTML to add formatting, graphics and other media, and links to other pages.

   The World Wide Web is a collective name for all the Web pages on the Internet.

2. At least three files: one for the text (which includes the HTML commands) and one for each graphics image. In some cases, you might need more files to add a background pattern, sound, or interactive features to the page.

3. Yes, or with any other word processor on any computer (as long as the word processor will save "plain text" or "ASCII" files). Note that many word processors also now allow you to save text in HTML format, and they will write some of the HTML for you. Chapter 23 will discuss the merits of that feature, but you should avoid using it while you're learning HTML with this book. Just save as plain text instead.

Activities

☐ At the end of each chapter in this book, you'll find some suggestions for optional activities to reinforce and expand what you learned in the chapter. However, because you're undoubtedly eager to get started learning HTML, let's skip the activities right now and dive right in to Chapter 2, "Creating a Web Page."

Hour **2**

Creating a Web Page

This chapter will guide you through the creation of your first Web page. The best way to follow along with this chapter is to actually create a Web page as you read, using the sample page developed here in the book as a model. If you're a little nervous about jumping right in, you might want to read this chapter once to get the general idea, and then go through it again at your computer while you work on your own page.

As mentioned in Chapter 1, "Welcome to HTML," you can use any text editor or word processor to create HTML Web pages. Though you'll eventually want to use an editor specially designed for HTML, for this chapter I recommend you use the editor or word processor you're most familiar with. That way you won't have to learn a new software program at the same time you're starting to learn HTML. Even a simple text editor like Windows Notepad will work just fine.

To Do:

Before you begin working with this chapter, you should start with some text that you want to put on a Web page.

1. Find (or write) a few paragraphs of text about yourself, your company, or the intended subject of your Web pages.

2. Be sure to save it as plain, standard ASCII text. Notepad and most simple text editors always save files as plain text, but you may need to choose it as an option if you're using a word processor. For most word processors, you'll see a check box labeled plain text or ASCII text when you select File | Save As....

3. As you go through this chapter, you will add HTML commands (called *tags*) to the text file, making it into a Web page. You can do this with the same text editor or word processor you used to type the text in the first place.

4. Always give files containing HTML tags a name ending in .htm or .html when you save them.

Tags That Every HTML Page Must Have

Figure 2.1 shows the text you would type and save to create the simplest possible HTML page. If you opened this file with a Web browser such as Netscape Navigator, you would see the page in Figure 2.2.

In Figure 2.1, as in every HTML page, the words starting with < and ending with > are actually coded commands. These coded commands are called *HTML tags* because they "tag" pieces of text and tell the Web browser what kind of text it is. This allows the Web browser to display the text appropriately.

 An HTML *tag* is a coded command used to indicate how part of a Web page should be displayed.

 In Figure 2.1, and most other figures in this book, HTML tags are printed darker than the rest of the text so you can easily spot them. When you type your own HTML files, all the text will be the same color (unless you are using a special HTML editing program that uses color to highlight tags, as HTMLED does).

Figure 2.1.

Every Web page you create must include the <HTML>, <HEAD>, <TITLE>, *and* <BODY> *tags.*

```
<HTML>
<HEAD>
<TITLE>My First Web Page</TITLE>
</HEAD>
<BODY>
Hello world!
</BODY>
</HTML>
```

Figure 2.2.

When you view the Web page in Figure 2.1 with a Web browser, only the actual title and body text show up.

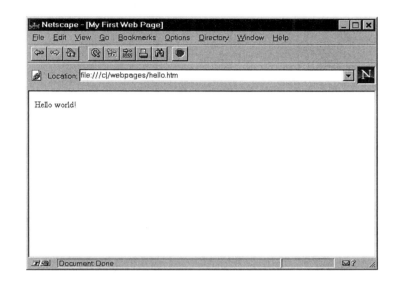

Most HTML tags have two parts: an *opening tag*, to indicate where a piece of text begins, and a *closing tag*, to show where the piece of text ends. Closing tags start with a / (forward slash) just after the < symbol.

For example, the <BODY> tag in Figure 2.1 tells the Web browser where the actual body text of the page begins, and </BODY> indicates where it ends. Everything between the <BODY> and </BODY> tags will appear in the main display area of the Web browser window, where you see "Hello world!" in Figure 2.2.

Netscape Navigator displays any text between <TITLE> and </TITLE> at the very top of the Netscape window, as in Figure 2.2. (Some older Web browsers display the title in its own special little box instead.) The title text will also be used to identify the page on the Netscape Navigator Bookmarks menu, or the Microsoft Internet Explorer Favorites menu, whenever someone selects Add Bookmark or Add to Favorites.

You will use the <BODY> and <TITLE> tags in every HTML page you create because every Web page needs a title and some body text. You will also use the other two tags shown in Figure 2.1, <HTML> and <HEAD>. Putting <HTML> at the very beginning of a document simply indicates that this is a Web page. The </HTML> at the end indicates that the Web page is over.

Don't ask me to explain why you have to put <HEAD> in front of the <TITLE> tag and </HEAD> after the </TITLE> tag. You just do. (Chapter 22, "HTML Tags for Site Management," reveals some other advanced header information that can go between <HEAD> and </HEAD>, but none of it is necessary for most Web pages.)

TIME SAVER

You may find it convenient to create and save a "bare-bones" page with just the opening and closing <HTML>, <HEAD>, <TITLE>, and <BODY> tags, similar to the document in Figure 2.1. You can then open that document as a starting point whenever you want to make a new Web page and save yourself from typing out all those "obligatory" tags every time.

(This won't be necessary if you use a dedicated HTML editing program, which will usually put these tags in automatically when you begin a new page.)

Paragraphs and Line Breaks

When a Web browser displays HTML pages, it pays no attention to line endings or the number of spaces between words. For example, the two verses in Figure 2.3 are both displayed exactly the same by Netscape Navigator in Figure 2.4, with a single space between all words. When the text reaches the edge of the Netscape window, it automatically wraps down to the next line, no matter where the line breaks were in the original HTML file.

Figure 2.3.

In HTML, it makes no difference how many spaces or lines you use when typing your text.

```
<HTML>
<HEAD><TITLE>Mother Goose's Melody</TITLE></HEAD>
<BODY>

Good people all     of every sort, Give ear
unto my song:

And if you find it     wondrous short, It cannot hold
you long.

<HR>

Good people all of every sort,
Give ear unto my song:
And if you find it wondrous short,
It cannot hold you long.

</BODY>
</HTML>
```

To control where line and paragraph breaks actually appear, you must use HTML tags. The <BR> tag forces a line break, and the <P> tag creates a paragraph break. The only practical difference between these two tags is that <P> inserts an extra blank line between paragraphs, and <BR> does not.

Figure 2.4.

The two verses in Figure 2.3 appear identical in a Web browser.

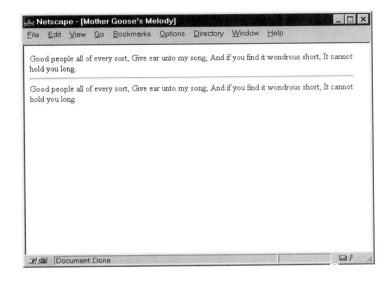

You might have also noticed the <HR> tag in Figure 2.3, which causes a horizontal "rule" line to appear in Figure 2.4. Inserting a horizontal rule with the <HR> tag also causes a line break, even if you don't include a <BR> tag along with it. For a little extra blank space above or below a horizontal rule, you can put a <P> tag before or after the <HR> tag.

Neither the <BR> line break tag nor the <HR> horizontal rule tag needs a closing </BR> or </HR> tag.

TIME SAVER

The <P> paragraph tag doesn't require a closing </P> tag at the end of the paragraph because a paragraph obviously ends whenever the next one begins.

You may occasionally see Web pages which do use the </P> tag to close paragraphs, but this is never necessary.

Figure 2.5 shows the <BR> and <P> tags being used to separate the lines and verses of a nursery rhyme and to separate two paragraphs of text commenting on the rhyme. Figure 2.6 is the resulting Web page.

Figure 2.5.
Use the <BR> tag for line breaks, and the <P> tag to skip a line between paragraphs.

```
<HTML>
<HEAD><TITLE>Tommy Thumb's Pretty Song Book</TITLE></HEAD>
<BODY>
When I was a little boy<BR>
I wash'd my<BR>Mother's Dishes.<BR>
I put my finger in my<BR>
Ear, and pull'd out<BR>Little fishes.<P>
My Mother call'd me<BR>Good boy,<BR>
And bid me pull out more,<BR>
I put my Finger<BR>In my Ear,<BR>
And pull'd out fourscore.<P>
The English chronicler John Aubrey (1627-97) claimed
this nursery rhyme was a cleaned-up version of
"an old filthy Rhythme used by base people."<P>
The second verse was most probably added
by a seventeenth-century play, <I>Love without Interest,
or The Man too hard for the Master.</I>
</BODY>
</HTML>
```

Figure 2.6.
The <BR> and <P> tags in Figure 2.5 become line and paragraph breaks on this Web page.

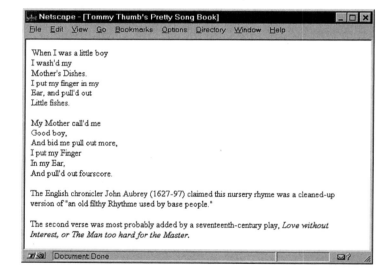

To Do:

Take a passage of text you have on hand and try your hand at formatting it as proper HTML.

1. Add <HTML><HEAD><TITLE>*My Title*</TITLE></HEAD><BODY> to the beginning of the text (using your own title for your page Instead of *My Title*).

2. Add </BODY></HTML> to the very end of the text.

3. Add <P> tags between paragraphs, and <BR> tags anywhere you want single-spaced line breaks.

2

4. Use <HR> to draw horizontal rules separating major sections of text, or wherever you'd like to see a line across the page.

5. Save the file as mypage.htm (using your own filename instead of mypage). If you are using a word processor, be sure to always save HTML files in plain text or ASCII format.

6. Open the file with Netscape Navigator or Microsoft Internet Explorer to see your Web page!

7. If something doesn't look right, go back to the text editor or word processor to make corrections and save the file again. You will then need to click on Reload (in Netscape Navigator) or Refresh (in Microsoft Internet Explorer) to see the changes you made to the Web page.

Headings

When you browse through Web pages on the Internet, you can't help but notice that most of them have a heading at the top which appears larger and bolder than the rest of the text. Figure 2.8 is a simple Web page, containing examples of the three largest heading sizes that you can make with HTML.

As you can see in Figure 2.7, the HTML to create headings couldn't be simpler. For a big level 1 heading, put an <H1> tag at the beginning and an </H1> tag at the end. For a slightly smaller level 2 heading, use <H2> and </H2> instead, and for a little level 3 heading, use <H3> and </H3>.

Theoretically, you can also use <H4>, <H5>, and <H6> to make progressively less important headings, but nobody uses these very much—after all, what's the point of a heading if it's not big and bold? Besides, most Web browsers don't show a noticeable difference between these and the already-small <H3> headings anyway.

JUST A MINUTE

On many Web pages these days, graphical images of ornately rendered letters and logos are often used in place of the ordinary text headings discussed in this chapter. You'll discover how to create graphics and put them on your pages in Part III, "Web Page Graphics." However, old-fashioned text headings are still widely used, and have two major advantages over graphics headings:

☐ Text headings transfer and display almost instantly, no matter how fast or slow the reader's connection to the Internet is.

☐ Text headings can be seen in *all* Web browsers and HTML-compatible software, even old DOS and UNIX programs that don't show graphics.

Figure 2.7.

Any text between the <H1> and </H1> tags will appear as a large heading. <H2> and <H3> make smaller headings.

```
<HTML>
<HEAD><TITLE>Orbit the Juggler's Home Page</TITLE></HEAD>
<BODY>
<H1>Orbit the Juggler</H1>
Using humorous storytelling and a variety of circus arts,
Peter "Orbit" King teaches the language of geometry and the
meaning of language.
<H2>Learn the ABCs and 123s of nature's own language.</H2>
This language is ancient because
it was first mentioned by Plato 2,400 years ago. It's also
brand new because it has been rediscovered in modern times
by scientists in the structure of everything from bacteria
to snowflakes, tornadoes to titanium. This brand new,
ancient way of thinking is particularly appropriate for
understanding and addressing the global economic,
social, and evironmental challenges that face us today.
<H3>And while you're at it, see over 60 ways to juggle!</H3>
Can you really develop new learning and communication skills
while watching Orbit juggle a hatchet, a quarter, and a
knife on a unicycle? (Yes, but please don't ask your math or
English teacher to repeat this lesson!)
</BODY>
</HTML>
```

Figure 2.8.

The <H1>, <H2>, and <H3> tags in Figure 2.7 make the three progressively smaller headings shown here.

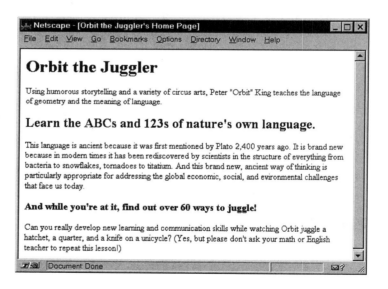

It's important to remember the difference between a *title* and a *heading.* These two words are often interchangeable in day-to-day English, but when you're talking HTML, <TITLE> gives the entire page an identifying name *which isn't displayed on the page itself.* The heading tags, on the other hand, cause some text on the page to be displayed with visual emphasis. There can only be one <TITLE> per page, but you can have as many <H1>, <H2>, and <H3> headings as you want, in any order that suits your fancy.

2

You'll learn to take complete control over the appearance of text on your Web pages in Part II, "Web Page Text." Yet headings provide the easiest and most popular way to draw extra attention to some important text.

Peeking at Other People's Pages

If you've even taken a quick peek at the World Wide Web, you know that the simple text pages described in this chapter are only the tip of the HTML iceberg. Now that you know the basics, you may surprise yourself with how much of the rest you can pick up just by looking at other people's pages on the Internet. As mentioned in Chapter 1, you can see the HTML for any page by selecting View | Document Source in Netscape Navigator, or View | Source in Microsoft Internet Explorer.

Don't worry if you aren't yet able to decipher what some HTML tags do, or exactly how to use them yourself. You'll find out all that in the next few chapters. However, sneaking a preview now will show you the tags you do know in action, and give you a taste of what you'll soon be able to do with your Web pages.

COFFEE BREAK

The HTML goodies at my *24-Hour HTML Café* are specially designed to be intuitive and easy to understand.

The HTML used in the main entrance page at `http://www.mcp.com/sams/books/235-8` may look a bit intimidating now, but you'll see how I developed this sophisticated site step-by-step as you work through each chapter of this book.

You can uncover the humble beginnings of the *24-Hour HTML Café* at

`http://www.mcp.com/sams/books/235-8/cafe2.htm`

which uses only the tags introduced in this chapter.

Summary

In this chapter, you've been introduced to the most basic and important HTML tags. By adding these coded commands to any plain text document, you can quickly transform it into a bona fide Web page.

The first step in creating a Web page is to put a few obligatory HTML tags at the beginning and end, including a title for the page. You then mark where paragraphs and lines end, and add horizontal rules and headings if you want. Table 2.1 summarizes all the tags introduced in this chapter.

Table 2.1. HTML tags covered in Chapter 2.

Tag	Function
`<HTML>...</HTML>`	Encloses the entire HTML document.
`<HEAD>...</HEAD>`	Encloses the head of the HTML document.
`<TITLE>...</TITLE>`	Indicates the title of the document. Used within `<HEAD>`.
`<BODY>...</BODY>`	Encloses the body of the HTML document.
`<P>...</P>`	A paragraph. The closing tag (`</P>`) is optional.
` `	A line break.
`<HR>`	A horizontal rule line.
`<H1>...</H1>`	A first-level heading.
`<H2>...</H2>`	A second-level heading.
`<H3>...</H3>`	A third-level heading.
`<H4>...</H4>`	A fourth-level heading (seldom used).
`<H5>...</H5>`	A fifth-level heading (seldom used).
`<H6>...</H6>`	A sixth-level heading (seldom used).

Q&A

Q Okay, so I've got this HTML Web page on my computer now. How do I get it on the Internet so everyone else can see it?

A Chapter 4, "Publishing Your HTML Pages," explains how to put your pages on the Internet as well as how to get them ready for publishing on a local network or CD-ROM.

Q I want "Fred's Fresh Fish" to appear both at the top of my page *and* on people's bookmark (or favorites) lists when they bookmark my page. How can I get it to appear both places?

A Make a heading at the top of your page with the same text as the title, like this:

```
<HTML><HEAD><TITLE>Fred's Fresh Fish</TITLE></HEAD>
<BODY><H1>Fred's Fresh Fish</H1>
...the rest of the page goes here...
</BODY></HTML>
```

Q I've seen Web pages on the Internet that don't have `<HTML>` tags at the beginning. I've also seen pages with some other weird tags in front of the `<HTML>` tag. You said pages always have to start with `<HTML>`. What's the deal?

2

A Many Web browsers will forgive you if you forget to put in the `<HTML>` tag, and display the page correctly anyway. Yet it's a very good idea to include it because some software does need it to identify the page as valid HTML.

In fact, the official standard goes one step further and recommends that you put a tag at the beginning that looks like this: `<!DOCTYPE HTML PUBLIC "-//IETF//DTD HTML//EN//3.2">` to indicate that your document conforms to the HTML 3.2 standard. No software that I've ever heard of pays any attention to this tag, however. It is not likely to be required in the near future, since so few of the millions of Web pages in the world include it.

Quiz

Questions

1. What four tags are required in every HTML page?

2. Insert the appropriate line break and paragraph break tags to format the following poems with a blank line between them:

   Good night, God bless you,
   Go to bed and undress you.

   Good night, sweet repose,
   Half the bed and all the clothes.

3. Write the HTML for the following to appear one after the other:

   ☐ A small heading with the words, "We are Proud to Present"

   ☐ A horizontal rule across the page

   ☐ A large heading with the one word "Orbit"

   ☐ A medium-sized heading with the words, "The Geometric Juggler"

   ☐ Another horizontal rule

4. Write a complete HTML Web page with the title "Foo Bar Home Page" and a heading at the top which reads "Happy Hour at the Foo Bar," followed by the words, "Come on down!" in regular type.

Answers

1. `<HTML>`, `<HEAD>`, `<TITLE>`, and `<BODY>` (along with their closing tags, `</HTML>`, `</HEAD>`, `</TITLE>`, and `</BODY>`).

2. ```
   Good night, God bless you,<BR>
   Go to bed and undress you.
   <P>
   Good night, sweet repose,<BR>
   Half the bed and all the clothes.
   ```

3. `<H3>We are Proud to Present</H3>`

   `<HR><H1>Orbit</H1>`

   `<H2>The Geometric Juggler</H2><HR>`

4. `<HTML><HEAD><TITLE>Foo Bar Home Page</TITLE></HEAD>`

   `<BODY><H1>Happy Hour at the Foo Bar</H1>`

   `Come on down!`

   `</B></BODY></HTML>`

Activities

- ☐ Even if your main goal in reading this book is to create Web pages for your business, you might want to make a personal Web page just for practice. Type a few paragraphs to introduce yourself to the world, and use the HTML tags you've learned in this chapter to make them into a Web page.

- ☐ You'll be using the HTML tags covered in this chapter so often that you'll want to commit them to memory. The best way to do that is to take some time now and create several Web pages before you go on. You can try creating some basic pages with serious information you want to post on the Internet, or just use your imagination and make some fun "joke" pages.

2
   ```

Hour 3

Linking to Other Web Pages

In the previous two chapters, you learned how to create an HTML page with some text on it. However, to make it a "real" Web page you need to connect it to the rest of the World Wide Web—or at least to your own personal or corporate "web" of pages.

This chapter will show you how to create *hypertext links*—those underlined words that take you from one Web page to another when you click on them with your mouse. You'll also learn to create links that go to another part of the same page.

Though the same HTML tag you'll learn in this chapter is also used to make graphics images into clickable links, graphical links aren't explicitly discussed here. You'll learn to create those in Chapter 9, "Putting Images on a Web Page." The more advanced technique of setting up several links from different regions of the same image is explained in Chapter 15, "Image Maps."

Linking to Another Web Page

The tag to create a link is called <A>, which stands for "anchor." (Don't even try to imagine the thought process of the person who came up with this strange name for a link between pages. As Thomas Carlyle once said, "The coldest word was once a glowing new metaphor.") You put the address of the page to link to in quotes after HREF=, like this:

```
<A HREF="http://netletter.com/dicko/welcome.htm">Click here!</A>
```

The link above would display the words Click here! in blue with an underline. When someone clicks on it, they would see the Web page named welcome.htm, which is located in the dicko folder on the Web server computer whose address is netletter.com—just as if they had typed the address into the Web browser by hand. (Internet addresses are also called *Uniform Resource Locators*, or *URLs* by techie types, by the way.)

HREF stands for Hypertext Reference and is called an *attribute* of the <A> tag. You'll learn more about attributes in Chapter 5, "Text Formatting and Alignment."

JUST A MINUTE

As you may know, you can leave out the http:// or http://www. at the front of any address when typing it into most Web browsers. You *cannot* leave that part out when you type an address into an <A HREF> link on a Web page, however.

TIME SAVER

One thing you *can* often leave out of an address is the actual name of the HTML page, because most computers on the Internet will automatically pull up the home page for a particular address or directory folder. For example, you can use http://netletter.com to refer to the page located at http://netletter.com/welcome.htm because my server computer knows welcome.htm is the page you should see first. (See Chapter 4, "Publishing Your HTML Pages.")

Figure 3.1 includes a number of <A> tags, which show up as underlined links in Figure 3.2. For example, clicking on the words "What happens to a Coke can if you freeze it?" in Figure 3.2 will take you to the page located at http://www.wp.com/marius/coke.html, as shown in Figure 3.3.

3

Figure 3.1.
Words between <A> and
</A> tags will become
links to the addresses
given in the HREF
attributes.

```
<HTML><HEAD><TITLE>Ingestibles Research</TITLE></HEAD>
<BODY>
<H1>Indigestible Ingestibles Research</H1>
Maybe we're all created equal, but you are what you eat
which makes some of us lower in saturated fat at least.<P>
Food is no longer just entertainment. It is science.
<A HREF="http://www.owlnet.rice.edu/~gouge/twinkies.html">
The T.W.I.N.K.I.E.S. Project</A> proves this conclusively,
but some questions still remain unanswered. Like
<A HREF="http://www.wp.com/marius/coke.html">What happens
to a Coke can if you freeze it?</A> and
<A HREF="http://www.texhoma.net/~mbrogden/MW/mw.html">
What significant factors differentiate the various
species of Milky Way candy?</A> And only recently has
modern science revealed
<A HREF="http://www.demon.co.uk/prodmon/imgsel4.html">
what snack cakes and meat pies look like when you x-ray
them.</A><P>Science of course leads to technology. <A HREF=
"http://www.research.digital.com/wrl/techreports/html/TN-13/">
Can common snack foods be used as a source of
household illumination?</A> And, more importantly, <A HREF=
"http://www.sci.tamucc.edu/~pmichaud/toast/toast.html">
Will Strawberry Pop-Tarts be the next high-tech weapon?</A>
Find out about these and other exciting technological advances
at <A HREF="http://www.chaco.com/useless/useless/food.html">
the contemporary food research archives.</A>
</BODY></HTML>
```

Figure 3.2.
The HTML in Figure
3.1 produces this page,
with links appearing as
blue or purple underlined
text.

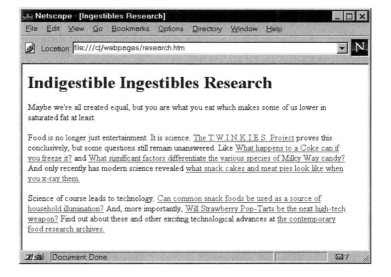

Figure 3.3.

Clicking on "What happens to a Coke can if you freeze it?" in Figure 3.2 retrieves this page from the Internet.

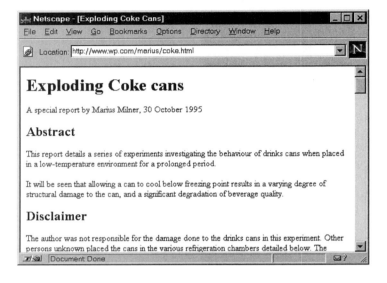

TIME SAVER

You can easily transfer the address of a page from your Web browser to your own HTML page using the Windows or Mac Clipboard. Just highlight the address in the Location, Address, Bookmark Properties, or Edit Favorites box in your Web browser, and select Edit | Copy (or press Ctrl+C). Then type `<A HREF="` and select Edit | Paste (Ctrl+V) in your HTML editor.

COFFEE BREAK

At the *24-Hour HTML Café*, you can explore a list of useful HTML learning resources on the Web from:

`http://www.mcp.com/sams/books/235-8/cafe3.htm`

Before you follow the links on that page, view the document's HTML source to see a simple example of how to put hypertext links to work.

Linking Between Your Own Pages

When you create a link from one page to another page on the same computer, it isn't necessary to specify a complete Internet address. If the two pages are in the same directory folder, you can simply use the name of the HTML file, like this:

```
<A HREF="pagetwo.htm">Click here to go to page 2.</A>
```

As an example, Figures 3.4 and 3.5 show a quiz page with a link to the answers page in Figures 3.6 and 3.7. The answers page contains a link back to the quiz page.

Figure 3.4.

Because this page links to another page in the same directory, the filename can be used in place of a complete address.

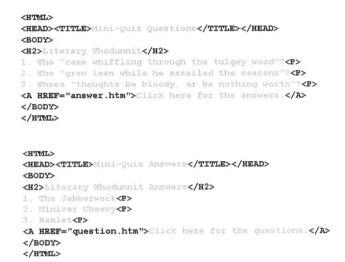

```
<HTML>
<HEAD><TITLE>Mini-Quiz Questions</TITLE></HEAD>
<BODY>
<H2>Literary Whodunnit</H2>
1. Who "came whiffling through the tulgey wood"?<P>
2. Who "grew lean while he assailed the seasons"?<P>
3. Whose "thoughts be bloody, or be nothing worth"?<P>
<A HREF="answer.htm">Click here for the answers.</A>
</BODY>
</HTML>
```

Figure 3.5.

This is the answer.htm *file, and Figure 3.4 is* question.htm, *which this page links back to.*

```
<HTML>
<HEAD><TITLE>Mini-Quiz Answers</TITLE></HEAD>
<BODY>
<H2>Literary Whodunnit Answers</H2>
1. The Jabberwock<P>
2. Miniver Cheevy<P>
3. Hamlet<P>
<A HREF="question.htm">Click here for the questions.</A>
</BODY>
</HTML>
```

Figure 3.6.

This is the question.htm *file listed in Figure 3.4 and referred to by the link in Figure 3.5.*

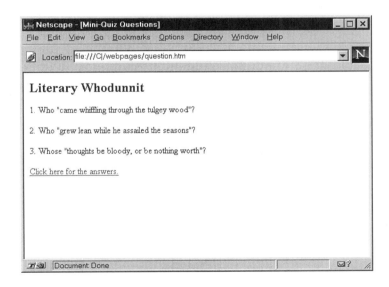

Figure 3.7.

"Click here for the answers" in Figure 3.6 takes you here. "Click here for the questions" takes you back to Figure 3.6.

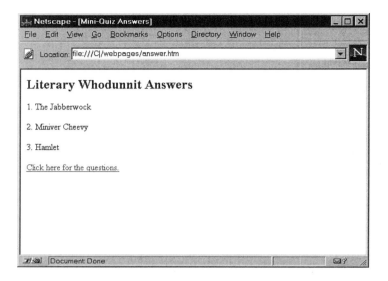

Using just filenames instead of complete Internet addresses saves you a lot of typing. And more importantly, the links between your pages will work properly no matter where the pages are located. You can test the links while the files are still right on your computer's hard drive. Then you can move them to a computer on the Internet, or to a CD-ROM or DVD disk, and all the links will still work correctly.

JUST A MINUTE

There is one good reason to sometimes use the complete address of your own pages in links. If someone saves one of your pages on his own hard drive, any links to your other pages from that page won't work unless he includes full Internet addresses.

I like to include a link with the full address of my main "home" page at the bottom of every page, and use simple filenames or relative addresses in all the rest of the links.

Relative Addresses

If you have many pages, you'll want to put them in more than one directory folder. In that case, you still shouldn't use the full Internet address to link between them. You can use relative addresses, which include only enough information to find one page from another.

NEW TERM   A *relative address* describes the path from one Web page to another, instead of a full (or "absolute") Internet address.

For instance, suppose you are creating a page named `zoo.htm` in a directory folder named `webpages` on your hard drive. You want to include a link to a page named `african.htm`, which is in a sub-folder named `elephants` within `webpages`. The link would look like this:

```
<A HREF="elephants/african.htm">Learn about African elephants.</A>
```

JUST A MINUTE

> Notice that the / (forward-slash) is always used to separate directory folders in HTML. Don't use the \ (backslash) normally used in Windows and DOS!

The `african.htm` page might contain a link back to the main `zoo.htm` page:

```
<A HREF="../zoo.htm">Return to the zoo.</A>
```

The double-dot (. .) is a special code which means "the folder containing the current folder." (The . . means the same thing in DOS, Windows, MacOS, and UNIX.)

You can then move these pages to another directory folder, disk drive, or Web server without changing the links, as long as you always put `african.htm` inside a sub-folder named `elephants`.

Relative addresses can span quite complex directory structures if necessary; Chapter 21, "Organizing Multiple Pages," offers more detailed advice for organizing and linking among large numbers of Web pages.

To Do:

You probably created a page or two of your own while working through Chapter 2, "Creating a Web Page." Now is a great time to add a few more pages and link them together.

☐ Use a home page as a main entrance and central "hub" to which all your other pages are connected. If you created a page about yourself or your business in Chapter 2, use that as your home page. You also might like to make a new page now for this purpose.

☐ On the home page, put a list of `<A HREF>` links to the other HTML files you've created (or plan to create soon). Be sure that the exact spelling of the filename, including any capitalization, is correct in every link.

☐ On every other page, include a link at the bottom (or top) leading back to your home page. That makes it simple and easy to navigate around your "site."

☐ You may also want to include a list of links to sites on the Internet, either on your home page or a separate "hotlist" page. People often include a list of their friends' personal pages on their own home page. (Businesses, however, should be careful not to lead potential customers away to other sites too quickly—there's no guarantee they'll come back!)

Remember to use only filenames (or relative addressing) for links between your own pages, but full Internet addresses for links to other sites.

Summary

The <A> tag is what makes hypertext "hyper." With it, you can create clickable links between pages, as well as links to specific anchor points on any page.

When creating links to other people's pages, include the full Internet address of each page in an <A HREF> tag. For links between your own pages, include just the filenames and enough directory information to get from one page to another.

Table 3.1 summarizes the two attributes of the <A> tag discussed in this chapter.

Table 3.1. HTML tags and attributes covered in Chapter 3.

Tag	Attribute	Function
<A>...</A>		With the HREF attribute, creates a link to another document or anchor; with the NAME attribute, creates an anchor that can be linked to.
	HREF="..."	The address of the document and/or anchor point to link to.
	NAME="..."	The name for this anchor point in the document.

Q&A

Q When I make links, some of them are blue and some of them are purple. Why? And how come most of the links I see on the Internet aren't blue and purple?

A A link will appear blue to anyone who hasn't recently visited the page it points to. Once you visit a page, any links to it will turn purple. These colors can be (and often are) changed to match any color scheme a Web page author wants, so many links you see on the Web won't be blue and purple. (Chapter 13, "Backgrounds and Color Control," tells how to change the colors of text and links on your Web pages.)

3

Q What happens if I link to a page on the Internet and then the person who owns that page deletes or moves it?

A That depends on how that person has set up his server computer. Usually, people will see a message when they click on the link saying "Page not found" or something to that effect. They can still click the back button to go back to your page.

Quiz

Questions

1. Your best friend from elementary school finds you on the Internet and says he wants to trade home page links. How do you put a link to his page at www.cheapsuits.com/~billybob/ on your page?

2. Your home page will be at http://www.mysite.com/home.htm when you put it on the Internet. Write the HTML code to go on that page so that when someone clicks on the words "All about me," they see the page located at http://www.mysite.com/mylife.htm.

3. You plan to publish a CD-ROM disc containing HTML pages. How do you create a link from a page in the \guide directory folder to the \guide\maine\katahdin.htm page?

4. How about a link from \guide\maine\katahdin.htm to the \guide\arizona\superstitions.htm page?

Answers

1. On your page, put:

    ```
    <A HREF="http://www.cheapsuits.com/~billybob/">
    My Buddy Billy Bob's Page of Inexpensive Businesswear</A>
    ```

2.  ```
    <A HREF="mylife.htm">All about me</A>
    ```

3.  ```
    <A HREF="maine/katahdin.htm">Mount Katahdin</A>
    ```

4.  ```
    <A HREF="../arizona/superstitions.htm">
    The Superstition Range</A>
    ```
    ```

Activities

☐ To make a formatted list of your favorite sites, select Go To Bookmarks and then select File | Save As in Netscape Navigator. You can then open that bookmark file in any HTML editor and add other text and HTML formatting as you wish.

Hour 4

Publishing Your HTML Pages

Here it is, the chapter you've been waiting for! Your Web pages are ready for the world to see, and this chapter explains how to get them to appear before the eyes of your intended audience.

The most obvious avenue for publishing Web pages is, of course, the Internet. Yet you may want to limit the distribution of your pages to a local *intranet* within your organization instead of making them available to the general public. You may also choose to distribute your Web pages on CD-ROMs, floppy disks, Zip disks, or the new DVD-ROM disks.

This chapter covers all of these options, and offers advice on designing your pages to work best with the distribution method you choose.

An *intranet* is a private network with access restricted to one organization, but which uses the same standards and protocols as the global public Internet.

To Do:

Before you read about publishing your pages, you should give some thought to which methods of distribution you will be using. You probably already know if you're going to be publishing on a corporate intranet, but the decision of whether to publish on the Internet or on disk can be harder to make.

☐ If you want your pages to be visible to as many people as possible all over the world, Internet publishing is a must. But don't rule out other distribution methods; you can easily adapt Internet-based pages for distribution on disks and/or local networks.

☐ If you want to reach a specific group of people who have computers, but may not be on the Internet yet, publish your pages on floppy disk (if there aren't very many of them) or CD-ROM (if you have an extensive site). But first, consider seriously whether you can present the same information on good old-fashioned paper.

☐ If you want to provide very large graphics, multimedia, or other content that would be too slow to transfer over today's modems, consider publishing on a CD-ROM. You can easily link the CD-ROM to an Internet Web site, and offer the CD-ROM to people who find you through the Internet, but want the "full experience."

Publishing Web Pages on Disk

Unless you were hired to create documents for a company intranet, you have probably assumed that the Internet is the best way to get your pages in front of the eyes of the world. But there are three major incentives for considering distribution on some form of disk instead:

☐ Currently, more people have disk drives than Internet connections.

☐ Disks can deliver information to the computer screen much faster than people can download it from the Internet.

☐ You can distribute disks to a select audience, whether or not they are connected to the Internet or any particular intranet.

In the not-too-distant future, as Web-enabled televisions and high-speed networks become more commonplace, these advantages may disappear. But for now, publishing on disk can be an excellent way to provide a bigger, faster, and more tightly targeted Web presentation than you could on today's Internet.

Publishing on 1.44MB floppy disks or 100MB Zip disks is simply a matter of copying files from your hard disk with any file management program. You just need to keep in mind that any links starting with http:// will only work if and when someone reading your pages is also

4

connected to the Internet. The cost is currently about $0.50 per floppy disk, or $10 per Zip disk, plus any delivery or mailing costs.

TIME SAVER

> Never use drive letters (such as C:) in <A HREF> link tags on your Web pages or they won't work when you copy the files to a different disk. Refer back to Chapter 3, "Linking to Other Web Pages," for more details on how to make links that will work both on disk and on the Internet.

Publishing on CD-ROM or the new DVD-ROM disks isn't much more complicated; you either need a drive (and accompanying software) capable of creating the disks, or you can send the files to a disk mastering and duplication company. Costs for CD-ROM duplication vary a lot depending on how many disks you need. For less than a hundred CD-ROMs, it may cost more than $10 per disk. But for thousands of copies, expect to pay less than $1 each plus delivery or mailing costs. DVD-ROM pricing hasn't settled down yet, but it will eventually be similar to CD-ROM pricing.

Setting Up an Internet Web Site

To make an HTML page part of the publicly accessible World Wide Web, you need to put it on a *Web server* (a computer permanently connected to the Internet and equipped to send out Web pages upon request). If you run your own Web server, this procedure is simply a matter of copying the file to the right directory. But most people use a Web server run by an Internet service provider (ISP) to host their pages.

Almost all service providers that offer Internet access also offer space to place your own personal Web pages for little or no additional cost. However, if you plan (or even hope) to attract large numbers of people, you should pay a little more money to get a fully supported business site with a major Internet service provider.

TIME SAVER

> Don't think that you have to use the same local company that provides you with Internet access to host your pages. If you run a busy business Web site, you may save a lot of money and get more reliable service from a company in another city. For example, I use a company in Vermont to access the Internet, but my Web site is hosted by a different company in Boston.
>
> To "comparison shop" the hosting services offered by various Internet service providers, go to the list of ISPs at:
>
> `http://thelist.com/`

Prices for a business site start well under $100 per month, but you usually pay more when lots of people start viewing your pages. For a site with about a hundred different Web pages, I have paid as little as $40 per month when a few thousand people looked at my pages, and as much as $2,000 per month when hundreds of thousands of people looked at my pages.

JUST A MINUTE

> One of the most important choices you'll need to make when you set up a Web site is the name you want to use as the address of the site.
>
> If you aren't willing to pay $100 up front and $50 a year to maintain your own domain name, the address of your site will include the name of your Internet service provider (example: `http://www.shore.net/~smith/`). If you're willing to pay for it, you can pick any name that isn't already in use by another company (example: `http://mister-smith.com/`).
>
> You can check to see if the name you want is already in use at
>
> `http://domain-registration.com/`
>
> (Or you can just enter the name in your Web browser to see if you get a page.) Once you find a name that isn't already taken, ask your Internet service provider to help you apply for that name as soon as possible.

Transferring Pages to a Web Server

When a Web server computer sends Web pages to people through the Internet, it uses an information exchange standard called Hypertext Transfer Protocol (HTTP). To upload a page to your Web site, however, you need software that uses an older communications standard called File Transfer Protocol (FTP).

NEW TERM *File Transfer Protocol* is the standard that your file transfer software must adhere to when sending files to a Web server. The server then sends those files out to anyone who asks for them using the Hypertext Transfer Protocol.

Netscape Navigator can receive files using both the HTTP and FTP standards. It can also send files using FTP, so you can use it to upload your pages to a Web server. Follow these steps:

1. Enter the address of your Web directory in Netscape Navigator's Location box, as in the following example:

   `ftp://myname:mypassword@myisp.net/home/web/wherever/`

   Put your username and password for accessing the site instead of *myname* and *mypassword*, your Internet service provider's address instead of *myisp.net*, and the top-level directory where your Web pages reside instead of */home/web/wherever/*.

4

2. Drag the icons for the HTML and graphics files you want to upload from any Windows 95 file management program (such as Windows Explorer) into the Netscape Navigator window.

3. A dialog box appears and asks you whether you want to upload the files. Click OK, and wait while the files are transferred.

4. Test your page by clicking on the HTML file you just uploaded in the FTP directory listing (in the Netscape window). You're on the Web!

Even though Netscape Navigator 2.0 or 3.0 can send files to any Web server on the Internet, specialized FTP programs such as WS_FTP or CuteFTP offer much more control for managing your Web pages. For example, Navigator doesn't give you any way to delete an old Web page that you want to get rid of, or change the name of a Web page on the server computer. You'll definitely want a specialized FTP program to maintain your Web site.

Figure 4.1 shows one of the most popular FTP programs, CuteFTP for Windows. You can download a free copy of CuteFTP (see the following "To Do:" section), though CuteFTP does require a modest registration fee for business users. (See the documentation that comes with the program for details.)

Similar programs are available for Macintosh computers (Fetch is a popular favorite), and FTP utilities come pre-installed on most UNIX computers. You can find these and other FTP programs at http://www.shareware.com.

Figure 4.1.

CuteFTP is a powerful and user-friendly FTP program that individuals can use for free.

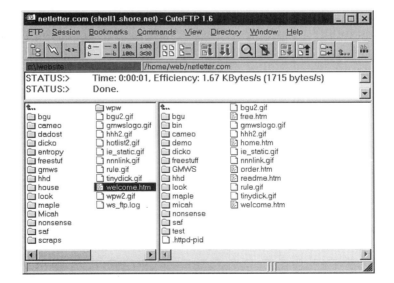

To Do:

I recommend that you download CuteFTP now and use it to send some files to your own Web site as you read on (if you have a Web site set up, that is).

☐ Go to the CuteFTP home page at `http://www.cuteftp.com/` and follow the Download CuteFTP links.

☐ Once the download is complete, run the self-extracting `.exe` program, which will install the CuteFTP program.

No matter which FTP program you choose, transferring your Web pages to a Web server involves the following steps. (The steps are illustrated here with CuteFTP, but other FTP programs work similarly.)

1. Before you can access the Web server, you must tell your FTP program its address, as well as your account name and password. In CuteFTP, select a category for your site in the FTP Site Manager window (Personal FTP Sites in Figure 4.2), and click Add site to access the FTP Site Edit dialog box in Figure 4.3.

Figure 4.2.

CuteFTP includes an intuitive FTP Site Manager, though most Web page authors only need a single FTP site entry.

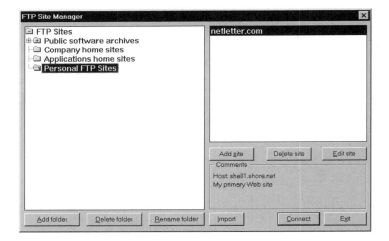

Figure 4.3.

Clicking on Add site or Edit site in Figure 4.2 brings up this dialog box.

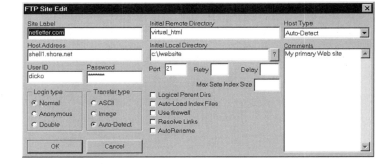

4

2. Here's how to fill in each of the items in Figure 4.3.

   Site Label is the name you'll use to refer to your own site. Nobody else will see this name, so enter whatever you want.

   Host Address is the FTP address of the Web server that you need to send your Web pages to. This usually (but not always) starts with ftp. Notice that it may or may not resemble the address that other people will use to view your Web pages. The Internet service provider that runs your Web server will be able to tell you the correct address to enter here.

   User ID and Password are also issued by the company that runs the Web server. Be aware that CuteFTP (and most other FTP programs) will remember your password automatically, which means that anyone who has physical access to your computer may be able to modify your Web site.

   You should set the Login type to Normal unless somebody important tells you otherwise. (The Anonymous setting is for downloading files from public FTP services that don't require user IDs or passwords.)

   Set the Transfer type to Auto-Detect. (This will automatically send HTML and other text files using a slightly different protocol than images and other non-text files, to ensure complete compatibility with all types of computers.)

   For the Initial Remote Directory, fill in the name of the main directory folder on the Web server where your Web pages will be located. The people who run your Web server will tell you the name of that directory. (In some cases, you don't need to enter anything here, because the Web server computer will automatically put you in the directory when you connect to it.)

   For the Initial Local Directory, enter the drive and directory folder on your computer's hard drive, where you keep your Web pages.

   Normally, you won't need to change the Port, Retry, Delay, Max Safe Index Size, and Host Type settings unless you experience problems with your connection. If that happens, have your service provider help you figure out the best settings. You should also make sure that Use firewall and the other check box options are unchecked unless someone in the know says to check them.

   You can enter any Comments or reminders to yourself that you like. Only you will see them.

3. When you click OK, you'll go back to the window shown in Figure 4.2. Make sure you are connected to the Internet, and click Connect to establish a connection with the Web server computer.

   Most server computers issue a short message to everyone who connects to them. Many FTP programs ignore this message, but CuteFTP presents it to you as shown in Figure 4.4. It seldom says anything important, so just click OK.

Figure 4.4.

CuteFTP displays the "boilerplate" message that some server computers send whenever you connect to them.

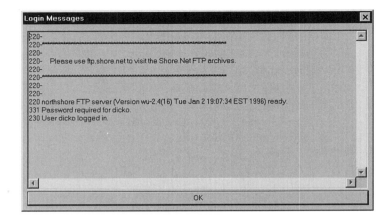

4. Once you're connected to the server, you'll see two lists of files, as shown earlier in Figure 4.1. The left window pane lists the files on your computer, while the right pane lists the files on the server computer.

   To transfer a Web page to the server, select the HTML file and any accompanying image files in the left window. (Remember that you can hold down the Ctrl key and click the mouse to select multiple files in any Windows program.) Then select Commands | Upload, as in Figure 4.5, or click on the Upload button on the toolbar.

   As you can see, the same menu contains commands to delete or rename files (on either your computer or the server), as well as commands to make and change directory folders.

TIME SAVER

Most Web servers have a special name for the file that should be sent if someone doesn't include a specific filename when they request a page. For example, if you go to http://netletter.com/, my Web server will automatically give you the welcome.htm file. Other Web servers use different names for the default file, such as index.html.

Be sure to ask your service provider the default filename so you can give your home page that name.

4

Figure 4.5.
To send files to the server, select Commands | Upload in CuteFTP.

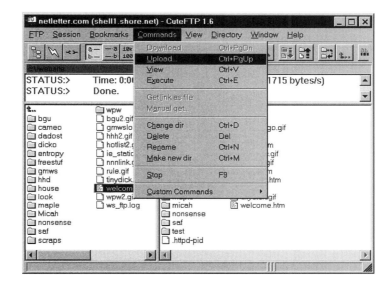

5. That's all there is to it! In most cases, you can immediately view the page you just put on the Web server using Netscape Navigator (see Figure 4.6) or Microsoft Internet Explorer.

Figure 4.6.
Most Web servers make pages immediately available on the Internet seconds after you upload them.

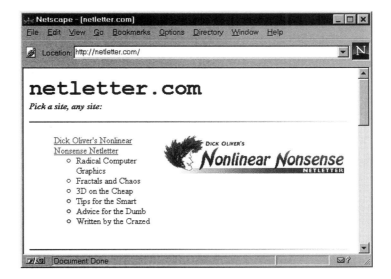

6. When you're done sending and modifying files on the Web server, select FTP | Disconnect to close the connection.

The next time you need to upload some Web pages, you won't need to fill in all the information in step 2. You can just click Connect, select the pages you want to send, and click on the Upload button.

JUST A MINUTE

> Most Web servers are set up so that any documents placed onto them are immediately made available to the entire World Wide Web. However, some require that users manually change file permission settings, which control who is allowed to access individual files. Your Internet service provider can tell you exactly how to change permission settings on their server and whether it's necessary to do so.

Putting Web Pages on an Intranet

The procedure outlined above for sending pages to a public Internet server is fairly standard. But the internal workings of private corporate intranets vary considerably from company to company. In some cases, you may need to use an FTP program to send files to an intranet server. In others, you may be able to transfer files using the same file management program you use on your own computer. You may also need to adjust permission settings, or make special allowances for the firewall that insulates a private intranet from the public Internet.

About all I can tell you here in this book about putting files on your company's intranet is to consult with your systems administrator. He can help you put your Web pages on the company server in the way that best ensures their accessibility and security.

Testing Your Pages

Whenever you transfer Web pages to a disk, Internet site, or intranet server, you should immediately test every page thoroughly.

The following checklist will help you make sure everything on your pages behaves the way you expected.

1. Before you transfer the pages, follow all of these ten steps to test the pages while they're on your hard drive. After you transfer the pages to the master disk or Web server, test them again—preferably through a 28.8Kbps modem connection, if your pages are on the Internet.

2. Do each of the following steps with the latest version of Netscape Navigator, the latest Microsoft Internet Explorer, and at least one older browser such as DOS Lynx or Netscape Navigator 2.0.

3. Make sure the computer you're testing with is set to a 16-color video mode, or at most a 256-color mode. (Pages look better in higher color modes, but you want to see the "bad news" of how they'll look to most people.)

4. If possible, use a computer with 800×600 resolution for testing purposes, but adjust the size of the browser window to exactly 640×480 pixels. On each page, use the Maximize button on the corner of the window to switch back and forth between full 800×600 resolution and 640×480 resolution. If pages look good at these two resolutions, they'll probably look fine at larger resolutions, too. (Additional testing at 1024×768 or 1600×1200 resolution isn't a bad idea, though.)

5. Turn off auto image loading in Netscape Navigator before you start testing, so you can see what each page looks like without the graphics. Check your ALT tag messages, then hit the Load Images button on the toolbar to load the graphics and review the page carefully again.

6. Use Microsoft Internet Explorer's Font Size button (the big A on the toolbar) to look at each page at all font sizes, to ensure that your careful layout doesn't fall to pieces.

7. Start at the home page and systematically follow every link. (Use the Back button to return after each link, then click the next link on the page.)

8. Wait for each page to completely finish loading, and scroll down all the way to make sure all images appear where they should.

9. If you have a complex site, it may help to make a checklist of all the pages on your site to make sure they are all tested.

10. Time how long it takes each page to load through a 28.8Kbps modem, preferably when connected through a different Internet service provider than the one who runs the Web server. Then multiply that time by two to find out how long 14.4Kbps modem users will need to wait to see the page. Is the information on that page valuable enough to keep them from hitting the Stop button and going elsewhere before the page finishes loading?

If your pages pass all those tests, then you can be pretty certain that they'll look great to every Internet surfer in the world.

Summary

This chapter gave you the basic knowledge you need to choose between the most common distribution methods for Web pages. It also guided you through the process of placing Web pages on a Web server computer using freely available file transfer software. Finally, it offered a checklist to help you thoroughly test your Web pages once they are in place.

Q&A

Q **When I try to send pages to my Web site from home, it works fine, but when I try it from the computer at work, I get error messages. Any idea what the problem might be?**

A The company where you work probably has a *firewall*, which is a layer of security protecting their local network from tampering via the Internet. You will need to set some special configuration options in your FTP program to help it get through the firewall when you send files. Your company's network administrator can help you with the details.

Q **I don't know which Internet service provider to pick to host my pages—there are so many! How do I choose?**

A Obviously, you should compare prices of the companies listed at `http://thelist.com` that provide hosting services, but you should also ask for the names of some customers with sites about the same size as you plan yours to be, and ask them (via e-mail) how happy they are with the company's service and support. Also, make sure that your provider has at least two major (T3 or bigger) links to the Internet, preferably provided to them by two different network companies.

Q **All the tests you recommend would take longer than creating my pages! Can't I get away with less testing?**

A If your pages aren't intended to make money or provide an important service, then it's probably not a big deal if they look funny to some people or produce errors once in a while. In that case, just test each page with a couple of different window and font sizes and call it good. However, if you need to project a professional image, there is no substitute for rigorous testing.

Q **I wanted to name my site `jockitch.com`, but Proctor and Gamble beat me to it. Is there anything I can do?**

A Well, if your company was named Jockitch, Inc., before Proctor and Gamble registered the word as a trademark, you could always try suing them. (Good luck.) Yet even if you don't have the budget to take on their lawyer army, there may be hope. Many new three-letter extensions for site names will probably soon be approved for use, so you may be able to get `jockitch.inc` or `jockitch.biz` (if P&G doesn't scoop you again).

4

Quiz

Questions

1. How do you put a few Web pages on a floppy disk?

2. Suppose your Internet service provider tells you to put your pages in the /top/ user/~elroy directory at ftp.bigisp.net, your username is elroy, and your password is rastro. You have the Web pages all ready to go in the \webpages folder on your C drive. Where do you put all that information in CuteFTP so you can get the files on the Internet?

3. What address would you enter in Netscape Navigator to view the Web pages you uploaded in Question 2?

4. If the following Web page is named mypage.htm, which files would you need to transfer to the Web server to put it on the Internet?

```
<HTML><HEAD><TITLE>My Page</TITLE></HEAD>
<BODY BACKGROUND="joy.gif">
<IMG SRC="me.jpg" ALIGN="right">
<H1>My Web Page</H1> Oh happy joy I have a page on the Web!<P>
<A HREF="otherpage.htm">Click here for my other page.</A>
</BODY></HTML>
```

Answers

1. Just copy the HTML files and image files from your hard drive to the disk. Anyone can then insert the disk in his computer, start his Web browser, and open the pages right from the floppy.

2. Click Add site in the FTP Site Manager window, then enter the information like this:

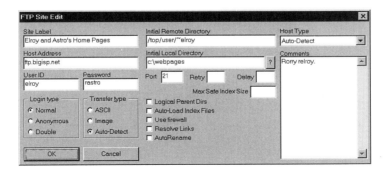

3. You can't tell from the information given in Question 2. A good guess would be `http://www.bigisp.net/~elroy/`, but you might choose a completely different domain name, such as `http://elroy-and-astro.com/`.

4. You would need to transfer all three of the following files into the same directory on the Web server:

   ```
   mypage.htm
   joy.jpg
   me.gif
   ```

   If you want the link on that page to work, you must also transfer `otherpage.htm` (and any image files that are referred to in that HTML file).

Activities

☐ So put your pages on the Internet already!

4

PART

II

Web Page Text

Hour

Hour **5**

Text Formatting and Alignment

As you discovered in Chapter 2, "Creating a Web Page," making your Web page can be as easy as typing some text and adding a few standard HTML tags to the beginning and end. In that chapter, you learned how to emphasize important text with headings. You also saw how to use paragraph breaks, line breaks, and horizontal rules to separate sections of text.

In this chapter, you will learn to control the appearance and arrangement of text on your pages. You'll learn to incorporate boldface, italics, and other special text formatting into your pages. You'll also see how to center text or align it to the right side of the page.

To do these things, you'll need a few more HTML tags. You'll also need to learn how to control optional settings (called *attributes*) for some of the tags you already know.

To Do:

Before you proceed, you should get some text to work with so you can practice formatting it as you read this chapter.

- ☐ Any text will do, but try to find (or type) some text that you want to put onto a Web page. The text from a company brochure or your personal resumé might be a good choice.
- ☐ If the text is from a word processor file, be sure to save it as plain text or ASCII text before you add any HTML tags.
- ☐ Add the `<HTML>`, `<HEAD>`, `<TITLE>`, and `<BODY>` tags (discussed in Chapter 2) before you use the tags introduced in this chapter to format the body text.

Emphasizing Text with Boldface and Italics

Way back in the age of the typewriter, we were content with plain text and an occasional underline for emphasis. But today, **boldface** and *italicized* text have become "de rigueur" in all paper communication. Naturally, you can add bold and italic text to your Web pages, too.

For boldface text, put the `<B>` tag at the beginning of the text and `</B>` at the end. Similarly, you can make any text italic by enclosing it between `<I>` and `</I>`. If you want bold italics, put `<B><I>` in front of it and `</I></B>` after it. You can also use italics within headings, but boldface usually won't show in headings because they are already bold.

The news article in Figure 5.1 uses the `<B>` and `<I>` tags extensively, and Figure 5.2 shows the resulting text as it appears in Netscape Navigator.

JUST A MINUTE

There are actually two ways to make text display as boldface; the `<B>` tag and the `<STRONG>` tag do the same thing in most Web browsers. Likewise, all popular browsers today interpret both `<I>` and `<EM>` as italics.

Many purists prefer the `<STRONG>` and `<EM>` tags because they imply only that the text should receive special emphasis, rather than dictating exactly how that effect should be achieved. Meanwhile, the vast majority of Web authors use the shorter and easier-to-remember `<B>` and `<I>` tags. I'll use `<B>` and `<I>` throughout this book, but if you like to be philosophically pure, by all means use `<STRONG>` and `<EM>` instead.

Figure 5.1.

Use the <B> tag for boldface text, and the <I> tag for italics.

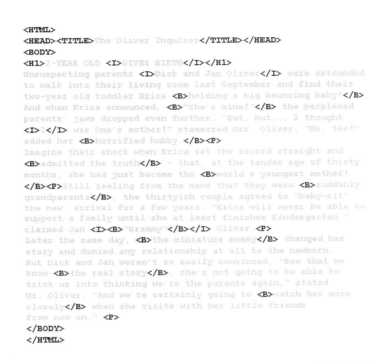

```
<HTML>
<HEAD><TITLE>The Oliver Inquirer</TITLE></HEAD>
<BODY>
<H1>2-YEAR OLD <I>GIVES BIRTH</I></H1>
Unsuspecting parents <I>Dick and Jan Oliver</I> were astounded
to walk into their living room last September and find their
two-year old toddler Erica <B>holding a big bouncing baby!</B>
And when Erica announced, <B>"She's mine!"</B> the perplexed
parents' jaws dropped even further. "But, but... I thought
<I>I</I> was Ona's mother!" stammered Mrs. Oliver. "Me, too!"
added her <B>horrified hubby.</B><P>
Imagine their shock when Erica set the record straight and
<B>admitted the truth</B> - that, at the tender age of thirty
months, she had just become the <B>world's youngest mother!
</B><P>Still reeling from the news that they were <B>suddenly
grandparents</B>, the thirtyish couple agreed to "baby-sit"
the new  arrival for a few years. "Erica will never be able to
support a family until she at least finishes Kindergarten,"
claimed Jan <I><B>"Grammy"</B></I> Oliver <P>
Later the same day, <B>the miniature mommy</B> changed her
story and denied any relationship at all to the newborn.
But Dick and Jan weren't so easily convinced. "Now that we
know <B>the real story</B>, she's not going to be able to
trick us into thinking we're the parents again," stated
Mr. Oliver. "And we're certainly going to <B>watch her more
closely</B> when she visits with her little friends
from now on." <P>
</BODY>
</HTML>
```

Figure 5.2.

The many <B> and <I> tags in Figure 5.1 certainly add plenty of emphasis to this Web page.

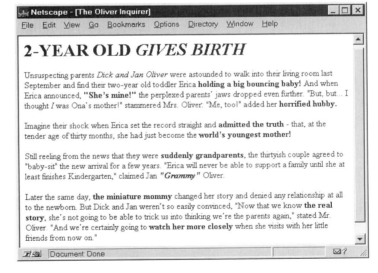

To Do:

Use headings, boldface, and italics to emphasize some of the text on your own Web page.

1. Use <H1>, <H2>, and <H3> to add any headings and sub-headings your page may need. (End each heading with </H1>, </H2>, or </H3>.)

2. If any of the text on your page should be in boldface, mark the beginning of it with <B> and the end with </B>. Use <I> and </I> to mark text to be italicized.

Character Formatting

In addition to <B>, <I>, <EM>, and <STRONG>, there are several other HTML tags for adding special formatting to text. Table 5.1 summarizes all of them (including the boldface and italic tags), and Figures 5.3 and 5.4 demonstrate each of them in action.

Table 5.1. HTML tags that add special formatting to text.

Tag	Function
<SMALL>	Small text
<BIG>	Big text
<SUPER>	Superscript
<SUB>	Subscript
<STRIKE>	Strikethrough (draws a line through text)
<U>	Underline
<TT>	Monospaced (typewriter) font
<PRE>	Monospaced font, preserving spaces and line breaks
<EM> or <I>	Emphasized (italic) text
<STRONG> or <B>	Strong (boldface) text

JUST A MINUTE

Use the <U> tag sparingly, if at all. People expect underlined text to be a link, and may get confused if you underline text that isn't a link.

Figure 5.3.

Each of the tags in Table 5.1 is used in this little poem.

```
<HTML><HEAD><TITLE>Text Test</TITLE></HEAD>
<BODY>
<BASEFONT SIZE=5>
<STRONG>The Script</STRONG><BR>
<EM>a text test</EM><P>
I <TT>typed</TT> a <SUP>super</SUP> script<BR>
of <SMALL>small</SMALL> union <STRIKE>strike</STRIKE> rhymes
<PRE>
s   o       m  y
preformatted
w    o    r    d s</PRE>
<SUB>sub</SUB> for <BIG>big</BIG> picket <U>lines</U>
</BODY></HTML>
```

Figure 5.4.

Here's what all character formatting from Table 5.1 and Figure 5.3 looks like.

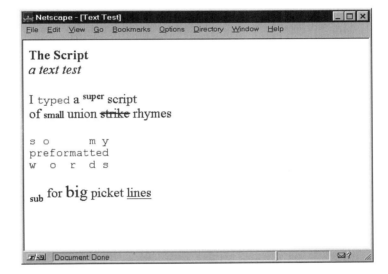

The <TT> tag usually changes the typeface to Courier New, a monospaced font. However, Web browsers let users change the monospaced <TT> font to the typeface of their choice (under Options | General Preferences | Fonts in Netscape Navigator 3.0 and View | Options | General | Font Settings in Microsoft Internet Explorer 3.0). The monospaced font may not even be monospaced for some users. However, the vast majority of people just stick with the standard fonts that their browser comes set up with, so you should design and test your pages with those default fonts, too. (The standard proportional font is usually Times New Roman, and the standard monospaced font is almost always Courier or Courier New.)

The <PRE> tag also causes text to appear in the monospaced font, but it also does something more unique and useful. As you learned in Chapter 2, multiple spaces and line breaks are normally ignored in HTML files. But <PRE> causes exact spacing and line breaks to be preserved. For example, without <PRE> the following text:

```
Qty     Description           Price        Total
1       Rubber chicken        $7.98        $7.98
2       Vibrating fake hand   $14.97       $29.94
12      Plastic cockroaches   $0.25        $3.00
                                           --------
                                           $40.92
```

would look like this:

Qty Description Price Total 1 Rubber chicken $7.98 $7.98 2 Vibrating fake hand $14.97 $29.94 12 Plastic cockroaches $0.25 $3.00 --------$40.92

Even if you added <BR> tags at the end of every line, the columns wouldn't line up properly. However, if you put <PRE> at the beginning of the invoice and </PRE> at the end, the columns would line up properly, and no <BR> tags would be needed.

There are fancier ways to make columns of text line up, and you'll learn all about them in Chapter 16, "Advanced Layout with Tables." The <PRE> tag gives you a quick and easy way to preserve the alignment of any monospaced text files that you might want to transfer to a Web page with a minimum of effort.

TIME SAVER

You can use the <PRE> tag as a quick way to insert vertical space between paragraphs or graphics without having to use a "spacer" image. For example, to put several blank lines between the words "Up" and "Down", you could type:

Up<PRE>

</PRE>Down

Text Alignment

Some HTML tags allow you to specify a variety of options, or *attributes,* along with the basic tag itself. For example, when you begin a paragraph with the <P> tag, you can specify whether the text in that paragraph should be aligned to the left margin, right margin, or center of the page.

To align a paragraph to the right margin, you can put ALIGN="right" inside the <P> tag at the beginning of the paragraph, like this:

```
<P ALIGN="right">
```

5

To center a paragraph, use:

```
<P ALIGN="center">
```

Similarly, the tag to align a paragraph to the left is:

```
<P ALIGN="left">
```

The word ALIGN is called an attribute of the <P> tag. You can use the ALIGN attribute with just about any HTML tag that contains text, including <H1>, <H2>, the other heading tags, and some tags you will meet later. There are many other attributes besides ALIGN. You will find out how to use them as you learn more HTML tags.

New Term *Attributes* are special code words used inside an HTML tag to control exactly what the tag does.

Just a Minute

> Keep in mind that sometimes the same attribute word can have different meanings when used with different tags. For instance, you will discover in Chapter 9, "Putting Images on a Web Page," that ALIGN="left" does something quite different when used with the <IMG> image tag than it does with the text tags discussed in this chapter.

When you want to set the alignment of more than one paragraph or heading at a time, you can use the ALIGN attribute with the <DIV>, or *division,* tag. By itself, <DIV> and its corresponding closing tag </DIV> actually don't do anything at all—which would seem to make it a peculiarly useless tag!

Yet if you include an ALIGN attribute, <DIV> becomes quite useful indeed. Everything you put between <DIV ALIGN="center"> and </DIV>, for example, will be centered. This may include lines of text, paragraphs, headings, images and all the other things that you'll learn how to put on Web pages in upcoming chapters. Likewise, <DIV ALIGN="right"> will right-align everything down to the next </DIV> tag.

5

Just a Minute

> When you look at Web pages that other people have created, you may see <CENTER> and </CENTER> used to center text. The <CENTER> tag is officially obsolete, and it may not work with future Web browsers, so you should always use <DIV ALIGN="center"> and </DIV> instead.

Figure 5.5 demonstrates the ALIGN attribute with both the <P> and <DIV> tags. <DIV ALIGN= "center"> is used to center two headings and some text at the top of the page, and all three ALIGN options are used with <P> tags to alter the alignment of the verse. The results are shown in Figure 5.6.

Figure 5.5.

The ALIGN *attribute allows you to left-justify, right-justify, or center text.*

```
<HTML>
<HEAD><TITLE>Tommy Thumb's Pretty Song Book </TITLE></HEAD>
<BODY>
<DIV ALIGN="center">
<H3>Selections from </H3>
<H2>Tommy Thumb's Pretty Song Book</H2>
<I>Published in 1744</I>
</DIV>
<P ALIGN="left">
I'll tell you a Story<BR>
Of Jacky Nory,<BR>
Will you have it now or anon?
<P ALIGN="center">
I will tell you another,<BR>
Of Jack and his Brother,
<P ALIGN="right">
And my Story's done.
</BODY>
</HTML>
```

Figure 5.6.

The alignment settings in Figure 5.5, as they appear in a Web browser.

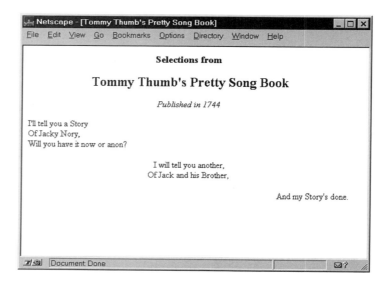

5

TIME SAVER

Whenever you don't use an ALIGN attribute, text will be aligned to the left. Therefore, there's usually no point in wasting your time typing ALIGN="left". For example, using <P> instead of <P ALIGN="left"> for the first paragraph in Figure 5.5 would have resulted in exactly the same Web page in Figure 5.6.

One place where you would need ALIGN="left" is when you want to left-align a single heading or paragraph within a larger region that has been centered or right-justified with <DIV ALIGN="center"> or <DIV ALIGN="right">.

For example, if you changed the <H2> tag in Figure 5.5 to <H2 ALIGN="left">, Tommy Thumb's Pretty Song Book would be left-aligned while Selections from and Published in 1744 would both still be centered.

COFFEE BREAK

To see how centering and text formatting can improve the look of a page, compare the new *24-Hour HTML Café* home page to the older versions introduced in previous chapters. The new page is:

http://www.mcp.com/sams/books/235-8/cafe5.htm

Summary

This chapter showed you how to make text appear as boldface, italic, or with other special formatting, such as superscripts, subscripts, or strikethrough text. You saw how to make everything line up properly in preformatted passages of monospaced text.

Finally, you learned that attributes are used to specify options and special behavior of many HTML tags, and you also learned to use the ALIGN attribute to center or right-justify text.

Table 5.2 summarizes the tags and attributes discussed in this chapter.

5

Table 5.2. HTML tags and attributes covered in Chapter 5.

Tag	Attribute	Function
`<EM>...</EM>`		Emphasis (usually italic).
`<STRONG>...</STRONG>`		Stronger emphasis (usually bold).
`<B>...</B>`		Boldface text.
`<I>...</I>`		Italic text.
`<TT>...</TT>`		Typewriter (monospaced) font.
`<PRE>...</PRE>`		Preformatted text (exact line endings and spacing will be preserved—usually rendered in a monospaced font).
`<BIG>...</BIG>`		Text is slightly larger than normal.
`<SMALL>...</SMALL>`		Text is slightly smaller than normal.
`<SUB>...</SUB>`		Subscript.
`<SUP>...</SUP>`		Superscript.
`<STRIKE>...</STRIKE>`		Puts a strikethrough line in text.
`<DIV>...</DIV>`		A region of text to be formatted.
	`ALIGN="..."`	Align text to CENTER, LEFT, or RIGHT. (May also be used with `<P>`, `<H1>`, `<H2>`, `<H3>`, and so on.)

Q&A

Q Other books talk about some text formatting tags that you didn't cover in this chapter, such as `<CODE>` and `<ADDRESS>`. Shouldn't I know about them?

A There are a number of tags in HTML to indicate what kind of information is contained in some text. The `<ADDRESS>` tag, for example, was supposed to be put around addresses. The only visible effect of `<ADDRESS>` in most browsers, however, is that the text is made italic. So Web page authors today usually just use the `<I>` tag instead. Similarly, `<CODE>` and `<KBD>` do essentially the same thing as `<TT>`. You may also read about `<VAR>`, `<SAMP>`, or `<DFN>` in some older HTML references, but nobody uses them in ordinary Web pages.

Q Some HTML pages I've seen use `ALIGN=CENTER` or `ALIGN=center` instead of `ALIGN="center"`. Which is correct?

A As with tags, it generally makes no difference whether attributes are in lowercase or uppercase. It also usually doesn't matter if you include the quotes around attribute

5

values like center. The only time you really do need the quotes is when the value contains a blank space or a character that has special meaning in HTML. In this book, I always include the quotes so that neither I nor you need to worry about when they're needed and when they're not.

Q **You mentioned that `<DIV ALIGN="center">` is a new tag that replaces the old `<CENTER>` tag. Won't my pages be incompatible with older Web browsers if I use the new tag?**

A Yes, but in practice the only incompatibility will be that some text appears left-aligned instead of centered. If this deeply concerns you, you can use both the old and new tags, like this:

```
<DIV ALIGN="center"><CENTER>This text will be centered in both old and new
browsers.</CENTER></DIV>.
```

Quiz

Questions

1. Write the HTML to produce the following:

   Come for ~~cheap~~ free H_2O on May 7th at 9:00PM

2. What's the difference between the following two lines of HTML?

   ```
   Deep <TT>S p a a c e</TT> Quest
   ```

   ```
   Deep <PRE>S p a a c e</PRE> Quest
   ```

3. What's the easiest way to center a single paragraph or heading?

4. How would you center everything on an entire page?

Answers

1. ```
   Come for <STRIKE>cheap</STRIKE> free H<SUB>2</SUB>O on May 7<SUPER><U>th</
   U></SUPER> at 9:00<SMALL>PM</SMALL>
   ```

2. The line using `<TT>` will look like this:

   ```
   Deep S p a a c e Quest
   ```

   The line using `<PRE>` will produce the following lines of text on the Web page (`<PRE>` always skips a line before and after the preformatted text):

   ```
   Deep
   S p a a c e
   Quest
   ```
   ```

3. Start it with `<P ALIGN="center">` (or `<H1 ALIGN="center">`, and so on).

4. Put `<DIV ALIGN="center">` immediately after the `<BODY>` tag at the top of the page, and `</DIV>` just before the `</BODY>` tag at the end of the page.

Activities

☐ Professional typesetters use small capitals for the "AM" and "PM" in clock times. They also use superscripts for dates like the "7th" or "1st". Use the `<SMALL>` and `<SUPER>` tags to typeset important dates and times correctly on your Web pages.

Hour 6

Font Control and Special Characters

This chapter gives you the power to decide what size, color, and typeface should be used to display any text on your Web pages. It also shows you how to create special symbols, such as the copyright mark and European language characters such as the é in Café.

Font Size and Color

To set the size and color of any text on a Web page, use the `<FONT>` tag:

```
<FONT SIZE=5 COLOR="purple">This text will be big and purple.</FONT>
```

The SIZE attribute can take any value from 1 (tiny) to 7 (fairly big), with 3 being the normal default size.

The COLOR attribute can take any of the following standard color names: black, white, red, green, blue, yellow, aqua, fuchsia, gray, lime, maroon, purple, navy, olive, silver, or teal.

JUST A MINUTE

The <BIG> and <SMALL> tags discussed in Chapter 5, "Text Formatting and Alignment," produce effects that you can also achieve with <FONT SIZE>. <FONT SIZE> gives you more precise control over the size, but <BIG> and <SMALL> may work with some older browsers that don't support the <FONT> tag.

The actual size and exact color of the fonts will depend on each reader's screen resolution and preference settings, but you can be assured that SIZE=6 will be a lot bigger than SIZE=2, and that COLOR="red" will certainly show its fire.

JUST A MINUTE

You'll learn more about controlling the color of the text on your pages in Chapter 13, "Backgrounds and Color Control." That chapter also shows you how to create your own custom colors and control the color of text links.

Choosing a Typeface

With the 3.0 versions of both Navigator and Internet Explorer, Netscape and Microsoft have added another extremely powerful form of font control: the <FONT FACE> attribute. This allows you to specify the actual typeface that should be used to display text—and has been the source of much rejoicing among Webmasters who are *awfully* sick of Times and Courier!

The page in Figures 6.1 and 6.2 uses these font controls to present a warmly welcoming homestyle site.

The code to set the typeface used for the headings in Figure 6.1 is:

```
<FONT FACE="Copperplate Gothic Bold" SIZE=5 COLOR="red">
```

If Netscape Navigator or Microsoft Internet Explorer can find a font named Copperplate Gothic Bold on a user's system, that font is used. Otherwise, they will use the default font (usually Times New Roman). Browsers other than Navigator 3.0 and Internet Explorer 3.0 will ignore the FONT FACE attribute and display the fonts they always use.

You can also specify a "second choice" font, for people who don't have your first choice font installed on their computer. For example, I used the following tag to choose the body text in Figure 6.1:

```
<FONT FACE="Lucida Handwriting, Comic Sans MS" SIZE=4 COLOR="maroon">
```

6

Figure 6.1.

The <FONT> tags give you control over the size, color, and typeface of any text.

```
<HTML>
<HEAD><TITLE>Maple Syrup from Sandiwood Farm</TITLE></HEAD>
<BODY>
<FONT FACE="Copperplate Gothic Bold" SIZE=6 COLOR="red">
Pure Maple Syrup<BR>
<FONT SIZE=5>A Vermont Tradition</FONT></FONT><P>
<FONT FACE="Lucida Handwriting, Comic Sans MS"
 SIZE=4 COLOR="maroon">
Every spring, when the snow turns to the texture of granulated
sugar and the warm morning sun melts the frost on the window
panes, the sugar maples come out of their long winter's sleep.
The result is one of Nature's most sumptous delights - fresh
maple sap, boiled down to a thick, rich syrup as sweet as
springtime itself.<P>
<FONT FACE="Copperplate Gothic Bold" SIZE=5 COLOR="red">
A Wholesome, Healthy Treat</FONT><P>
Vermont maple syrup is healthier and lower in calories than
refined sugar, and is better for the planet since it involves
less industrial waste in its production. We invite you to
<A HREF="http://netletter.com/maple/syrup.htm">
see how our family produces syrup at Sandiwood farm.</A><P>
</BODY></HTML>
```

Figure 6.2.

If you have the Copperplate Gothic Bold and Lucida Handwriting fonts installed on your computer, they will be used to display the page in Figure 6.1.

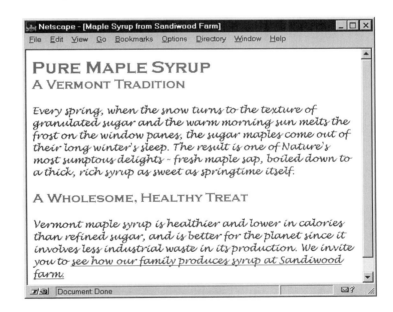

Anyone who has Comic Sans MS (a very common font) installed, but doesn't have Lucida Handwriting (a slightly less common font), will see the body text as it appears in Figure 6.3.

Figure 6.3 also shows what the headings look like to people who don't have the Copperplate Gothic Bold font.

Figure 6.3.

Someone without the two fonts specified in Figure 6.1 (but with Comic Sans MS) would see this instead of Figure 6.2.

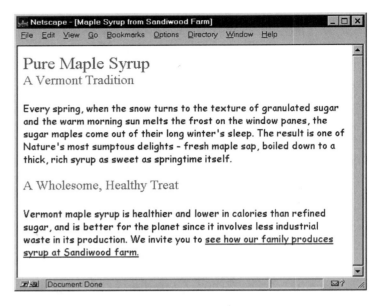

Currently, only fonts that each user happens to have on his or her system will show up, and you have no control over which fonts are installed. Furthermore, the exact spelling of the font names is important, and many common fonts go by several slightly different names. Extensions to HTML will soon support a new, highly compact font format that can be automatically downloaded along with your pages to solve these problems. For now, you just have to stick to the most common fonts and make sure your pages still look acceptable in Times New Roman.

Figure 6.4 shows the most common TrueType fonts, many of which are also available in PostScript format. Microsoft offers a number of these fonts available for free download from this site:

```
http://www.microsoft.com/truetype/
```

Microsoft has also included these fonts (and variations on them) in Windows and other popular software packages, as indicated in Figure 6.4.

TIME SAVER

To make all the text in Figure 6.4 larger, I put <BASEFONT SIZE=5> just after the <BODY> tag. (I did the same thing in Figure 6.5, too.) <BASEFONT> is just a time-saving tag for setting the overall size of all text in a document. The size of all headings will also be relative to the <BASEFONT SIZE>. This tag can't take any attributes other than SIZE, and doesn't require a closing </BASEFONT> tag.

6

Figure 6.4.

*The most popular
TrueType fonts are good
bets for inclusion in your
Web pages. (Arial is
especially reliable.)*

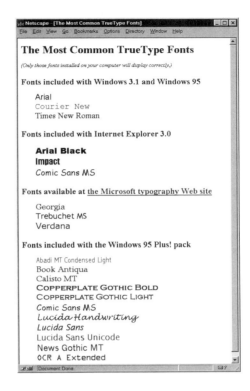

If you want to use a font on your Web page that isn't on this list, don't be afraid to do so! The user will never see an error message if the font can't be found; the worst thing that could happen is that the user won't see your special font, but will still see the text in the next best font that can be found. If one of the fonts in Figure 6.4 has a similar feel to the one you want, include it as a "second choice" as I did with Comic Sans MS in the preceding example.

To Do:

All the Web pages associated with a single "site" should usually use the same fonts and text color scheme. You don't need to be a professional typographer to make good font choices if you follow the guidelines below.

If you are a professional typographer, you know how to break these rules and still make a page look great. If you try to deviate from them without much experience, however, your pages are likely to stand out as very "unprofessional" looking, even to people who can't articulate exactly why.

☐ Always choose a typeface with *serifs* (those little beveled points on the edges of the letters) for the main body of your text. The serif typefaces that a significant number of people are likely to have installed are Times New Roman, Georgia, Book Antiqua, and Calisto MT.

☐ For headings, choose a heavy typeface without serifs, such as Arial Black, Impact, or Copperplate Gothic Bold. For captions and other short passages of text, either use your body text font or a "light" version of your heading font, such as Arial or Copperplate Gothic Light.

Medium-weight fonts without serifs are suitable for both headings and short passages of text. These include Arial, Trebuchet MS, Verdana, Lucida Sans, Lucida Sans Unicode, and News Gothic MT.

☐ Use one color for all body text, and either the same color or a "stronger" complementary color for all headings and captions. Unless you are an experienced graphics designer, stay with a dark color such as black, blue, maroon, olive, or purple for body text, and put it on a contrasting, light background. If you want a wilder color, headings (and graphics images) are the best place for it.

☐ Use ornamental fonts like Comic Sans MS, Lucida Handwriting, and OCR A Extended very sparingly and for main headings or highly stylistic pages only. Better yet, reserve these fonts for use in graphics images where you can also accent them with textures, shadows, or other effects.

☐ If your company has a standard set of TrueType or PostScript fonts for all communications, specify those fonts as the first choice in your `<FONT FACE>` tags. However, you should always include one or two "second choice" fonts from Figure 6.4 as well.

Special Characters

Most fonts now include special characters for European languages, such as the accented e in Café. There are also a few mathematical symbols and special punctuation marks such as the circular • bullet.

You can insert these special characters at any point in an HTML document by looking up the appropriate codes in Table 6.1. (This table includes only the most commonly used codes for English-language usage. You'll find a complete table of all special characters for European language fonts in Appendix B, "HTML Quick Reference.")

For example, the word Café would look like this:

```
Caf&#233;
```

6

Each symbol also has a mnemonic name that might be easier to remember than the number. Another way to write Café, for instance, is:

```
Caf&eacute;
```

Notice that there are also codes for the angle brackets (< >), quote symbol ("), and ampersand (&) in Table 6.1. You need to use the codes if you want these symbols to appear on your pages, because the Web browser will otherwise interpret them as HTML commands.

In Figures 6.5 and 6.6, several more of the symbols from Table 6.1 and Appendix B are shown in use.

Figure 6.5.

Special character codes begin with &# and end with ;.

```
<HTML><HEAD><TITLE>International Alphabet</TITLE></HEAD>
<BODY>
<H1>The International Alphabet</H1>
<H2>A, B, C, D, E, F, G <BR>
and then there's &Aring; &Ccedil; &Egrave; and &Eacute;<BR>
H, I, and &Iuml; (did I forget &ETH;?) <BR>
J, K, L, M, N, O, P, <BR>
I mean N, &Ntilde; O, &Otilde; and &Ouml;<BR>
(oh, and &Ocirc; and &Oslash; too.) <BR>
P, Q, R, S, T, U, V, <BR>
and &Ucirc; and &Uacute; and (um, let's see...)<BR>
W, X, Y, &Yacute; and Z.</H2>
</BODY></HTML>
```

Figure 6.6.

This is how the HTML page in Figure 6.5 will look in most (not all) Web browsers.

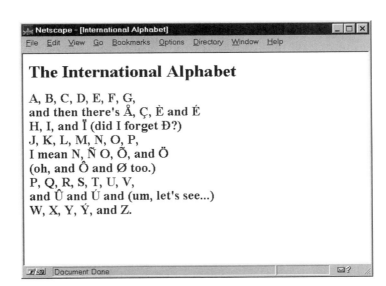

TIME SAVER

Looking for the copyright (©) or registered trademark (®) symbols? The codes you need are © and ® respectively.

To create an unregistered trademark (™) symbol, use <SUPER>TM</SUPER> or <SMALL><SUPER>TM</SUPER></SMALL> for a smaller version.

Table 6.1 lists some of the special characters you might need to use on your Web page.

Table 6.1. Important special characters.

Character	Numeric Code	Code Name	Description
"	&#34;	&quot;	Quotation mark
&	&#38;	&amp;	Ampersand
<	&#60;	&lt;	Less than
>	&#62;	&gt;	Greater than
¢	&#162;	&cent;	Cent sign
£	&#163;	&pound;	Pound sterling
¦	&#166;	¦ or brkbar;	Broken vertical bar
§	&#167;	&sect;	Section sign
©	&#169;	&copy;	Copyright
®	&#174;	&reg;	Registered trademark
°	&#176;	&deg;	Degree sign
±	&#177;	&plusmn;	Plus or minus
²	&#178;	&sup2;	Superscript two
³	&#179;	&sup3;	Superscript three
·	&#183;	&middot;	Middle dot
¹	&#185;	&sup1;	Superscript one
¼	&#188;	&frac14;	Fraction one-fourth
½	&#189;	&frac12;	Fraction one-half
¾	&#190;	&frac34;	Fraction three-fourths
Æ	&#198;	&AElig;	Capital AE ligature
æ	&#230;	&aelig;	Small ae ligature
É	&#201;	&Eacute;	Accented capital E
é	&#233;	&eacute;	Accented small e
×	&#215;		Multiply sign
÷	&#247;		Division sign

JUST A MINUTE

Some older Web browsers will not display many of the special characters in Table 6.1. Some fonts may also not include all of these characters.

See Table B.1 in Appendix B for a complete list of special symbols and European language characters.

The Future of Web Fonts

There are two major advances in the works which promise to revolutionize Web page typography. Neither of these advances is ready for widespread use today, but you should be aware of them and plan on learning about them when the revolution hits.

Cascading Style Sheets (CSS) will be part of the next HTML standard, but they work very differently from normal HTML. You will be able to create a special document containing only information about the fonts and formatting to be used on a Web page. This document, called a *style sheet*, can then be linked to any number of Web pages so they will all have a consistent style.

Style sheets offer two huge time-saving advantages. Because a single style sheet may control the appearance of many pages, you can change the look and feel of your entire Web site just by changing a single style sheet. For complex Web sites, this might save you from spending hours modifying each page individually. The second big advantage of style sheets is that they will allow more precise control over the appearance of your pages than any previous version of HTML. You will be able to set the exact line spacing, font metrics, margins, and paragraph indentation for any text. You'll also have the ability to put colored boxes behind any text, and wield more control over multiple-column text than you can today.

When you want a document, or a part of a document, to be a little different, you can put style information at any point in that document to override part of its style sheet. (The idea is that styles "cascade" down from the style sheet to the document, and then to specific parts of the document. At any point in that cascade, new styles may "flow in." That's why they're called "cascading style sheets.")

6

JUST A MINUTE

If you'd like to start learning about style sheets today, Microsoft Internet Explorer 3.0 supports some of the simpler aspects of HTML style sheets. The Internet Explorer Web site at http://www.microsoft.com/ie/ offers a quick style sheet tutorial.

Upcoming versions of Microsoft Internet Explorer and Netscape Navigator promise full support of the new CSS standard.

The other revolutionary advance in typography that's afoot is *font embedding*. This will allow you to retrieve the actual typeface along with a Web page, so even people who don't have the correct font preinstalled on their computer will see it on the page.

There has been a standard for embedding TrueType fonts in documents for a while, but it doesn't yet include some features that are necessary for it to work with Web pages. The most important feature to be added is *font compression*, which minimizes the file size of fonts so they can be transferred over the Internet quickly. Transferring only the letterforms actually used in a document and allowing font publishers to control how the font can be reused are also key features to make font embedding a reality.

The upcoming *OpenType* font standard will also combine both TrueType and PostScript (the two competing font formats) into a single standard.

Support for font embedding should appear in Netscape Navigator and Microsoft Internet Explorer at the same time as style sheet support. These two technologies together will dramatically expand your ability to control the appearance of your Web pages.

COFFEE BREAK

At the *24-Hour HTML Café*, I chose Georgia as the main font for body text. Because I wanted to use fonts that most people don't have installed for headings, I used Paint Shop Pro to render all headings as graphics. When embedded fonts become a reality, I may choose to replace some of the graphics at the Café with regular headings that use the Parisian and Present Script fonts.

In the meantime, check it out at:

http://www.mcp.com/sams/books/235-8/cafe6.htm

(You'll also notice that I used one of the codes discussed under the Special Characters section to finally spell Café with the accent-acute it deserves!)

If you go to the address above and still see most of the text as Times New Roman, you don't have Georgia installed on your computer yet. I highly recommend that you download it from Microsoft by going to http://www.microsoft.com/truetype/ and following the "free Web fonts" link. Georgia will be included with future versions of Microsoft Internet Explorer, and is likely to become a popular font on the Web due to its excellent readability and stylish appearance at low resolutions.

While you're at Microsoft, pick up Verdana, Trebuchet, and whatever new free fonts they have, too. Then go back to the *24-Hour HTML Café* for links to some sample pages that use them.

6

Summary

This chapter has shown you how to control the size, color, and typeface of any section of text on a Web page. This chapter also provided an overview of some exciting advances in font control that are just around the bend, including HTML style sheets and font embedding.

Table 6.2 summarizes all the tags and attributes covered in this chapter. (See Table B.1 in Appendix B for special character codes.)

Table 6.1 Summary of tags and attributes covered in Chapter 6.

Tag	Attribute	Function
`<FONT>...</FONT>`		Controls the appearance of the enclosed text.
	`SIZE="..."`	The size of the font, from 1 to 7. Default is 3. Can also be specified as a value relative to the current size; for example, +2.
	`COLOR="..."`	Changes the color of the text.
	`FACE="..."`	Name of font to use if it can be found on the user's system. Multiple font names can be separated by commas, and the first font on the list that can be found will be used.
`<BASEFONT>`		Sets the default size of the font for the current page.
	`SIZE="..."`	The default size of the font, from 1 to 7.

Q&A

Q How do I find out the exact name for a font that I have on my computer?

A On a Windows or Macintosh computer, open the Control Panel and click on the Fonts folder. The TrueType fonts on your system will be listed. Use the exact spelling of font names when specifying them in the `<FONT FACE>` tag. Windows 95 users can view all the characters in any font with the Character Map utility, usually located in the Accessories folder.

To find the name of PostScript fonts in Windows if you use Adobe Type Manager, run the ATM Control Panel.

Q How do I put Kanji, Arabic, Chinese, and other non-European characters on my pages?

A First of all, everyone who you want to be able to read these characters on your pages must have the appropriate language fonts installed. They must also have selected that language character set and font under Options | General Preferences | Fonts in Netscape Navigator or View | Options | General | Fonts in Microsoft Internet Explorer. You can use the Character Map accessory in Windows 95 (or a similar program in other operating systems) to get the numerical codes for each character in any language font. If the character you want has a code of 214, use Ö to place it on a Web page.

The best way to include a short message in an Asian language (such as `We speak Tamil—Call us!`) is to include it as a graphics image. That way everyone will see it, even if they use English as their primary language for Web browsing.

Quiz

Questions

1. How would you say, "We're having our annual Nixon Impeachment Day SALE today!" in normal-sized blue text, but with the word "SALE" at the largest possible size in bright red?

2. How would you make all text on a page green and a little larger than normal, but make all headings yellow?

3. How do you say "© 1996, Webwonks Inc." on a Web page?

Answers

1. ```
   <FONT COLOR="blue">We're having our annual Nixon Impeachment Day
   <FONT COLOR="red" SIZE=7>SALE</FONT> today!</FONT>
   ```

2. Put the following at the beginning of the Web page:

   ```
   <BODY TEXT="green"><BASEFONT SIZE=4>
   ```

   Then make each heading look like this:

   ```
   <H1><FONT COLOR="yellow">Heading goes here</FONT></H1>
   ```

3. ```
   &copy; 1996, Webwonks Inc.
   ```

   The following would also produce the same result:

   ```
   &#169; 1996, Webwonks Inc.
   ```

6

Activities

☐ Go through all the Web pages you've created so far, and ask yourself if they would look significantly better if you used a different typeface or font color. Use the <FONT> tag to enhance the pages that would benefit from it most, and leave the rest alone.

6

Hour 7

Arranging Text in Lists

When you present information on paper (or with a good old-fashioned overhead projector) you probably often include lists of numbered steps or "bullet points." You've also undoubtedly written many indented lists to organize information such as terms and their definitions or the outline of a business plan. Because lists are so common, HTML provides tags which automatically indent text and add numbers or bullets in front of each listed item.

In this chapter, you'll find out how to format numbered lists, bulleted lists, and a variety of other indented lists. You will also see how the HTML tags for creating lists can be used for almost any other type of indentation you want on your Web pages.

To Do:

You can make the most of this chapter if you have some text that needs to be indented correctly to be presentable.

☐ Any type of outline, "bullet points" from a presentation, numbered steps, glossary, or list of textual information from a database will serve as good material to work with.

☐ If the text you'll be using is from a word processor or database program, be sure to save it to a new file in plain text or ASCII format. You can then add the appropriate HTML tags to format it as you go through this chapter.

The Three Types of HTML Lists

There are three basic types of HTML lists. All three are shown in Figure 7.2, and Figure 7.1 reveals the HTML to construct them:

☐ The numbered list at the top is called an *ordered list*. It begins with the <OL> tag and ends with a closing </OL> tag. Numbers and line breaks appear automatically at each <LI> tag, and the entire list is indented.

☐ The bulleted list is called an *unordered list*. It opens with the <UL> tag and closes with </UL>. It looks just like an ordered list, except that bullets appear at each <LI> tag instead of numbers.

☐ The list of terms and their meanings is called a *definition list*. It starts with the <DL> tag and ends with </DL>. The <DT> tag goes in front of each term to be defined, with a <DD> tag in front of each definition. Line breaks and indentation appear automatically.

 Ordered lists are indented lists that have numbers or letters in front of each item.

 Unordered lists are indented lists with a special bullet symbol in front of each item.

 Definition lists are indented lists without any number or symbol in front of each item.

JUST A MINUTE

Remember that different Web browsers can display Web pages quite differently. The HTML standard doesn't specify exactly how Web browsers should format lists, so people using older Web browsers may not see the same indentation that you see.

Software of the future may also format HTML lists differently, though all current Web browsers now display lists in almost exactly the same way.

Figure 7.1.

Use <OL> and <LI> for ordered lists, <UL> and <LI> for unordered lists, and <DL>, <DT>, and <DD> for definition lists.

```
<HTML><HEAD><TITLE>The Joy of Gluing </TITLE></HEAD><BODY>
Tips for successful gluing:
<OL>
<LI>Always apply glue to clean, dry surfaces
<LI>For faster drying, increase the temperature
<LI>Clamp glue joints for safety
</OL>
Favorite synthetic glues:
<UL>
<LI>Acrylic Resin
<LI>Cyanoacrylate Ester
<LI>Polyethyline Hot Melt
</UL>
Favorite animal glues:
<DL>
<DT>Albumin glue
<DD>Made from blood and protein, used in plywood
<DT>Bone glue
<DD>Made from bones, used in cardboard boxes
<DT>Fish glue
<DD>Made from fish oil and skin, good for photo mounting
</DL>
</BODY></HTML>
```

Figure 7.2.

The three types of HTML lists, as they appear in Netscape Navigator.

Lists Within Lists

Although definition lists are officially supposed to be used for defining terms, many Web page authors use them anywhere they'd like to see some indentation. In practice, you can indent any text simply by putting <DL><DD> at the beginning of it and </DL> at the end.

7

You can indent items further by *nesting* one list inside another, like this:

```
<DL><DD>This item will be indented
<DL><DD>This will be indented further
<DL><DL><DD>And this will be indented very far indeed
</DL></DL></DL></DL>
```

Just make sure you always have the same number of closing `</DL>` tags as opening `<DL>` tags.

Ordered and unordered lists can also be nested inside one another, down to as many levels as you wish. In Figure 7.3, a complex indented outline is constructed from several unordered lists. You'll notice in Figure 7.4 that Netscape Navigator automatically uses a different type of bullet for each of the first three levels of indentation, making the list very easy to read.

Figure 7.3.

You can build elaborate outlines by placing lists within lists.

```
<HTML><HEAD><TITLE>Germanic Languages</TITLE></HEAD><BODY>
<UL><LI>West Germanic Languages
    <UL><LI>English
        <UL><LI>British
            <UL><LI>BBC
                <LI>Cockney
                <LI>Dubliner
            </UL>
            <LI>American
            <UL><LI>Newscaster
                <LI>Drawl
                <LI>Jive
            </UL>
        </UL>
        <LI>Dutch
        <UL><LI>Hollander
            <LI>Flemish
            <LI>Afrikaans
        </UL>
    </UL>
    <LI>East Germanic Languages
    <UL><LI>Gothic
        <LI>German
        <LI>Yiddish
    </UL>
</UL>
</BODY></HTML>
```

As shown in Figure 7.4, Netscape Navigator will normally use a solid disc for the first-level bullet, a hollow circle for the second-level bullet, and a solid square for all deeper levels. However, you can explicitly choose which type of bullet to use for any level by using `<UL TYPE="disc">`, `<UL TYPE="circle">`, or `<UL TYPE="square">` instead of `<UL>`.

You can even change the bullet for any single point in an unordered list by using the TYPE attribute in the `<LI>` tag. For example, the following would display a hollow circle in front of the words "Extra" and "Super," but a solid square in front of the word "Special."

7

```
<UL TYPE="circle">
<LI>Extra
<LI>Super
<LI TYPE="square">Special
</UL>
```

Figure 7.4.

Multi-level unordered lists are neatly indented and bulleted for readability.

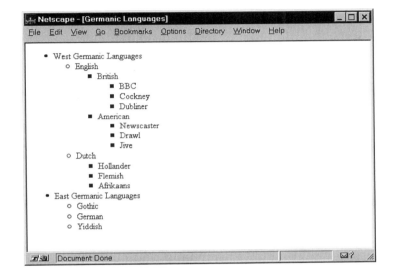

JUST A MINUTE

Netscape Navigator is the only Web browser that currently lets you control the appearance of list bullets. All bullets will appear as solid discs in Microsoft Internet Explorer 3.0.

The TYPE attribute also works with ordered lists, but instead of choosing a type of bullet you choose the type of numbers or letters to place in front of each item. Figure 7.5 shows how to use roman numerals (TYPE="I"), capital letters (TYPE="A"), and lowercase letters (TYPE="a"), along with ordinary numbers in a multi-level list. In Figure 7.6, you can see the resulting nicely formatted outline.

Though Figure 7.5 uses only the TYPE attribute with the <OL> tag, you can also use it for specific <LI> tags within a list (though it's hard to imagine a situation where you would want to). You can also explicitly specify ordinary numbering with TYPE="1", and you can make lowercase roman numerals with TYPE="i".

Here's one more seldom-used but handy-when-you-need-it trick: You can start an ordered list with any number (or letter) with the START attribute. <OL START="3">, for example, starts a numbered list at 3 instead of 1. Individual points can be renumbered with the VALUE attribute (<LI VALUE="12">, for example).

7

JUST A MINUTE

Note that you must always use numbers with the START and VALUE attributes. To make a list that starts with the letter C, for example, you need to type <OL TYPE="A" START="3">.

Figure 7.5.

The TYPE *attribute lets you make multi-tiered lists with both numbered and lettered points.*

```
<HTML><HEAD><TITLE>Sure-Fire Business Plan</TITLE></HEAD>
<BODY>
<OL TYPE="I"><LI>Invent Something
    <OL><LI>Find Some Geniuses
        <OL TYPE="A"><LI>Look for Nerdy Names in:
            <OL TYPE="a"><LI>Cambridge, MA Phone Book
                <LI>IBM Research Labs Lay-Off Roster
                <LI>"Nanotechnology Today" Subscriber List
            </OL>
            <LI>Send Friends to Look in:
            <OL TYPE="a"><LI>Some Big Libraries
                <LI>CalTech Dorms
                <LI>Restrooms at a Science Convention
            </OL>
        </OL>
        <LI>Hire Them to Design and Build It
        <OL TYPE="A"><LI>Take Out a Loan
            <LI>Wave Cash Under Their Noses
            <LI>Rent a Big House with a Lab in the Back
        </OL>
    </OL>
    <LI>Market It Big Time
    <OL><LI>Run Lots of TV Ads
        <LI>Open a Web Site
        <LI>Rake In the Green
    </OL>
</OL>
</BODY></HTML>
```

COFFEE BREAK

By combining ordered, unordered, and definition lists within one another, you can organize the most complex information in a readable and attractive way. To get your creative juices flowing, I've created a "list of lists" for you to browse through before you begin organizing your own HTML lists.

To check it out, go to the *24-Hour HTML Café List-O-Mania* page at

`http://www.mcp.com/sams/books/235-8/listlist.htm`

Have some fun while you're there by trying to figure out what the real titles of the sample lists might be, based on the information they contain. Answers are given—as a nested HTML list, of course—at the end of the page.

You can also see how a list was used to enhance the *24-Hour HTML Café* welcome page during the early stages of its development, at

`http://www.mcp.com/sams/books/235-8/cafe7.htm`

Figure 7.6.

A well-formatted outline can make almost any plan look plausible.

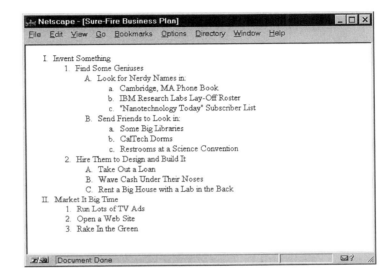

```
Netscape - [Sure-Fire Business Plan]
File   Edit   View   Go   Bookmarks   Options   Directory   Window   Help

   I.  Invent Something
          1.  Find Some Geniuses
                 A.  Look for Nerdy Names in:
                        a.  Cambridge, MA Phone Book
                        b.  IBM Research Labs Lay-Off Roster
                        c.  "Nanotechnology Today" Subscriber List
                 B.  Send Friends to Look in:
                        a.  Some Big Libraries
                        b.  CalTech Dorms
                        c.  Restrooms at a Science Convention
          2.  Hire Them to Design and Build It
                 A.  Take Out a Loan
                 B.  Wave Cash Under Their Noses
                 C.  Rent a Big House with a Lab in the Back
   II.  Market It Big Time
          1.  Run Lots of TV Ads
          2.  Open a Web Site
          3.  Rake In the Green

Document: Done
```

To Do:

Take a list or two of your own, and try to find the best way to present the information so that it can be easily understood.

☐ Which type of list or combination of list types best suits your list? Use ordered lists only for lists that have a natural order to them. Try to avoid more than seven bullet points in a row in any unordered list, or the list will be hard to read. Use definition lists whenever indenting is sufficient to convey the structure of your information.

☐ Start each list (or new level within a multi-tiered list) with an <OL>, <UL>, or <DL>. Start each point within the list with <LI>. Use the TYPE attribute if you want non-standard bullets or letters instead of numbers.

☐ If you want a blank line between list items, put a <P> tag next to each <LI> tag.

☐ Be very careful to close every <OL> list with </OL>, and to make sure that each <UL> or <DL> has a corresponding </UL> or </DL>. Unclosed lists can make pages look very strange, and can even cause some Web browsers not to display the list at all.

Summary

In this chapter, you learned to create and combine three basic types of HTML lists: *ordered lists, unordered lists,* and *definition lists.* Lists can be placed within other lists to create outlines and other complex arrangements of text.

7

Table 7.1 lists all the tags and attributes covered in this chapter.

Table 7.1. HTML tags and attributes covered in Chapter 7.

Tag	Attribute	Function
`<OL>...</OL>`		An ordered (numbered) list.
	`TYPE="..."`	The type of numerals used to label the list. Possible values are A, a, I, i, 1.
	`START="..."`	The value with which to start this list.
`<UL>...</UL>`		An unordered (bulleted) list.
	`TYPE="..."`	The bullet dingbat used to mark list items. Possible values are DISC, CIRCLE, and SQUARE.
`<LI>`		A list item for use with `<OL>` or `<UL>`.
	`TYPE="..."`	The type of bullet or number used to label this item. Possible values are DISC, CIRCLE, SQUARE, A, a, I, i, 1.
	`VALUE="..."`	The numeric value this list item should have (affects this item and all below it in `<OL>` lists).
`<DL>...</DL>`		A definition list.
`<DT>`		A definition term, as part of a definition list.
`<DD>`		The corresponding definition to a definition term, as part of a definition list.

Q&A

Q I used `<UL TYPE="square">`, but the bullets still came out round, not square.

A Are you using Netscape Navigator version 2.0 or higher? Alternate bullet types don't show up in any other Web browser yet, but they probably will in future versions.

Q I've seen pages on the Internet that use three-dimensional looking little balls or other special graphics for bullets. How do they do that?

A That trick is a little bit beyond what this chapter covers. You'll find out how to do it yourself in Chapter 9, "Putting Images on a Web Page."

7

Quiz

Questions

1. Write the HTML to create the following ordered list:

   X. Xylophone

   Y. Yak

   Z. Zebra

2. How would you indent a single word and put a square bullet in front of it?

3. Use a definition list to show that the word "glunch" means "a look of disdain, anger, or displeasure" and the word "glumpy" means "sullen, morose, or sulky."

4. Write the HTML to create the following indentation effect:

   Apple pie,

      pudding,

         and pancake,

   All begin with an A.

Answers

1. `<OL TYPE="A" START="24"><LI>Xylophone<LI>Yak<LI>Zebra</OL>`

   The following alternative will also do the same thing:

   `<OL TYPE="A"><LI VALUE="24">Xylophone<LI>Yak<LI>Zebra</OL>`

2. `<UL TYPE="square"><LI>Supercalifragilisticexpealidocious</UL>`

   (Putting the TYPE="square" in the <LI> tag would give the same result, because there's only one item in this list.)

3. `<DL>`

   `<DT>glunch<DD>a look of disdain, anger, or displeasure`

   `<DT>glumpy<DD>sullen, morose, or sulky`

   `</DL>`

4. `<DL><DT>Apple pie,<DD>pudding,<DL><DD>and pancake,</DL>`
   `All begin with an A.</DL>`

   Note that blank lines will appear above and below and pancake, in Microsoft Internet Explorer, but not in Netscape Navigator.

7

Activities

☐ Try producing an ordered list outlining the information you'd like to put on your Web pages. This will give you practice formatting HTML lists, and also give you a head start on thinking about the issues covered in Part VI, "Building a Web Site."

Hour 8

Intra-Page and E-mail Links

In Chapter 3, "Linking to Other Web Pages," you learned to use the <A> tag to create links between HTML pages. This chapter shows you how to use the same tag to allow readers to jump between different parts of a single page. This gives you a convenient way to put a table of contents at the top of a long document, or at the bottom of a page you can put a link that returns you to the top. You'll see how to link to a specific point within a separate page, too.

This chapter also tells you how to embed a live link to your e-mail address in a Web page, so readers can instantly compose and send a message to you from within most Web browsers.

Using Named Anchors

Figure 8.1 demonstrates the use of intra-page links. To see how such links are made, take a look the first `<A>` tag in Figure 8.1:

```
<A NAME="top"></A>
```

This is a different use of the `<A>` anchor tag; all it does is give a name to the specific point on the page where the tag occurs. The `</A>` tag must be included, but no text is necessary between `<A>` and `</A>`.

Now look at the *last* `<A>` tag in Figure 8.1:

```
<A HREF="#top">Return to top of document.</A>
```

The # symbol means that the word `"top"` refers to a named anchor point within the current document, rather than a separate page. So when a reader clicks on `Return to top of document.`, the Web browser will display the part of the page starting with the `<A NAME="top">` tag.

Figure 8.1.

An `<A>` tag with a NAME *attribute acts as a marker, so `<A>` tags with* HREF *attributes can link to that specific point on a page.*

```
<HTML><HEAD><TITLE>U.S. Bill of Rights</TITLE></HEAD>
<BODY>
<A NAME="top"></A><H1>THE BILL OF RIGHTS (1791)</H1>
<H2>Amendments to the United States Constitution</H2>
<A HREF="#first">
I. Freedom of religion, speech, assembly, and petition</A>
<BR><A HREF="#second">
II. Right to bear arms</A>
<BR><A HREF="#third">
III. Freedom from forced quartering of soldiers</A>
<BR><A HREF="#fourth">
IV. Right to security from search and seizure</A>
<BR><A HREF="#fifth">
V. Right to due process of law</A>
<BR><A HREF="#sixth">
VI. Right to jury trial in criminal cases</A>
<BR><A HREF="#seventh">
VII. Right to jury trial in common law cases</A>
<BR><A HREF="#eighth">
VIII. Freedom from excessive bail, fines or punishments</A>
<BR><A HREF="#ninth">
IX. Acknowledgement of other rights</A>
<BR><A HREF="#tenth">
X. Delegation of other powers to the states and people</A>

<A NAME="first"></A><H2>Amendment I</H2>
Congress shall make no law respecting an establishment of
religion, or prohibiting the free exercise thereof; or
abridging the freedom of speech, or of the press; or the
right of the people peaceably to assemble, and to petition
the government for a redress of grievances.
<A NAME="second"></A><H2>Amendment II</H2>
A well regulated militia, being necessary to the security
of a free state, the right of the people to keep and bear
arms, shall not be infringed.

...amendments III through IX go here...

<A NAME="tenth"></A><H2>Amendment X</H2>
The powers not delegated to the United States by the
Constitution, nor prohibited by it to the states, are
reserved to the states respectively, or to the people.
<P><A HREF="#top">Return to top of document.</A>
</BODY></HTML>
```

Here's an easy way to remember the difference between these two different types of <A> tags: <A HREF> is what you click on, and <A NAME> is where you go when you click there.

NEW TERM An *anchor* is a named point on a Web page. The same tag is used to create hypertext links and anchors (which explains why the tag is named <A>).

Similarly, each of the <A HREF> links in Figure 8.1 makes an underlined link leading to a corresponding <A NAME> anchor. Clicking on "II. Right to bear arms" in Figure 8.2, for instance, takes you to the part of the page shown in Figure 8.3.

Figure 8.2.

The <A NAME> tags in Figure 8.1 don't appear at all on the Web page. The <A HREF> tags appear as underlined links.

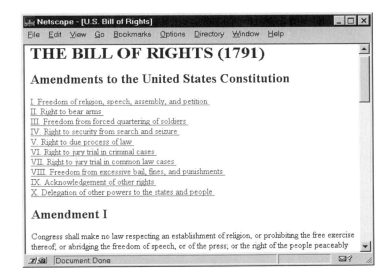

Figure 8.3.

Clicking on "II. Right to bear arms" in Figure 8.2 takes you down to "Amendment II" on the same page.

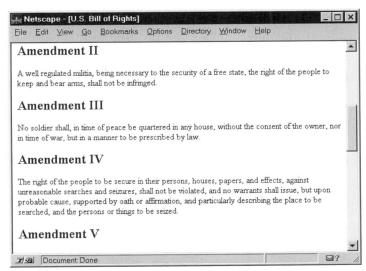

To Do:

Now that you have several pages of your own linked together, you might want to add an index at the top of your home page so people can easily get an overview of what your pages have to offer.

- ☐ Place <A NAME> tags in front of each major topic on your home page, or any long page you make.

- ☐ Copy each of the major topic headings to a list at the top of the page, and enclose each heading in an <A HREF> linking to the corresponding <A NAME> tag.

Linking to a Specific Part of Another Page

You can even link to a named anchor on another page by including the address or name of that page followed by # and the anchor name.

Figure 8.4 shows several examples, such as this one:

```
<A HREF="articles.htm#two">II. The President</A>
```

Clicking on "II. The President" (in Figure 8.5) will bring up the page named articles.htm, and go directly to the point where <A NAME="two"> occurs on that page.

Figure 8.4.

To link to a specific part of another page, put both the page address and anchor name in the <A HREF> tag.

```
<HTML><HEAD><TITLE>U.S. Constitution</TITLE></HEAD>
<BODY>
<H3>THE CONSTITUTION OF THE UNITED STATES OF AMERICA</H3>
We the people of the United States, in order to form a
more perfect union, establish justice, insure domestic
tranquility, provide for the common defense, promote the
general welfare, and secure the blessings of liberty to
ourselves and our posterity, do ordain and establish this
Constitution for the United States of America.<P>
<A HREF="articles.htm#one">I. The Congress</A><BR>
<A HREF="articles.htm#two">II. The President</A><BR>
<A HREF="articles.htm#three">III. The Courts</A><BR>
<A HREF="articles.htm#four">IV. The States</A><BR>
<A HREF="articles.htm#five">V. Amendment</A><BR>
<A HREF="articles.htm#six">VI. Application</A><BR>
<A HREF="articles.htm#seven">VII. Ratification</A><P>
<A HREF="rights.htm">The Bill of Rights (1791)
</A><BR><A HREF="amends.htm">
Other Amendments (1798-1971)</A>
</BODY></HTML>
```

8

Figure 8.5.

The page listed in Figure 8.4. The first seven links all go to different parts of a page named `articles.htm`.

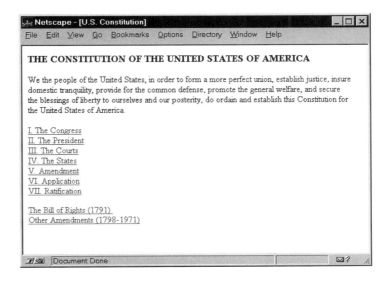

CAUTION

Be sure to only include the # symbol in <A HREF> link tags. Don't put a # symbol in the <A NAME> tag, or links to that name won't work.

COFFEE BREAK

One of the most common uses for the <A NAME> tag is creating an alphabetical index. The bad news for anyone with an alphabetical list that they want to index is that typing out 26 links to 26 anchors is a rather tedious endeavor. The good news is that I've already done it for you and dropped off the indexed page at the *24-Hour HTML Café:*

`http://www.mcp.com/sams/books/235-8/alpha.htm`

You can just save this document to your hard drive, and then cut-and-paste your own alphabetical information after each letter.

While you're at the Café, stop by

`http://www.mcp.com/sams/books/235-8/cafe8.htm`

to see how the progress on the "construction site" is going. This page uses <A HREF> tags to link all the sample pages discussed so far in the book and <A NAME> tags to provide an index at the top.

Linking Your E-mail Address to a Web Page

In addition to linking between pages and between parts of a single page, the `<A>` tag allows you to link to your e-mail address. This is the simplest way to enable readers of your Web pages to "talk back" to you. Of course, you could just tell them your e-mail address and trust them to type it into whatever e-mail program they use if they want to say something to you. But you can make it almost completely effortless for them to send you a message by providing a clickable link to your e-mail address instead.

An HTML link to my e-mail address would look like this:

```
<A HREF="mailto:dicko@netletter.com">Send me an e-mail message.</A>
```

The words `Send me an e-mail message.` will appear just like any other `<A>` link (as underlined text in the color you set for links in the `LINK` or `VLINK` attributes of the `<BODY>` tag). In most Web browsers, when someone clicks on the link they get a window where they can type in a message, which will be immediately sent to you.

If you want people to see your actual e-mail address (so they can make note of it or send a message using a different e-mail program), type it both in the `HREF` attribute and as part of the message between the `<A>` and `</A>` tags.

For example, the HTML in Figure 8.6 is an e-mail directory page for my little "Mom and Pop software shop," Cedar Software. The resulting page in Figure 8.7 shows the principal officers with a clickable e-mail link for each.

When someone clicks on the top link in Figure 8.7 in Netscape Navigator 3.0, a separate window (see Figure 8.8) will open with spaces for him to enter a subject line and e-mail message. The e-mail address from the link will be automatically entered for him, and he can simply click on the mail button to send the message.

TIME SAVER

It is customary to put an e-mail link to the Web page author at the bottom of every Web page. Not only does this make it easy for customers or others to contact you, it also gives them a way to tell you about any problems with the page that your testing may have missed.

Figure 8.6.
*Links to e-mail addresses
use the same <A> tag as
links to Web pages.*

```
<HTML>
<HEAD><TITLE>Cedar Software E-Mail Directory</TITLE></HEAD>
<BODY>
<H1>Cedar Software E-Mail Directory</H1>
<UL>
<LI><A HREF="mailto:dick@netletter.com">
    <I>Dick Oliver, President</I><BR>
    dick@netletter.com</A><P>
<LI><A HREF="mailto:jan@netletter.com">
    <I>Jan Oliver, Chief Advisor</I><BR>
    jan@netletter.com</A><P>
<LI><A HREF="mailto:erica@netletter.com">
    <I>Erica Oliver, Senior VP of Toddling</I><BR>
    erica@netletter.com</A><P>
<LI><A HREF="mailto:ona@netletter.com">
    <I>Ona Oliver, Junior VP of Toddling</I><BR>
    ona@netletter.com</A><P>
<LI><A HREF="mailto:molly@netletter.com">
    <I>Molly Stubbs, Toddler Supervisor</I><BR>
    molly@netletter.com</A><P>
<LI><A HREF="mailto:pippin@netletter.com">
    <I>Pippin, Office Dustmop</I><BR>
    pippin@netletter.com</A><P>
<LI><A HREF="mailto:lucy@netletter.com">
    <I>Lucy, Dustmop Assistant</I><BR>
    lucy@netletter.com</A><P>
<LI><A HREF="mailto:dandyo@netletter.com">
    <I>Dandy, Company Horse</I><BR>
    dandy@netletter.com</A><P>
</UL>
</BODY></HTML>
```

Figure 8.7.
The `"mailto:"` *links in
Figure 8.6 look just like*
`http://` *links on the
page.*

Figure 8.8.

Clicking on the top link in Figure 8.7 brings up this e-mail window within Netscape Navigator.

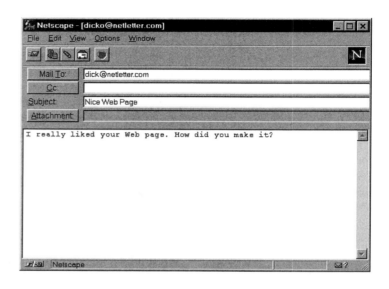

Summary

This chapter has shown you two uses for the <A> tag not covered in Chapter 3. You saw how to create named anchor points within a page and how to create links to a specific anchor. You also saw how to link to your e-mail address so readers can easily send you messages.

Table 8.1 summarizes the two attributes of the <A> tag discussed in this chapter.

Table 8.1. HTML tags and attributes covered in Chapter 8.

Tag	Attribute	Function
<A>...</A>		With the HREF attribute, creates a link to another document or anchor; with the NAME attribute, creates an anchor that can be linked to.
	HREF="..."	The address of the document and/or anchor point to link to.
	NAME="..."	The name for this anchor point in the document.

Q&A

Q Can I put both HREF and NAME in the same <A> tag? Would I want to for any reason?

A You can, and it might save you some typing if you have a named anchor point and a link right next to each other. But it's generally better to use <A HREF> and <A NAME> separately to avoid confusion, because they play very different roles in an HTML document.

Q What happens if I accidentally spell the name of an anchor wrong, or forget to put the # in front of it?

A If you link to an anchor name that doesn't exist within a page (or you misspell the anchor name), the link just goes to the top of that page.

Q What if I use a different company to handle my e-mail than my Web pages? Will my e-mail links still work?

A Yes. You can put any e-mail address on the Internet into a link, and it will work fine. The only situation where e-mail links won't work is when the person who clicks on the link hasn't set up the e-mail part of their Web browser properly, or is using an older version that isn't capable of sending e-mail.

Quiz

Questions

1. Write the HTML to make it possible for someone clicking on the words "About the authors" at the top of the page to skip down to a list of credits at the bottom of the page.

2. Suppose your company has three employees, and you want to create a company directory page listing some information about each of them. Write the HTML for that page, and the HTML to link to one of the employees from another page.

3. If your e-mail address is bon@soir.com, how would you make the text "goodnight greeting" into a link that people can click on to compose and send you an e-mail message?

Answers

1. At the top of the page, put:

   ```
   <A HREF="#credits">About the authors</A>
   ```

   And at the beginning of the credits section, put:

   ```
   <A NAME="credits"></A>
   ```

2. The company directory page would look like this:

   ```
   <HTML><HEAD><TITLE>Company Directory</TITLE></HEAD>
   <BODY><H1>Company Directory</H1>
   <A NAME="jones"><H2>Jane Jones</H2>
   Ms. Jones is our accountant... etc.
   <A NAME="smith"><H2>Sam Smith</H2>
   Mr. Smith is our salesman.. etc.
   <A NAME="bharwahniji"><H2>R.K. Satjiv Bharwahniji</H2>
   Mr. Bharwahniji is our president... etc.
   </BODY></HTML>
   ```

   A link to one employee's information from another page would look like this (if the above file was named `directory.htm`):

   ```
   <A HREF="directory.htm#bharwahniji">About our president</A>
   ```

3. Type the following on your Web page:

   ```
   Send me a <A HREF="mailto:bon@soir.com">goodnight greeting</A>!
   ```

Activities

☐ When you link back to your home page from other pages, you might want to skip some of the introductory information at the top of the home page. Using a link to a named anchor just below that introductory information will avoid presenting it to people who have already read it, making your pages seem less repetitive. Also, if any pages on your site are longer than two screens of information when displayed in a Web browser, consider putting a link at the bottom of the page back up to the top.

☐ Look through your Web pages and consider whether there are any places in the text where you'd like to make it easy for people to respond to what you're saying. Include a link right there to your e-mail address. Especially if you're running a business, you can never provide too many opportunities for people to contact you and tell you what they need or think about your products.

8

PART

III

Web Page Graphics

Hour

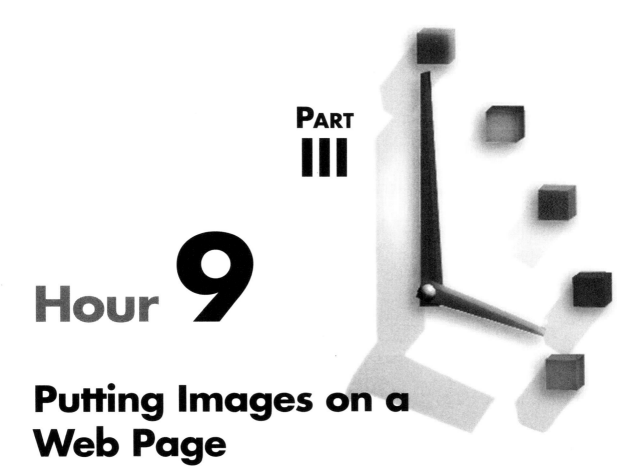

Hour **9**

Putting Images on a Web Page

In Chapters 1 through 8, you learned to create Web pages containing text. However, you'd be hard-pressed to find many Web pages these days that don't also include graphics images. This chapter shows you how easy it is to put graphics on your pages with HTML.

Chapter 10, "Creating Web Page Images," will help you come up with some good graphics of your own, and Chapter 11, "Making Pages Display Quickly," will show you how to make your graphical pages appear onscreen as fast as possible. I also save the technical details you need to know about computer graphics files for Chapter 10.

To Do:

You should get two or three images ready now so you can try putting them on your own pages as you follow along with this chapter.

If you have some image files already saved in the GIF or JPEG format (the filenames will end in .gif or .jpg), use those. Otherwise, you can just grab some graphics that I've put on the Internet for you to practice with. Here's how:

1. Enter the following address into your Web browser:

   `http://www.mcp.com/sams/books/235-8/sample/images.htm`

   You should see a page with four images of hats and stars at the bottom.

2. Save the images to your computer's hard drive by clicking on each image with the right mouse button (or holding down the mouse button if you use a Macintosh computer), then selecting Save Image As... from the pop-up menu.

   Put them on your hard drive in whichever folder you use for creating Web pages.

JUST A MINUTE

If you aren't using Netscape Navigator or Microsoft Internet Explorer for Windows 95, you may need to call up each of the images individually at the following addresses, and select File | Save As... to save each one:

`http://www.mcp.com/sams/books/235-8/sample/hat.gif`
`http://www.mcp.com/sams/books/235-8/sample/magic.gif`
`http://www.mcp.com/sams/books/235-8/sample/magic2.gif`
`http://www.mcp.com/sams/books/235-8/sample/star.gif`

3. As you read this chapter, use the hat and star image files to practice putting images on your pages. (You'll find out how to find or create the perfect images for your Web pages in the next chapter.)

COFFEE BREAK

At the *24-Hour HTML Café*, you'll find live links to many graphics and multimedia hotlists and hot sites where you can find ready-to-use graphics. To access these links, go to:

`http://www.mcp.com/sams/books/235-8/hotlist.htm#graphics`

The familiar Web search engines and directories such as Yahoo! (`http://www.yahoo.com/`), Excite (`http://www.excite.com`), and InfoSeek (`http://www.infoseek.com/`) can become a gold mine of graphics images, just by leading you to sites related to your own theme. They can also help you discover the oodles of sites specifically dedicated to providing free and cheap access to reusable media collections.

Placing an Image on a Web Page

To put an image on a Web page, first move the image file into the same directory folder as the HTML text file. Then insert the following HTML tag at the point in the text where you want the image to appear (using the name of your image file instead of *myimage.gif*):

```
<IMG SRC="myimage.gif">
```

Figure 9.1, for example, inserts the image named house.jpg between the first and second paragraphs of text. Whenever a Web browser displays the HTML file in Figure 9.1, it will automatically retrieve and display the image file shown in Figure 9.2.

Figure 9.1.

Use the IMG tag to place an image on a Web page.

```
<HTML><HEAD><TITLE>The Olivers' House</TITLE></HEAD>
<BODY>
Deep in the wilds of Elmore, Vermont lies the lair
of the rare and secretive <I>Familia Oliveria</I>.<P>
<IMG SRC="house.jpg" ALT="Our Humble Abode">
<P>Each winter, the male of the species disappears into
his octagonal office <I>(left)</I>, and comes out only
for skiing, sliding, and trips to the mailbox.
The female and young dwell in the main house <I>(right)</I>,
though she occasionally switches places with the male to
ship orders in the office while he cooks exotic food and
attends to the offspring. Once each week, local residents
have the rare opportunity to spot the elusive Olivers as
they gather food in their aging Toyota.<P>
</BODY></HTML>
```

Figure 9.2.

When a Web browser displays the HTML page in Figure 9.1, it adds the image named house.jpg.

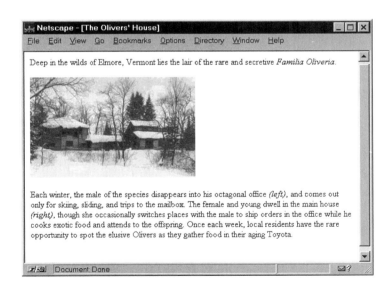

If you guessed that IMG stands for "image," you're right. SRC stands for "source," which is a reference to the location of the image file. (As discussed back in Chapter 1, "Welcome to HTML," a Web page image is always stored in a separate file from the text, even though it will appear to be part of the same "page.")

Just as with the <A HREF> tag (covered in Chapter 3, "Linking to Other Web Pages"), you can specify any complete Internet address as the <IMG SRC>. Or you can specify just the filename if an image will be located in the same directory folder as the HTML file. You may also use relative addresses such as photos/birdy.jpg or ../smiley.gif.

JUST A MINUTE

Theoretically, you can include an image from any Internet Web page within your own pages. For example, you could include the hat image from my "Sample Images" page by putting the following on your Web page:

<IMG SRC="http://www.mcp.com/sams/books/235-8/sample/hat.gif">

The image would be retrieved from my server computer whenever your page was displayed.

However, even though you could do this, you shouldn't do it! Not only is it bad manners (it costs most people money whenever you pull something from their server computer), it can also make your pages display more slowly. If someone gives you permission to use an image from one of their pages, always transfer a copy of that image to your computer, and use a local file reference such as <IMG SRC="hat.gif">.

Labeling an Image

The <IMG> tag in Figure 9.1 includes a short text message: ALT="Our Humble Abode". The ALT stands for alternate text because this message will appear in place of the image in older Web browsers that don't display graphics.

The message you put in the ALT attribute will be seen by some people who are using the latest Web browser software, too. Many people—especially those with slow modems—turn off the Auto Load Images option in Netscape Navigator, so they can see the text on Web pages without wasting time downloading images they don't care about. When automatic image loading is off, the ALT message appears instead of an image. Clicking on that message causes the image to be downloaded and displayed, and clicking on the image download button (fifth from the left on the toolbar) causes all images on the page to appear. Figure 9.3 shows the same page as Figure 9.2, with Auto Load Images turned off.

9

Figure 9.3.

Anyone who turns off Auto Load Images in Netscape Navigator will see the ALT *message instead of the image.*

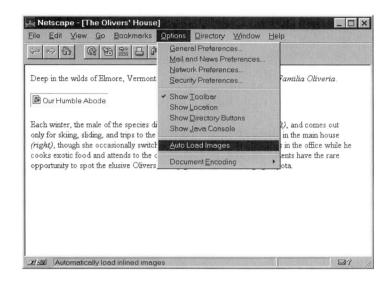

Microsoft Internet Explorer also allows people to turn off graphics (by deselecting View | Options… | General | Show Pictures) so that users have to click on the ALT message to see the actual image. Internet Explorer 3.0 also displays the ALT message whenever someone holds the mouse over a graphic image without clicking.

Both Netscape Navigator and Microsoft Internet Explorer also display the ALT message before retrieving and displaying an image, even when automatic graphics loading is turned on. If the image file is large, or there are a lot of images on the same page, the ALT message may be on the screen quite a while before it is replaced by the image.

You should generally include a suitable ALT attribute in every <IMG> tag on your Web pages, keeping in mind the variety of situations where people might see that message. A very brief description of the image is usually best, but Web page authors sometimes put short advertising messages or subtle humor in their ALT messages. For small or unimportant images, it's fine to omit the ALT message altogether.

Horizontal Image Alignment

As discussed in Chapter 5, "Text Formatting and Alignment," you can use <DIV ALIGN="center">, <DIV ALIGN="right">, and <DIV ALIGN="left"> to align part of page to the center, right margin, or left margin. Both text and images are affected these tags.

For example, the first <IMG> tag in Figure 9.4 occurs between a <DIV ALIGN="center"> tag and the closing </DIV> tag. You can see in Figure 9.5 that this causes the image (as well as the text above it) to be centered on the page.

Figure 9.4.

Use the ALIGN *attribute with the* DIV *and* IMG *tags to control horizontal image alignment.*

```
<HTML><HEAD><TITLE>The Olivers and Their House</TITLE></HEAD>
<BODY>
<DIV ALIGN="center">
Deep in the wilds of Elmore, Vermont lies the lair
of the rare and secretive <I>Familia Oliveria</I>.<P>
<IMG SRC="house.jpg" ALT="Our Humble Abode"></DIV>
<IMG SRC="dicko.gif" ALIGN="left" ALT="Dick">
Each winter, the male of the species disappears into
his octagonal office <I>(left)</I>, and comes out only
for skiing, sliding, and trips to the mailbox.
<IMG SRC="jano.gif" ALIGN="right" ALT="Jan">
The female and young dwell in the main house <I>(right)</I>,
though she occasionally switches places with the male to
ship orders in the office while he cooks exotic food and
attends to the offspring. Once each week, local residents
have the rare opportunity to spot the elusive Olivers as
they gather food in their aging Toyota.
</BODY></HTML>
```

Figure 9.5.

While <DIV ALIGN> *only affects the placement of text and images,* <IMG ALIGN> *also causes text to flow around images.*

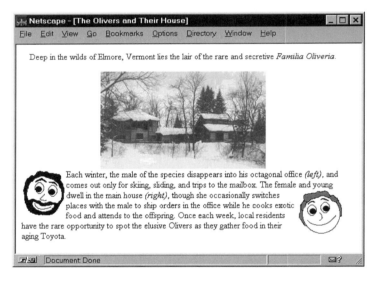

You can also make text wrap around images, as it does around the two cartoon images at the bottom of Figure 9.5. You do this by including an ALIGN attribute within the <IMG> tag itself, as shown in the second and third <IMG> tags in Figure 9.4.

<IMG ALIGN="left"> aligns the image to the left and causes text to wrap around the right side of it. And as you'd expect, <IMG ALIGN="right"> aligns the image to the right and causes text to wrap around the left side of it.

You can't use <IMG ALIGN="center"> because text won't wrap around a centered image. You must use <DIV ALIGN="center"> if you want an image to be centered on the page, as I did with the top image in Figures 9.4 and 9.5.

9

Note that ALIGN means something different in an <IMG> tag than it does in a <DIV> tag. <IMG ALIGN="right"> will align an image to the right and cause any text that follows to wrap around the image. <DIV ALIGN="right">, on the other hand, just controls the alignment and never causes text to wrap around images.

Vertical Image Alignment

Sometimes, you may want to insert a small image right in the middle of a line of text. Or you might like to put a single line of text next to an image as a caption. In either case, it would be handy to have some control over how the text and images line up vertically. Should the bottom of the image line up with the bottom of the letters? Or should the text and images all be arranged so their middles line up? You can choose between these and several other options:

- ☐ To line up the top of an image with the top of the tallest image or letter on the same line, use <IMG ALIGN="top">.
- ☐ To line up the bottom of an image with the bottom of the text, use <IMG ALIGN="bottom">.
- ☐ To line up the bottom of an image with the bottom of the lowest image or letter on the same line, use <IMG ALIGN="absbottom">. (If there are some larger images on the same line, ALIGN=absbottom might place an image lower than ALIGN=bottom.)
- ☐ To line up the middle of an image with the middle of the text, use <IMG ALIGN="middle">.
- ☐ To line up the middle of an image with the overall vertical center of everything on the line, use <IMG ALIGN="absmiddle">. This might be higher or lower than ALIGN="middle", depending on the size and alignment of other images on the same line.

All these options are shown in Figure 9.6, and you can see how they affect two different lines of images and text in Figure 9.7. Notice that the large hat image in the top line radically affects where the small stars with ALIGN="top" and ALIGN="absbottom" are placed. The second line doesn't have a big image in it, so the effect of ALIGN="top" and ALIGN="absbottom" are much less dramatic.

If you don't include any ALIGN attributes in an <IMG> tag, the image will line up with the bottom of any text next to it. That means you never actually have to type in ALIGN="bottom" because it does the same thing.

In fact, you probably won't use any of the vertical alignment settings much. The vast majority of Web page images use either `ALIGN="left"`, `ALIGN="right"`, or no `ALIGN` attribute at all. So don't worry about memorizing all the options listed above—you can always refer to this book if you ever do need them!

Figure 9.6.

You can control vertical alignment of images with the ALIGN *attribute.*

```
<HTML>
<HEAD><TITLE>Image Alignment Magick Tricks</TITLE></HEAD>
<BODY>
<H1 ALIGN="center">
IMAGE ALIGNMENT<P>
<IMG SRC="magic.gif" ALIGN="middle">
<IMG SRC="star.gif" ALIGN="bottom">M
<IMG SRC="star.gif" ALIGN="top">A
<IMG SRC="star.gif" ALIGN="absmiddle">G
<IMG SRC="star.gif" ALIGN="absbottom">I
<IMG SRC="star.gif" ALIGN="absmiddle">C
<IMG SRC="star.gif" ALIGN="top">K
<IMG SRC="star.gif" ALIGN="bottom">
<P>
<IMG SRC="star.gif" ALIGN="bottom">T
<IMG SRC="star.gif" ALIGN="top">R
<IMG SRC="star.gif" ALIGN="absmiddle">I
<IMG SRC="star.gif" ALIGN="absbottom">C
<IMG SRC="star.gif" ALIGN="absmiddle">K
<IMG SRC="star.gif" ALIGN="top">S
<IMG SRC="star.gif" ALIGN="bottom">
</H1>
</BODY></HTML>
```

Figure 9.7.

The top, middle, and bottom of each line depend on the size of the text and images on that line.

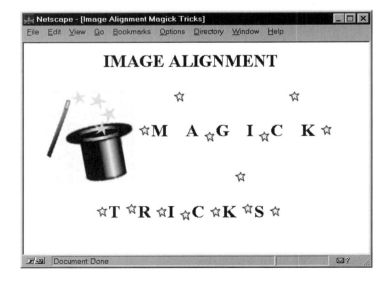

9

To Do:

Try adding some images to your Web pages now, and experiment with all the different values of ALIGN. To get you started, here's a quick review of how to add the magic hat image to any Web page.

☐ Copy the magic.gif image file to the same directory folder as the HTML file.

☐ With a text editor, add <IMG SRC="magic.gif"> where you want the image to appear in the text.

☐ If you want the image to be centered, type <DIV ALIGN="center"> before the <IMG> tag and </DIV> after it. To wrap text around the image instead, add ALIGN="right" or ALIGN="left" to the <IMG> tag.

If you have time for a little more experimentation, try combining multiple images of various sizes (such as the star and the magic hats) with various vertical alignment settings for <IMG ALIGN>.

Images That Are Links

With the same <A HREF> tag used to make text links, you can make any image into a clickable link to another page. Figures 9.8 and 9.9 show a sample page. Clicking on the big button (or the words "To Balance the U.S. Federal Budget") retrieves the page located at http://garnet.berkeley.edu:3333/budget/budget-1.html on the Internet.

Figure 9.8.

Any images (and/or text) between <A HREF> and </A> tags become clickable links.

```
<HTML><HEAD><TITLE>Slash the Budget!</TITLE></HEAD>
<BODY>
<H1 ALIGN="center">Slash the Budget!</H1>
Now you too can look like a fool by cutting essential
government programs and still piling up billions of
dollars worth of federal deficit! Think you're smarter
than Bill, George, Ron, Gerry, Jimmy, and Dick put together?
Here's your big chance to prove it:<P ALIGN="center">
<A HREF=
"http://garnet.berkeley.edu:3333/budget/budget-1.html">
<IMG SRC="button.gif" ALT="Click Here"><BR>
To Balance the U.S. Federal Budget</A>
</BODY></HTML>
```

Figure 9.9.

The words "Click Here" are part of the `button.gif` *image referred to by the* `<IMG SRC>` *tag in Figure 9.8.*

Normally, Web browsers draw a colored rectangle around the edge of each image link. Like text links, the rectangle will usually appear blue to people who haven't visited the link recently, and purple to people who have visited it.

Chapter 13, "Backgrounds and Color Control," explains how to change the link colors, and Chapter 14, "Page Design and Layout," explains how to eliminate or change the size of the rectangle drawn around image links.

All the same rules and possibilities discussed in Chapter 3 and Chapter 8, "Intra-Page and E-mail Links," apply to image links exactly as they do for text links. (You can link to another part of the same page with `<A HREF="#name">` and `<A NAME="name">`, for example.)

COFFEE BREAK

The addition of images can make an enormous difference in the impact a page has on the people who visit it. I added a few graphics to our developing *24-Hour HTML Café* site at:

`http://www.mcp.com/sams/books/235-8/cafe9.htm`

To appreciate the improvement, compare this to the site with the same text content at:

`http://www.mcp.com/sams/books/235-8/cafe8.htm`

In the next chapter, you'll find out how to build (or borrow) your own great graphics like these.

Summary

This chapter has shown you how to use the `<IMG>` tag to place graphics images on your Web pages. You learned to include a short text message to appear in place of the image as it loads, and for people who choose not to download graphics automatically. You also learned to control the horizontal and vertical alignment of each image, and how to make text wrap around the left or right side of an image.

Finally, you learned how to make images into "buttons" that link to other pages using the same `<A>` tag introduced in Chapter 3.

Table 9.1 summarizes the attributes of the `<IMG>` tag covered in this chapter.

Table 9.1. HTML attributes covered in Chapter 9.

Attribute	Function
`SRC="..."`	The address or filename of the image.
`ALT="..."`	A text message that may be displayed in place of the image.
`ALIGN="..."`	Determines the alignment of the given image. If `LEFT` or `RIGHT`, the image is aligned to the left or right column, and all following text flows beside that image. All other values, such as `TOP`, `MIDDLE`, `BOTTOM`, `ABSMIDDLE`, or `ABSBOTTOM`, determine the vertical alignment of this image with other items in the same line.

Q&A

Q I found a nice image on a Web page on the Internet. Can I just use Save Image As... to save a copy and then put the image on my Web pages?

A It's easy to do that, but unfortunately it's also illegal in most countries. You should get written permission from the original creator of the image first. Most Web pages include the e-mail addresses of their authors, which makes it a simple matter to ask for permission—a lot simpler than going to court, anyway!

Q How long of a message can I put after `ALT=` in an `<IMG>` tag?

A Theoretically, as long as you want. But practically, you should keep the message short enough so that it will fit in less space than the image itself. For big images, ten words may be fine. For small images, a single word is better.

Q **How do I control both the horizontal and vertical alignment of an image at once?**

A The short answer is that you can't. For example, if you type `<IMG ALIGN="right" ALIGN="middle" SRC="myimage.gif">`, the `ALIGN="middle"` will be ignored.

There are ways around this limitation, however. Chapter 14 will explain how to position text and images exactly where you want them in both the horizontal and vertical directions.

Quiz

Questions

1. How would you insert an image file named `elephant.jpg` at the very top of a Web page?

2. How would you make the word "Elephant" appear whenever the actual `elephant.jpg` image couldn't be displayed by a Web browser?

3. Write the HTML to make the `elephant.jpg` image appear on the right side of the page, with a big headline reading "Elephants of the World Unite!" on the left side of the page next to it.

4. Write the HTML to make a tiny image of a mouse (named `mouse.jpg`) appear between the words "Wee sleekit, cow'rin," and the words "tim'rous beastie."

5. Suppose you have a large picture of a standing elephant named `elephant.jpg`. Now make a small image named `fly.jpg` appear to the left of the elephant's head, and `mouse.jpg` appear next to the elephant's right foot.

Answers

1. Copy the image file into the same directory folder as the HTML text file, and type `<IMG SRC="elephant.jpg">` immediately after the `<BODY>` tag in the HTML text file.

2. Use the following HTML: `<IMG SRC="elephant.jpg" ALT="Elephant">`

3. `<IMG SRC="elephant.jpg" ALIGN="right">`
   `<H1>Elephants of the World Unite!</H1>`

4. `Wee sleekit, cow'rin,<IMG SRC="mouse.jpg">tim'rous beastie`

5. `<IMG SRC="fly.jpg" ALIGN="top">`
   `<IMG SRC="elephant.jpg">`
   `<IMG SRC="mouse.jpg">`

9

Activities

☐ Try using any small image as a "bullet" to make lists with more flair. If you also want the list to be indented, use the <DL> definition list and <DD> for each item (instead of <UL> and <LI>, which would give the standard boring bullets). Here's a quick example, using the star.gif file from my sample images page:

```
<DL><DD><IMG SRC="star.gif">A murder of crows
<DD><IMG SRC="star.gif">A rafter of turkeys
<DD><IMG SRC="star.gif">A muster of peacocks</DL>
```

Hour 10

Creating Web Page Images

You don't have to be an artist to put high-impact graphics and creative type on your Web pages. You don't need to spend hundreds or thousands of dollars on software, either. This chapter tells you how to create the images you need to make visually exciting Web pages. It also explains how to make those images appear as quickly as possible, even for people using slow modems to access them. (Chapter 11, "Making Pages Display Quickly," presents more techniques for speeding up the display of your graphics, too.)

TIME SAVER

One of the best ways to save time creating the graphics and media files is, of course, to avoid creating them altogether. Any graphic or media clip you see on any site is instantly reusable as soon as the copyright holder grants (or sells) you the right to copy it.

Grabbing a graphic from any Web page is as simple as clicking it with the right mouse button, and picking Save Image As in Netscape Navigator or Save Picture As in Microsoft Explorer. Extracting a background image from a page is just as easy: Right-click the background and choose Save Background As.

Choosing Graphics Software

You can use almost any computer graphics program to create graphics images for your Web pages, from the simple Paintbrush program that comes free with Microsoft Windows to an expensive professional program such as Adobe Photoshop. If you have a digital camera or scanner attached to your computer, it probably came with some graphics software capable of creating Web page graphics.

If you already have some software that you think might be good for creating Web graphics, try using it to do everything described in this chapter. If it can't do some of the tasks covered here, it probably won't be a good tool for Web graphics.

To Do:

One excellent and inexpensive program that does provide everything you're likely to need is Paint Shop Pro from JASC, Inc. If you are using a Windows computer, I highly recommend that you download a free, fully functional evaluation copy of Paint Shop Pro before reading the rest of this chapter.

(Macintosh users should download BME at `http://www.softlogik.com` instead, because Paint Shop Pro is currently available for Windows only.)

1. Start your Web browser, and go to `http://www.jasc.com/pspdl.html`.

2. Follow the directions to transfer the latest version of Paint Shop Pro onto your hard drive. (As of this writing, the file you need is called `psp41.zip`.)

3. You will need a program capable of handling Zip archives in order to install Paint Shop Pro. If you don't have such a program, go to `http://www.winzip.com` and follow the instructions there to download and install WinZip.

4. Use WinZip (or an equivalent program) to remove the Paint Shop Pro installation programs from the Zip file, and put them in a directory folder of their own.

5. Run the `pspsetup.exe` program to install Paint Shop Pro.

JUST A MINUTE

The Paint Shop Pro software you can get online is a fully functional shareware evaluation copy. If you agree with me that it's essential for working with Web page images, please be prompt about sending the $69 registration fee to the program's creators at JASC Software. (The address is in the online help in the software.) I'm confident that you're not going to find any other graphics software even close to the power and usability of Paint Shop Pro for anywhere near $69. (In fact, I have all the leading super-expensive commercial graphics programs from Photoshop on down, and Paint Shop Pro is the best by far for day-to-day work with Web graphics.)

10

Almost all the graphics you'll see in this book were created with Paint Shop Pro, and this chapter uses Paint Shop Pro to illustrate several key Web graphics techniques you'll need to know. Of course, there are so many ways to produce images with Paint Shop Pro, I can't even begin to explain them all. If you'd like a quick but complete tutorial on using Paint Shop Pro to make high-impact Web page graphics, pick up a copy of the Que Publishing book *Creating Your Own Web Page Graphics*, by Andy Shafran and Dick Oliver (yep, that's me).

Graphics Basics

Two forces are always at odds when you post graphics and multimedia on the Net. Your eyes and ears want everything to be as detailed and accurate as possible, but your clock and wallet want files to be as small as possible. Intricate, colorful graphics mean big file sizes, which can take a long time to transfer, even over a fast connection.

So how do you maximize the quality of your presentation while minimizing file size? To make these choices, you need to understand how color and resolution work together to create a subjective sense of quality.

The *resolution* of an image is the height and width measured in pixels (the individual dots that make up a digital image). Large, high-resolution images take longer to transfer and display than small, low-resolution images. Resolution is usually written as the width times the height; a 300×200 image, for example, is 300 dots wide and 200 dots high.

NEW TERM *Resolution* is the number of individual dots, or *pixels*, that make up an image.

You might be surprised to find that resolution isn't the most significant factor determining the storage size (and transfer time) of an image file. This is because images used on Web pages are always stored and transferred in *compressed* form. The mathematics of image compression is complex, but the basic idea is that repeating patterns or large areas of the same color can be squeezed out when the image is stored on a disk. This makes the image file much smaller, and allows it to be transferred faster over the Internet. The original appearance of the image can then be restored by the Web browser program when the image is displayed.

NEW TERM *Image compression* is the mathematical manipulation that images are put through to squeeze out repetitive patterns. It makes them load and display much faster.

In the rest of this chapter, you'll learn exactly how to create graphics with big visual impact and small file sizes. The techniques you'll use to accomplish this depend on the contents and purpose of each image. There are as many uses for Web page graphics as there are Web pages, but four types of graphics are by far the most common:

- ☐ Photos of people, products, or places
- ☐ Graphical banners and logos for the tops of pages
- ☐ Snazzy-looking buttons or icons to link between pages
- ☐ Background textures or *paper* to go behind pages

The last of these will be covered in Chapter 13, "Backgrounds and Color Control." But you can learn to create the other three kinds of graphics right now.

Preparing Photographic Images

To put photos on your Web pages, you'll need some kind of scanner or digital camera. You'll often need to use the custom software that comes with your scanner or camera to save pictures on your hard drive. Note, however, that you can control any scanner that is compatible with the TWAIN interface standard directly from Paint Shop Pro and most other graphics programs—see the software documentation for details.

TIME SAVER

If you don't have a scanner or digital camera, any Kodak film-developing store can transfer photos from 35mm film to a CD-ROM for a modest fee. You can then use Paint Shop Pro to open and modify the Kodak Photo CD files.

Once you have the pictures, you can use Paint Shop Pro (or a similar graphics program) to get them ready for the Web.

You want Web page graphics to be as compact as possible, so you'll usually need to crop or reduce the size of scanned images. Follow these steps to crop an image in Paint Shop Pro:

1. Click on the rectangular selection tool on the tools palette. (The tools palette is shown on the left in Figure 10.1. You can drag it wherever you want it, so it may be in a different place on your screen.)

2. Click on the top-left corner of the part of the image you want to keep, and hold down the mouse button while you drag down to the lower-right corner (see Figure 10.1).

3. Select Image | Crop.

Figure 10.1.
Use the rectangular selection tool to crop images as tightly as possible.

Even after cropping, your image may be larger than it needs to be for a Web page. Generally, a complex photograph should be no more than 300×300 pixels, and a simpler photo can look fine at 100×50 or so.

TIME SAVER

Notice that in Paint Shop Pro the resolution of the current image is shown at the bottom-right corner of the window. The image may look larger or smaller than it really is, because Paint Shop Pro automatically adjusts the image to fit in the window while you're working on it. To see the image at the size it will appear on a Web page, select View | Normal Viewing (1:1).

Most graphics programs offer two different ways to change the resolution of an image, and one technique gives much nicer-looking results than the other. The names of these techniques vary from program to program, but in Paint Shop Pro you should always use the Image | Resample command (instead of Image | Resize). You'll get the Resample dialog box, shown in Figure 10.2.

You'll almost always want Custom size and Maintain aspect ratio selected. When you enter the width (in pixels) which you'd like the image to be, the height will be calculated automatically to keep the image from squishing out of shape.

Figure 10.2.

*To change the size
of a photographic image,
always use Image |
Resample.*

Many photographs will require some color correction to look their best on a computer screen. Like most photo editing programs, Paint Shop Pro offers many options for adjusting the brightness, contrast, and color balance of an image.

Most of these options are pretty intuitive to use, but the most important and powerful one may be unfamiliar if you're not an old graphics pro. Whenever an image appears too dark or too light, select Colors | Adjust | Gamma Correction. For most images, this works better than Colors | Adjust | Brightness and Contrast, because it doesn't "wash out" bright or dark areas.

As shown in Figure 10.3, you can click on the small arrow buttons in the Gamma Correction dialog box to adjust the correction factor until the image looks about right. (Numbers above 1 make the image lighter, and numbers between 1 and 0 make the image darker.)

10

Figure 10.3.
Gamma Correction is the best way to fix images that are too dark or too light.

Most of the other image editing tools in Paint Shop Pro offer small preview windows like the one in Figure 10.3, so a little playful experimentation is the best way to find out what each of them does.

Controlling JPEG Compression

Photographic images look best when saved in the JPEG file format. When you're finished adjusting the size and appearance of your photo, select File | Save As and choose the JPG-JPEG-JFIF Compliant file type with Standard Encoding, as shown in the bottom half of Figure 10.4.

Figure 10.4 also shows the File Preferences dialog box you'll see when you click the Options button. You can control the compression ratio for saving JPEG files by adjusting the compression level setting between 1 percent (high quality, large file size) and 99 percent (low quality, small file size).

In Chapter 11 you'll see how various JPEG compression levels affect the quality of typical images.

Figure 10.4.

Paint Shop Pro allows you to trade reduced file size for image quality when saving JPEG images.

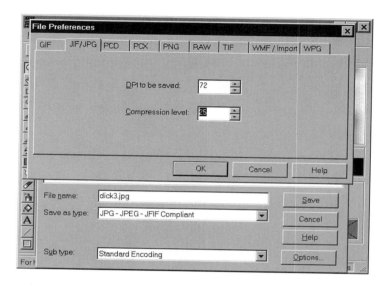

Creating Banners and Buttons

Graphics that you create from scratch, such as banners and buttons, involve different considerations than photographs.

The first decision you need to make when you produce a banner or button is how big it should be. Almost everyone accessing the Web now (or in the foreseeable future) has a computer with one of three screen sizes. The most common resolution for notebook computers and televisions is 640×480 pixels. The resolution of most desktop computers today is 800×600 pixels, and 1024×768 pixels is the preferred resolution of most new computers and future laptops. You should generally plan your graphics so that they will always fit in the smallest of these screens, with room to spare for scrollbars and margins.

This means that full-sized banners and title graphics should be no more than 600 pixels wide. Photos and large artwork should be from 100 to 300 pixels in each dimension, and smaller buttons or icons should be 20 to 100 pixels tall and wide.

Figure 10.5 shows the dialog box you get when you select File | New to start a new image. You should always begin with 16.7 Million Colors (24 Bit) as the Image type. You can always change the size of the image later with Image | Crop or Image | Enlarge Canvas, so don't worry if you aren't sure *exactly* how big it needs to be.

For the Background color, choose White to match the background that most Web browsers ordinarily use for Web pages. (You'll see how to change the background color of a page in Chapter 13. When you know you'll be making a page with a non-white background, you can choose a different background color here, too.)

Figure 10.5.

You need to know the approximate size of an image before you start working on it.

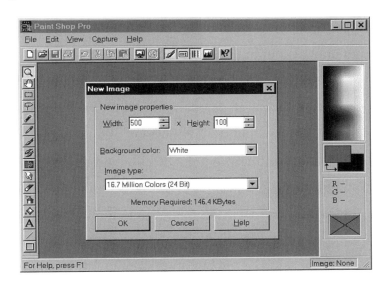

When you enter the width and height of the image in pixels and click OK, you are faced with a blank canvas—an intimidating sight if you're as art-phobic as most of us! Fortunately, computer graphics programs such as Paint Shop Pro make it amazingly easy to produce professional-looking graphics for most Web page applications.

To make the title banner and buttons in Figure 10.6, for instance, all I did was pick colors from the color palette on the right, click on the text tool on the left, choose a font and size, and position each word where I thought it looked nice. I used the Image | Special Effects | Buttonize menu option to automatically add three-dimensional shading to the edges of the buttons. Other sophisticated effects like drop shadows, sunburst gradient fills, and textured papers are equally effortless.

Figure 10.6.

Many sharp-looking Web page images can be created with minimal artistic skill or computer graphics experience.

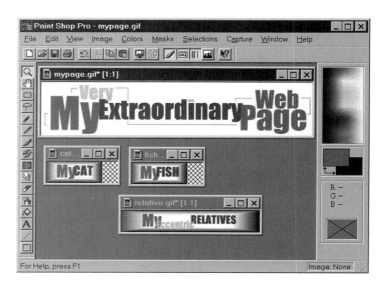

Reducing the Number of Colors

One of the most effective ways to reduce the download time for an image is to reduce the number of colors. This can drastically reduce the visual quality of photographic images, but works great for most banners, buttons, and other icons.

In Paint Shop Pro, you can do this by selecting Colors | Reduce Color Depth. (Most other graphics programs have a similar option.) The software will automatically find the best palette of 16 or 256 colors for approximating the full range of colors in the image.

JUST A MINUTE

> Even if you use only two or three colors in an image, you should still select Colors | Reduce Color Depth | 16 Colors before you save it. If you don't, the image file will waste some space leaving room for lots of colors even though very few are actually in use.

When you reduce the number of colors in an image, you will see a dialog box with several choices (see Figure 10.7). For Web page images, you will almost always want to choose an Optimized palette, and Nearest color instead of Error diffusion or any form of dithering.

10

Figure 10.7.
Reducing the number of colors in an image can dramatically decrease file size without changing the appearance of the image much.

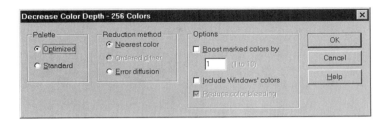

TIME SAVER

Dithering (called *error diffusion* in Paint Shop Pro) means using random dots or patterns to intermix palette colors. This can make images look better in some cases, but usually should be avoided for Web page graphics. Why? Because it substantially increases the information complexity of an image, and that almost always results in much larger file sizes and slower downloads. So, listen to your Great Uncle Oliver and "don't dither!"

There is a special file format for images with a limited number of colors, called the Graphics Interchange Format (GIF). To save a GIF image in Paint Shop Pro, select File | Save As and choose GIF-CompuServe as the image type.

Interlaced GIFs and Progressive JPEGs

Both the GIF and JPEG image file formats offer a nifty feature to make images appear faster than they possibly could otherwise. An image can be stored in such a way that a "rough draft" of the image appears quickly, and then the details are filled in as the download finishes. This has a profound psychological effect, because it gives people something "complete" to look at, instead of drumming their fingers waiting for a large image to pour slowly onto the screen.

A file stored with this feature is called an *interlaced GIF* or *progressive JPEG*. Despite the two different names, the visual results are similar with either format.

An *interlaced GIF* file is an image that will appear blocky at first, then more and more detailed as it finishes downloading. Similarly, a *progressive JPEG* file appears blurry at first, then gradually comes into focus.

Most graphics programs that can handle GIF files enable you to choose whether to save them interlaced or noninterlaced. In Paint Shop Pro, for example, you can choose the Version 89a-Interlaced Sub type on the Save As dialog box, just before you save a GIF file (see Figure 10.8).

To save a progressive JPEG file, choose the JPG-JPEG-JFIF Compliant image type and the Progressive Encoding Sub type.

Figure 10.8.

Paint Shop Pro lets you save interlaced GIF images, which appear to display faster when loading.

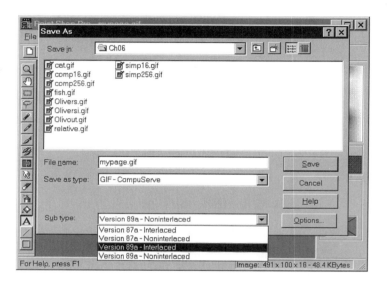

JUST A MINUTE

The progressive JPEG standard is quite new and is supported only by Netscape Navigator version 2.0 or higher and Microsoft Internet Explorer version 3.0 or higher.

Browsers that don't support progressive JPEG will *not* display the file as if it were just a regular JPEG—they will display nothing at all or a message saying the file isn't recognizable. Interlaced GIFs, on the other hand, will appear correctly even in older browsers that don't support two-stage display.

Figure 10.9 shows a Web page with a title banner saved in the interlaced GIF format being downloaded from the Internet. Notice that the banner appears blocky. If this weren't an interlaced GIF, only the top half of the image would be showing at this point in the download.

Figure 10.10 shows the same page a few seconds later, when the download is complete.

10

Figure 10.9.

The banner at the top of this page looks blocky because the interlaced GIF file isn't done loading yet.

Figure 10.10.

The same page as in Figure 10.9, after all images are done loading.

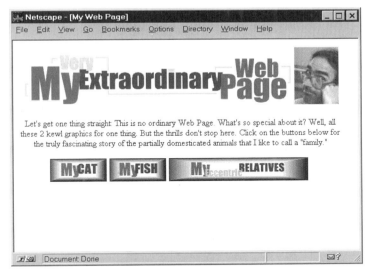

JUST A MINUTE

Image files smaller than about 3KB will usually load so fast that nobody will ever see the interlacing or progressive display anyway. In fact, very small images may actually load *more slowly* when interlaced. So save these tricks for larger images only.

To Do:

Well don't just sit there reading, grab that mouse and crank up Paint Shop Pro! I can't tell you what graphics best convey the mood and spirit you'd like for your site. But here are a few pitfalls to avoid and shortcuts to take as you navigate the uncharted territory of your own Web graphics:

- ☐ Stick with a few thematic colors on each page and throughout all your pages. Beginning "Web artists" tend to get carried away with the millions of colors your computer can produce.

- ☐ To save time, make a simple, unlabelled button or icon and use it as a starting point for all your links. This will also give your pages a consistent look.

- ☐ Use one font in all titles and buttons. Okay, two fonts, tops. The "ransom note" look is definitely passé.

- ☐ Keep your first graphics direct and to the point. Remember, you'll learn much more about backgrounds, colors, fonts, and layout tricks in the chapters to come!

COFFEE BREAK

Adding graphics to your pages opens up vast horizons of artistic possibility, and it can often be challenging to come up with an attractive, practical design for your Web page graphics.

To help your creative juices start flowing (and perhaps keep them from flowing too wildly), I've provided a number of sample pages with thematic images almost anyone could produce in Paint Shop Pro or an equivalent graphics program. To browse through these pages, go to

`http://www.mcp.com/sams/books/235-8/cafe10.htm`

and click on the Great Graphics Ideas link.

Summary

In this chapter, you learned the basics of preparing graphics for use on Web pages. You saw how to download and use the popular graphics program Paint Shop Pro to work with photos, banners, buttons, and other Web page images. You also found out how to decide between the various graphics file formats used for Web page graphics, and how to make images that appear in stages for the illusion of speed.

Don't miss Chapter 11, "Making Pages Display Quickly," for more graphics speed-up tricks.

10

Q&A

Q **I've heard that I need Photoshop to do Web graphics well. Is it true?**

A Adobe Photoshop is the most popular commercial graphics program for creating Web page graphics, and it is arguably the most powerful as well. But unless you're an experienced graphics professional (in which case you already own Photoshop), you'll probably find it much easier—and a lot less expensive—to learn and use Paint Shop Pro. Note that Paint Shop Pro does support all Photoshop-compatible plug-ins and add-on programs, too.

Q **Shouldn't I just hire a graphics artist to design my pages for me instead of learning all this stuff?**

A If you have plenty of money and need a visually impressive site—or if you think that ugly building with chartreuse trim that people are always complaining about actually looks pretty nice—hiring some professional help might not be a bad idea. But remember that you probably know what you want more than anyone else does, which often counts more than artistic skills in producing a good Web page.

Q **I've produced graphics for printing on paper. Is making Web page graphics much different?**

A Yes. In fact, many of the rules for print graphics are reversed on the Web. Web page graphics have to be low-resolution, while print graphics should be as high-resolution as possible. White washes out black on computer screens, while black bleeds into white on paper. Also, someone may stop a Web page when only half the graphics are done. So try to avoid falling into old habits if you've done a lot of print graphics design.

Quiz

Questions

1. Suppose you have a scanned picture of a horse that you need to put on a Web page. How big should you make it, and in what file format should you save it?

2. Your company logo is a black letter Z with a red circle behind it. What size should you draw (or scan) it, and what file format should you save it in for use on your Web page?

3. Should you save a 100×50 pixel button graphic as an interlaced GIF file?

Answers

1. Depending on how important the image is to your page, as small as 100×40 pixels or as large as 300×120 pixels. The JPEG format, with about 50-percent compression, would be best.

2. About 100×100 pixels is generally good for a logo, but a simple graphic like that will compress very well so you could make it up to 300×300 pixels if you want. Save it as a 16-color GIF file.

3. No. A small file like that will load just as fast or faster without interlacing.

Activities

☐ If you have an archive of company (or personal) photos, look through it to find a few that might enhance your Web site. Scan them (or send them out to be scanned) so that you'll have a library of graphics all ready to draw from as you produce more pages in the future.

☐ Before you start designing graphics for an important business site, try spicing up your own personal home page. This will give you a chance to learn Paint Shop Pro (or your other graphics software) so you'll look like you know what you're doing when you tackle it at work.

10

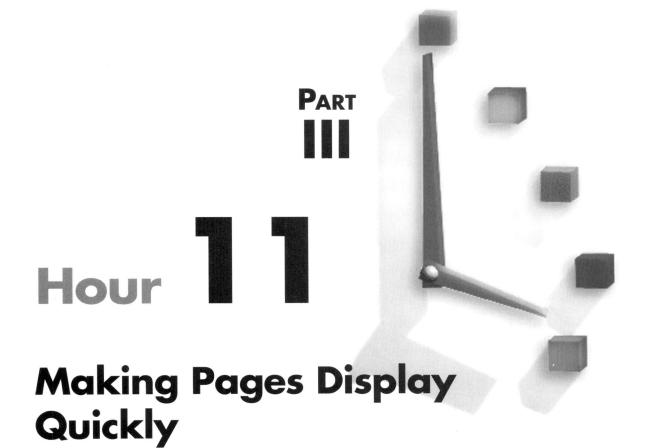

Hour **11**

Making Pages Display Quickly

This chapter teaches you how to ensure that your Web pages will appear as quickly as possible when people try to read them. This is essential for making a good impression with your pages, especially with people who will be accessing them through modem connections to the Internet.

Balancing Image File Size and Quality

The single most important and effective thing you can do to speed up the display of your pages is to make your graphics files as small as possible.

In Chapter 10, "Creating Web Page Images," you learned how to set the compression level for JPEG images and select the number of colors for GIF images. With both types of graphics files, you need to try to find a balance between acceptable image quality and maximum speed.

Figure 11.1 compares the results of saving two graphics files at various GIF- and JPEG-quality settings (keep in mind that the differences are more obvious in color). The numbers in parentheses are the file sizes. For example, the top-left image in Figure 11.1 is 15K, and the top-right image is 3K.

If you examine these images closely (you can look at them in color at http://www.mcp.com/sams/books/235-8/ch06/compress.htm), you'll probably decide that 50-percent JPEG compression provides a good compromise of quality and size for the COMPLEXITY image. The SIMPLICITY image would both look and compress best as a 16-color GIF.

Figure 11.1.

Simple images usually look best and load fastest as 16-color GIF files, while 50-percent JPEG compression is good for most complex graphics.

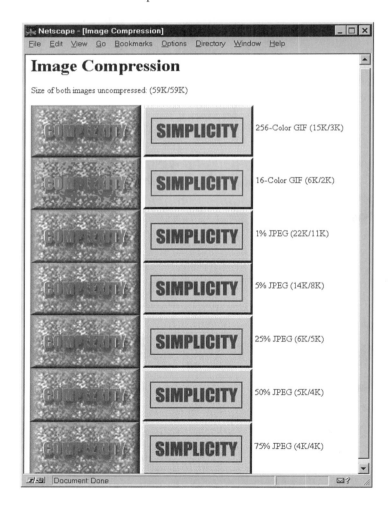

To estimate how long it will typically take for your images to download, you can assume that a standard 28.8Kbps modem with a good connection to a Net site can pull about 2KB per second on average. If you were surfing the Net, would you rather wait nearly half a minute to see this image in its full glory, or watch it pop onto your screen at 75-percent quality in less than six seconds?

Remember that many people are still accessing the Net through 14.4Kbps or slower modems. As a general rule, any Web page that includes more than 50KB worth of graphics should be accessed only from another, less graphics-intensive page. Links to the graphics-intensive page should warn readers so they can turn automatic graphics downloading off if they are using a slow dial-up modem connection.

Specifying Image Width and Height

Because text moves over the Internet much faster than graphics, most Web browsers will display the text on a page before the images. This gives people something to read while they're waiting to see the pictures, which makes the whole page seem to come up much faster.

You can make sure that everything on your page appears as quickly as possible and in the right places by explicitly stating the width and height of each image. That way, a Web browser can leave the right amount of space for that image as it lays out the page and come back to get the actual image file later.

For each image on your page, use Paint Shop Pro or another graphics program to find out the exact width and height in pixels. (In Paint Shop Pro, this information appears at the bottom-right corner of the main window when you move the mouse over any part of an image.) Then include those dimensions in the <IMG> tag like this:

```
<IMG SRC="myimage.gif" WIDTH=200 HEIGHT=100>
```

TIME SAVER

The width and height you specify for an image don't have to match the actual width and height of the image. The Web browser program will try to squish or stretch the image to whatever size you specify.

This usually makes images look very ugly, but there is one excellent use for it: You can save a very small, totally transparent image and use it as any size "spacer" by specifying the width and height of the blank region you want to create on your page.

Providing a Preview Image

You can also speed things up by providing a small image file to be displayed while someone is waiting for a full-sized image file to download.

Put the name of the smaller file after the word LOWSRC in the same image tag as the full-sized SRC image:

```
<IMG SRC="bigfile.gif" LOWSRC="tinyfile.jpg">
```

What happens here is that the Web browser makes its first pass through your document, and when it sees your LOWSRC tag, it loads that (presumably smaller) image first. Then it makes a second pass through your document and loads the main image.

Though this attribute was originally designed with the intention that the LOWSRC image would be a low-resolution or highly compressed version of the SRC image, you can also use two entirely different images to get a two-frame animation effect.

Figure 11.2 is an HTML page that uses the WIDTH, HEIGHT, and LOWSRC attributes in an <IMG> tag. Figure 11.3 shows the LOWSRC and SRC images. The LOWSRC image is only two colors and contains less detail, so its GIF file is only 3KB and will load in less than 2 seconds through a 28.8Kbps modem. The SRC image file, with 256 colors and lots of detail, is 35KB—taking about ten times as long to download.

Figure 11.2.

Always include the width and height of all images. Use LOWSRC *to include a small image to display while a large image loads.*

```
<HTML>
<HEAD><TITLE>The Olivers</TITLE></HEAD>
<BODY>
<IMG SRC="olivers.gif" LOWSRC="olivout.gif"
 ALIGN="left" WIDTH=250 HEIGHT=350>
These are the Olivers. You don't have to like them.
But they like you. Why? Because you bought one of
Dick Oliver's books. That means that the Olivers can
pay their mortgage this month, which is a friendly
sort of feeling indeed. So we'd like to welcome you
as an official honorary member of the Oliver family.
</BODY>
</HTML>
```

Figure 11.3.

Though these two images are the same width and height, the left image compresses into a much smaller GIF file.

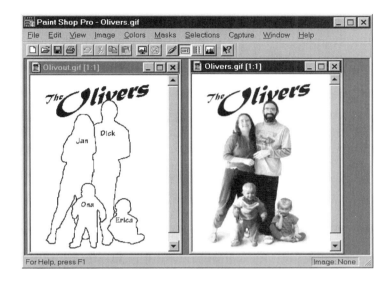

Figures 11.4 through 11.7 show the page from Figure 11.2 as it will look to someone viewing it on the Internet. It appears in four stages:

0–2 seconds (Figure 11.4):
> The text appears with a small icon and rectangle as a placeholder for the image. If I hadn't included WIDTH and HEIGHT attributes in the <IMG> tag, the text would be in the wrong place at first and would then jump over suddenly, making it hard to read.

2–4 seconds (Figure 11.5):
> The LOWSRC image appears. Because I saved it as an interlaced GIF image (see Chapter 10), it fades in gradually over the course of a couple seconds.

4–20 seconds (Figure 11.6):
> The SRC image replaces the LOWSRC image. I didn't save the SRC image as an interlaced GIF, because I wanted it to "wipe out" the LOWSRC image in a single pass.

About 20 seconds (Figure 11.7):
> The page is complete. Because most people will have just finished reading the text at this time, they won't feel like they had to wait at all!

If someone comes back to a page more than once in the same day, the Web browser will usually only show the LOWSRC image the first time. After that, it will be able to quickly pull the SRC image out of its memory.

Figure 11.4.

When WIDTH *and* HEIGHT *attributes are included in an* <IMG> *tag, the browser draws a rectangular placeholder for an image before loading it.*

Figure 11.5.

Next, the LOWSRC *image is displayed (if one was specified).*

Figure 11.6.
The SRC *image gradually replaces the* LOWSRC *image as it downloads.*

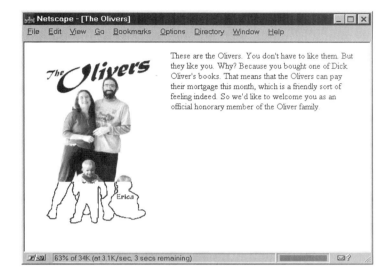

Figure 11.7.
If the page is loaded again by the same person a little while later, they won't see the LOWSRC *image at all.*

COFFEE BREAK

When you have multiple graphics elements without WIDTH and HEIGHT attributes on a page, it can be especially disconcerting to watch it reshuffle elements while loading. To see the difference, compare the following two versions of the *24-Hour HTML Café* page:

```
http://www.mcp.com/sams/books/235-8/cafe10.htm
http://www.mcp.com/sams/books/235-8/cafe11.htm
```
The latter page also uses LOWSRC images for a groovy effect while loading.

Summary

This chapter helped you choose the number of colors and compression level of images so they load fast and still look good. You also learned how to make sure people always have text or a preview image to look at while waiting for the larger images on your page.

Table 11.1 summarizes the tags and attributes discussed in this chapter.

Table 11.1. HTML tags and attributes covered in Chapter 11.

Tag	Attribute	Function
<IMG>		Inserts an inline image into the document.
	SRC="..."	The address of the image.
	WIDTH="..."	The width, in pixels, of the image. If WIDTH is not the actual width, the image is scaled to fit.
	HEIGHT="..."	The height, in pixels, of the image. If HEIGHT is not the actual height, the image is scaled to fit.
	LOWSRC="..."	The path or URL of an image that will be loaded first, before the image specified in SRC. The value of LOWSRC is usually a smaller or lower resolution version of the actual image.

Q&A

Q This may be a dumb question, but how do I tell if my image is "complex" (suitable for JPEG compression) or "simple" (suitable for GIF compression)?

A Try reducing the number of colors to 16. If the image still looks fine, it's probably best to use GIF compression. If it looks terrible with so few colors, try saving it both as a 50-percent JPEG and a 256-color GIF. Then compare the file sizes to see which one is smaller.

11

Q My 16-color GIF image looks great in Paint Shop Pro, but lousy in Netscape Navigator. Did I do something wrong?

A Netscape Navigator usually uses a different method for mixing the colors of 16-color images than it does for 256-color images, which can sometimes make 16-color graphics look really bad. Here's a cheap solution: In Paint Shop Pro, reduce the number of colors in your image to 16, then increase the number of colors to 256 before you save it as a GIF. The image file will still be as small as a 16-color GIF, but Netscape Navigator will use the 256-color dithering method for displaying it. That often makes it look a lot better.

Q How do I make a "smaller" copy of an image for use with the LOWSRC tag?

A There are three easy ways: One is to save the image as a JPEG file with very high compression. Another is to reduce the number of colors to 16 (or even 2), and save the file as a GIF. The third way is to resize the image to a lower resolution (say, 50×20 instead of 200×80). The Web browser will "stretch" the small LOWSRC image to fit in the same space as the big SRC image, as long as you include WIDTH=200 HEIGHT=80 in the <IMG> tag.

See Chapter 10 for detailed instructions on how to do all three of these things in Paint Shop Pro.

Quiz

Questions

1. What compression level setting is generally best for most JPEG images?
2. How could you display a picture of a wolf briefly, then replace it with a picture of a man (without using GIF animation)?
3. What four attributes should you always include in every <IMG> tag as a matter of habit?

Answers

1. 50-percent compression.
2. `<IMG SRC="man.jpg" LOWSRC="wolf.jpg">`
3. SRC, ALT, WIDTH, and HEIGHT. For example:

   ```
   <IMG SRC="fred.jpg" ALT="Fat Fred" WIDTH=300 HEIGHT=100>
   ```

Activities

☐ For large images (any graphics file over 15KB), it's worth a little experimentation to find the exact compression ratio or number of colors that gives you the minimum acceptable quality. Save it at all the settings shown in Figure 11.1, and compare them in Netscape Navigator or Microsoft Internet Explorer.

☐ Black-and-white images make the smallest files, so many sites use a 2-color version of a color graphic as the LOWSRC image. If simply reducing the colors of an image doesn't yield a good LOWSRC image, try using Paint Shop Pro's Emboss or Trace Contour effects first.

11

Hour 12

Creating Animated Graphics

There are several ways to add some movement to a Web page, and most of them are covered in the most advanced chapter in this book—Chapter 20, "Scripting, Applets, and ActiveX." However, you can actually add animation to standard GIF images, and it's so easy to do that the technique doesn't even qualify as "advanced."

GIF animations are a great way to make simple animated icons and add a little motion to spice up any Web page. In this chapter, you'll learn how to create GIF animations and how to optimize them for the fastest possible display.

Software for Making Web Page Animations

Alchemy Mindworks' GIF Construction Set is a nifty little utility designed especially for assembling GIF animations. There are a few other GIF animation programs available, including both freeware and advanced commercial software packages. However, GIF Construction Set offers the best mix of great features, ease of use, and low price.

(For Macintosh users, I recommend GifBuilder, which is available free at `http://www.shareware.com`. Another good GIF animation program for the Mac is Gif.gIF.giF at `http://www.cafe.net/peda/ggg/`)

To Do:

You can download a free evaluation copy of GIF Construction Set from the Internet. I recommend that you do so now so that you can try your hand at building an animation or two as you read this chapter.

1. If you are using Windows 95 or NT, download this file:

   `ftp://ftp.mindworkshop.com/pub/alchemy/gifcon32.exe`

   If you're using Windows 3.1 or 3.11, download this file instead:

   `ftp://ftp.mindworkshop.com/pub/alchemy/gifcon.exe`

2. Run the file you downloaded. It will extract and install GIF Construction Set automatically.

Building a GIF Animation

The first step in creating a GIF animation is to create a series of images to be displayed one after the other. You can use any graphics software you like to make the images. You don't even need to use software that supports GIF to make the images; GIF Construction Set can import BMP, JPEG, PCX, TIFF, and almost any other graphics file format you throw at it.

TIME SAVER

The fastest way to create a simple GIF animation with GIF Construction Set is to select File | Animation Wizard. This will start an "interview" that leads you through all the steps discussed below.

You also can create scrolling text and a number of transition effects automatically with the Edit | Banner and Edit | Transition menu options. These commands provide an easy way to add some quick animation effects to still images.

In this chapter, however, I show you how to create animations "by hand," without using the Wizard or automatic effects. This will give you a head start when you want to use the advanced animation tricks discussed toward the end of the chapter.

Before you assemble an animation with GIF Construction Set, you may want to open the images you'd like to include from another graphics program so you can refer to them as you put the animation together. Figure 12.1 shows the four images for this example open in Paint Shop Pro with the GIF Construction Set program in the foreground.

Figure 12.1.

Use Paint Shop Pro or any other graphics program to produce the individual "frames" of your animation.

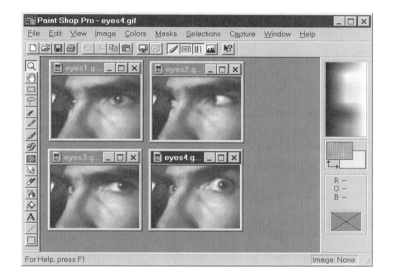

To Do:

You may want to create a few frames for your own animation and use them to follow along with the numbered steps below.

You'll find it easier to build and modify animations if you give the images for each animation similar names. You might name the images for a dog animation dog1.gif, dog2.gif, dog3.gif, and so on.

The following numbered steps show you how to make a simple GIF animation.

1. To start a new animation, start GIF Construction Set and select File | New. At the top of the white area, HEADER GIF89a Screen (640×480) should appear. This is the first "block" in the GIF file, to which you will be adding additional image blocks and control blocks that will be listed below it.

2. Click the Edit button, and the dialog box in Figure 12.2 appears. Enter the screen width and depth (height) of the largest image you want to use in the animation and click OK. (Not sure how big your images are? Paint Shop Pro displays the width and depth of the current image in the lower-left corner of the screen.)

12

Figure 12.2.

*GIF Construction Set
runs in a fairly small
window, allowing you to
see other applications,
such as Paint Shop Pro,
at the same time.*

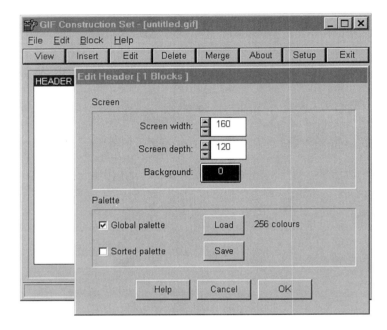

3. If you want the animation to loop continuously when viewed in Netscape Navigator, click the Insert button and then click LOOP. This inserts a special control block telling it to immediately restart the animation every time it finishes. If you want to create an animation that plays only once and then stops (leaving the last image on display), skip this step.

4. Click Insert, then Image, and then choose the first image in the animation. This is also the image that will be displayed by browsers that don't support GIF animation.

5. A dialog box will appear, saying, "The palette of the image you have imported does not match the global palette for this file." To make your animated GIF file as small as possible, select Use this image as the global palette for the first image you insert. Then select Remap to global palette if you see this dialog box when inserting subsequent images.

6. Press the up arrow once, or click LOOP, Insert, and Control, in that order. This inserts a control block in front of the image. Click Edit to get the Edit Control Block dialog box shown in Figure 12.3. You can enter a time delay to wait between this image and the next. (The other options are explained later in this chapter.)

12

Figure 12.3.

Control blocks enable you to make images transparent and to insert a time delay between images.

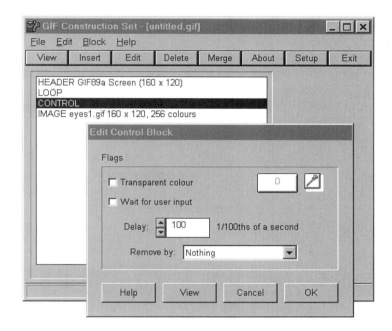

7. Repeat steps 4 through 6 for every image in the animation. Remember that the control block for an image has to appear *just above* the image block in the list. However, you need to insert the image first and then go back to edit the control block to add transparency.

   A little confusing? Don't worry, you'll be an old pro at it by the end of this chapter. In the meantime, if you make a mistake, you can highlight any block and click Delete to get rid of it.

8. When all the images and control blocks are inserted in the right order (as in Figure 12.4), select File | Save As to save the animation. Be sure to give it a name ending in `.gif`!

9. Using your favorite Web page editor, make an HTML document with an `<IMG>` tag referring to the GIF file you just saved as the SRC (for example, `<IMG SRC="lookani.gif">`). Load the document in Netscape Navigator or Microsoft Internet Explorer to see the results.

   You can also preview the animation within GIF Construction Set by clicking View at any time during the construction process.

12

Figure 12.4.

The images will be listed in order, with a small preview of the current frame to the right.

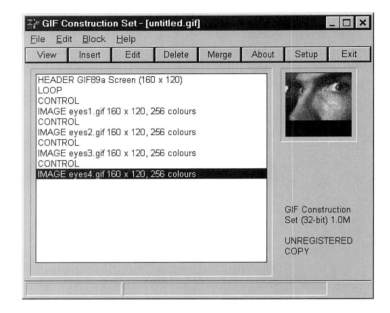

I obviously can't illustrate the animated effect of flipping back and forth between two images with a printed figure in a book. However, you can load the document at http://www.mcp.com/sams/books/235-8/ch12/look.htm to see this and another simple GIF animation.

Multiple Animations on One Page

Figures 12.5 through 12.7 show a page I created for the CD-ROM to accompany *Web Page Wizardry* from Sams.net Publishing. *Web Page Wizardry* is an excellent choice if you want to learn about more advanced animation and multimedia techniques after you finish this book.

This page is also online at http://www.mcp.com/sams/books/235-8/ch12/wpw.htm. If you view it with Netscape Navigator version 2.0 or higher, or with Microsoft Internet Explorer 3.0, you'll notice that all the icons are animated; a vision appears in the crystal ball, the scepter flashes, the cauldron bubbles, and the book pages turn. These icons are actually four separate multi-image GIFs, and the HTML code for this snazzy action-filled page looks just like an ordinary static Web page.

12

Figure 12.5.

At first glance, this looks like a page full of regular GIF images.

```
<HTML><HEAD><TITLE>Web Page Wizardry</TITLE></HEAD>
<BODY BACKGROUND="bubsmoke.jpg">
<DIV ALIGN="center">
<IMG SRC="wpwtitle.gif"><P>
<IMG SRC="visions.gif">
<IMG SRC="actions.gif">
<IMG SRC="spacer.gif">
<IMG SRC="spacer.gif">
<IMG SRC="brews.gif">
<IMG SRC="spacer.gif">
<IMG SRC="pages.gif">
<BR>
<IMG SRC="vistext.gif">
<IMG SRC="acttext.gif">
<IMG SRC="brwtext.gif">
<IMG SRC="spacer.gif">
<IMG SRC="pagtext.gif">
</DIV>
</BODY></HTML>
```

Figure 12.6.

Viewed in a modern Web browser, however, the page in Figure 12.5 becomes an animated scene full of action.

Figure 12.7.

Notice the differences between this shot and the one in Figure 12.6. It's alive!

A Hand-Crafted Animation

I could have created all this animation in Paint Shop Pro or another shareware graphics program, but I decided to bring in the heavy artillery and create it in Adobe Photoshop instead. Not only does Photoshop offer more advanced drawing and coloring tools, but more importantly, it also lets you keep various parts of an image in separate layers that you can modify independently. This feature (which is also found in a number of other commercial graphics editors) makes drawing simple animation a breeze.

By way of example, let me explain how I created the spell book that flips its own pages. To start, I sketched the first image from scratch and then drew five views of the turning page on separate layers, as shown in Figure 12.8.

TIME SAVER

To make "layered" animations like this in Paint Shop Pro, start by drawing the basic image (in this case the book), and using Edit | Copy and Edit | Paste | As New Image to create multiple copies of it. Then add the details for each image (in this case the turning page) separately.

12

Figure 12.8.

Photoshop makes it easy to build animation because you can just draw the changes from frame to frame and use transparency to show or hide it at will.

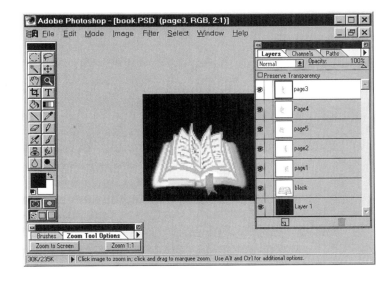

After I drew all the pages, I turned on each layer one at a time (keeping the book and background layers always on) and used Photoshop's File | Save a Copy command to save each view as a separate true-color BMP file.

Transparent Animations

You can make the background transparent by editing the control block in front of each image and choosing Transparent colour and Remove by: Background when you edit the control block (see Figure 12.9). You can use the eyedropper tool (mentioned earlier) to pick the transparent color, or you can click on the number next to the eyedropper to pick the color directly from the global or local palette (see Figure 12.10).

To make sure you have picked the right color to be transparent, you can click the View button to preview the animation.

JUST A MINUTE

Note that the background color used during the preview can be set by selecting File | Setup and picking a color under Edit view mode background.

12

Figure 12.9.

If you want the animation to have a transparent color, insert and edit a control block before each image.

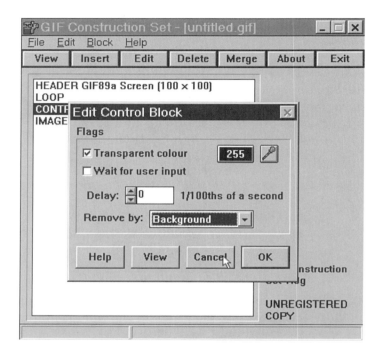

Figure 12.10.

To pull up this color-picking palette, click the number next to the eyedropper tool (255 in Figure 12.9).

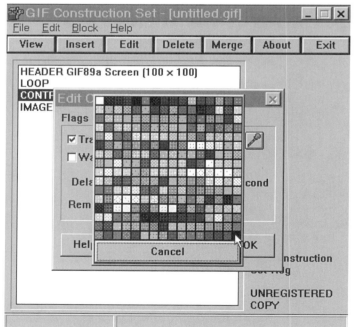

Doing the Loop

In the first example in this chapter, I mentioned that you can make an animation loop continuously by clicking Insert, then on Loop in GIF Construction Set. However, there's one more thing you need to know to create a successful looped animation, and it isn't at all obvious. Because of the way that Netscape Navigator processes and displays multi-image GIF files, you will often find that the first frame of a looping animation is skipped or only half displayed, making a noticeable jerk or some other subtle-but-annoying effect.

The way to avoid this is to always repeat the first image at the end of any fast-moving animation. This way, the jerk becomes invisible because it occurs between two identical images. For example, Figure 12.11 shows the complete pages.gif animation. This actually contains only six separate images—the seventh one is a repeat of the first.

Repeating the first image does increase the size of the GIF file, so it's a good idea to try the animation without the first image repeat to see if you're happy with the results. If you are, the only reason to consider repeating the first image is that a few older browsers will display only the last image in the animation. (Most older browsers, however, will display the first image.)

Figure 12.11.

For smooth animation, it often helps to make the first and last images identical.

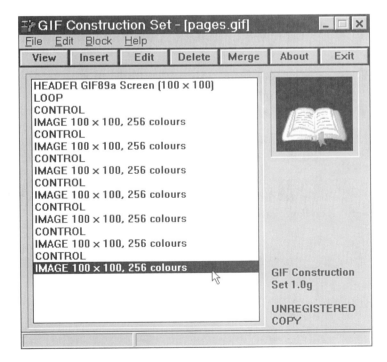

TIME SAVER

One more tip on looping: If you highlight the LOOP block and click the Edit button, you can set the number of iterations for the animation to repeat before stopping. This doesn't actually work in Netscape Navigator 2.0, but it does work in Navigator 3.0 and Microsoft Explorer 3.0.

COFFEE BREAK

Once you get started with Web page animation, it's hard not to get carried away. I couldn't resist adding a flashing neon sign for the *24-Hour HTML Café*, which you can see at:

http://www.mcp.com/sams/books/235-8/cafe12.htm

You'll also find links to a number of other animation-enhanced pages.

While you're browsing, you might want to check out the GIF Construction Set demonstration page at:

http://www.mindworkshop.com/alchemy/gcsdemo.html

It contains a number of snazzy animations which show off features of GIF Construction Set (and animated GIFs in general) that this short chapter didn't have enough space to discuss.

Summary

This chapter introduced you to animated GIF images, which are the easiest and quickest way to add some action to your Web pages. You found out where to get GIF Construction Set, an excellent shareware program for putting together GIF animations. You also saw how to control the timing of each frame in an animation, and make animations partially transparent.

GIF animations can be placed on Web pages using the same <IMG> tag as ordinary, unmoving images. All the <IMG> attributes and options discussed in Chapter 9, "Putting Images on a Web Page," also work with animated images.

12

Q&A

Q   **I've seen quite a few animations on the Web that show a three-dimensional object rotating. Can I make those with GIF Construction Set?**

A   Yes, but you'll also need some kind of 3D modeling and rendering software to create the individual frames.

You also may have seen interactive, three-dimensional virtual reality scenes and objects embedded in Web pages. Those are something completely different from GIF animations, made with a special language called the Virtual Reality Modeling Language, or VRML. For more information on VRML, refer to *Web Page Wizardry: Wiring Your Site for Sound and Action*, from Sams.net Publishing.

Q   **My GIF animation looks great in Microsoft Internet Explorer, but runs way too fast in Netscape Navigator. What's up?**

A   When you don't include a time interval between frames, some Web browsers (such as Explorer 3.0 and Navigator 2.0) leave a short pause between frames anyway, which is usually what you want. Navigator 3.0, however, will run the animation as fast as it can, which usually makes it look psychotic.

The solution is to always include a time interval in the control block before every image in the animation.

Q   **I've seen moving marquee-type signs on Web pages. Are those GIF animations?**

A   Sometimes they are and sometimes they aren't. There are several ways to make text move across an area on a Web page. One of the easiest ways is to use GIF Construction Set, which can make several types of fancy marquees from a simple string of text that you type in. See the GIF Construction Set online help for details.

Note that GIF animations are only one way to make marquees. Java applets or ActiveX controls are often used to make marquees as well (see Chapter 20). Some versions of Microsoft Internet Explorer even support a special <MARQUEE> tag, but it is likely to become obsolete soon.

Q   **I have a Windows AVI video clip. Can I turn it into a GIF animation?**

A   Yes. The Microsoft Web site (http://www.microsoft.com/) has a little program you can download called Microsoft GIF Animator that will do the trick. A more advanced video editing program that supports AVI and GIF files is VideoCraft from Andover Advanced Technologies (http://www.andatech.com/).

You can also embed AVI files directly into Web pages, as discussed in Chapter 20.

12

Quiz

Questions

1. If you want your logo to bounce up and down on your Web page, how would you do it?
2. How would you make a quarter-of-a-second pause between each frame of the animation?
3. Which of the following should you normally choose in the Edit Control dialog box for each frame of a transparent animation, under Remove by?

> Nothing
> Leave as is
> Background
> Previous Image

Answers

1. Use Paint Shop Pro or another graphics program to make a few images of the logo at various heights (perhaps squishing when it reaches a line at the bottom). Then assemble those images using GIF Construction Set, and save them as a multi-image GIF animation file named bounce.gif. You can then place that animation on a Web page using the <IMG SRC="bounce.gif"> tag, just like any GIF image.
2. When you build the animation in GIF Construction Set, insert a control block before each image, and click the Edit button to edit each control block. Enter 25 as the time delay (in centiseconds).
3. Remove by: Background is what you'll almost always want, but feel free to experiment with the others to see what they do.

Activities

☐ GIF Construction Set can make slide shows of dissimilar images by automatically generating transition effects, such as fading between pictures. It can also automatically add a number of special effects to still or moving text. If you take a little time to explore the advanced features of this program, I'm sure you'll find it time well spent.

☐ Don't forget that GIF Construction Set is shareware, and that the free copy you downloaded is for evaluation purposes. If you like it (and who wouldn't!?), be sure to send Alchemy Mindworks their well-earned $20 registration fee at the address you see when you exit the program.

12

PART
IV

Web Page Design

Hour

Hour 13

Backgrounds and Color Control

Nearly every sample Web page in Chapters 1 through 12 has a white background and black text. In this chapter, you'll find out how to make pages with the background and text colors of your choice. You'll also discover how to make your own custom background graphics, and how to let the background show through parts of any image you put on your Web pages.

To Do:

The black-and-white figures printed in this book obviously don't convey colors very accurately, so you may want to view the sample pages online at:

`http://www.mcp.com/sams/books/235-8/examples.htm#chapter13`

You can also try the colors on your own Web pages as you read about how to make them.

Background and Text Colors

To specify the background color for a page, put BGCOLOR="blue" inside the <BODY> tag. Of course, you can use many other colors other than blue. You can choose from the 16 standard Windows colors: black, white, red, green, blue, yellow, magenta, cyan, purple, gray, lime, maroon, navy, olive, silver, and teal. (You can call magenta "fuschia" and cyan "aqua" if you prefer.)

You can also specify colors for text and links in the <BODY> tag. For example, in Figure 13.1 you'll notice the following <BODY> tag:

```
<BODY BGCOLOR="red" TEXT="yellow" LINK="white" VLINK="gray" ALINK="green">
```

As you probably guessed, TEXT="yellow" makes the text yellow. There are three separate attributes for link colors:

- LINK="white" makes links that haven't been visited recently white.
- VLINK="gray" makes recently visited links gray.
- ALINK="green" makes links briefly blink green when someone clicks on them.

Because I used pure red as the background color in the graphics images, they blend right into the background of the Web page.

TIME SAVER

> Here's a neat trick: If you make the VLINK color the same as the BGCOLOR color, links to pages that a visitor has already seen will become invisible. This can make your page seem "smart"—offering people only links to places they haven't been. (Note, however, that it may also annoy anybody who wants to return to a page they've already seen!)

Figures 13.1 and 13.2 illustrate how color can be used in combination with links.

If the 16 named colors don't include the exact hue you're after, you can mix your own custom colors by specifying how much red, green, and blue light should be mixed into each color.

The format is #rrggbb, where rr, gg, and bb are two-digit hexadecimal values for the red, green, and blue components of the color. If you're not familiar with hexadecimal numbers, don't sweat it. Just remember that FF is the maximum, 00 is the minimum, and use one of the following codes for each component:

- FF means full brightness
- B0 means 75-percent brightness
- 80 means 50-percent brightness

- [ ] `40` means 25-percent brightness
- [ ] `00` means none of this color component

Figure 13.1.

You can specify colors for the background, text, and links in the <BODY> tag of any Web page.

```
<HTML><HEAD><TITLE>Buy Stuff Here</TITLE></HEAD>
<BODY BGCOLOR="red"
 TEXT="yellow" LINK="white" VLINK="grey" ALINK="green">
<IMG SRC="buystuff.gif"><P>
Got some dough you'd love to blow?
Well, well, well baby have you come to the right place!<P>
If you're talking big <IMG SRC="money.gif" ALIGN="middle">
in a big way, you're talking our language.
We've got it all, and we'll take it all.
Right here, right now. So
<A HREF="link.htm"> click here now </A>
or call us on our dime:<P>
<IMG SRC="buyhere.gif" ALIGN="right">
</BODY></HTML>
```

Figure 13.2.

On a color screen, this page has a red background, yellow body text, and white link text, as specified in Figure 13.1.

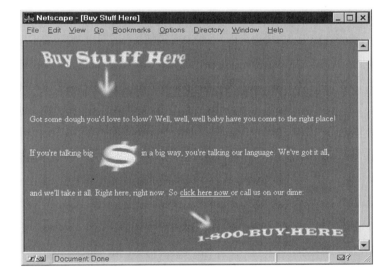

For example, bright red is `#FF0000`, dark green is `#004000`, bluish-purple is `#8000B0`, and medium-gray is `#808080`. As another example, the custom colors in Figure 13.3 specify a deep indigo background with steel blue text and a fuschia link that turns white after it's been visited (see Figure 13.4).

For a very handy chart showing the hexadecimal color codes, along with the colors they create, go to

`http://www.pheonix.net/~jacobson/rgb.html`

13

Figure 13.3.

For exact control of colors, you can use hexadecimal color codes instead of English color names.

```
<HTML><HEAD><TITLE>Hi-Ku</TITLE></HEAD>
<BODY BGCOLOR="#400040"
 TEXT="#8080FF" LINK="#FF00FF" VLINK="#FFFFFF">
<H2><I>modern moments</I></H2>
<H3><I>hi-tech haiku</I></H3>
<DIV ALIGN="center"><I>
pick up and you know<BR>
from the pause before the voice<BR>
telemarketer
<P>
CDs never change<BR>
but every time I play one<BR>
it's not quite the same
<P>
traffic jam? no prob<BR>
I've got a cel modem and<BR>
lots of batt life left<P>
</DIV><P ALIGN="right">
<A HREF="http://netletter.com/dicko/hiku.htm">more</A>
</BODY></HTML>
```

Figure 13.4.

On a color screen, the background on this page is indigo, with silvery blue text.

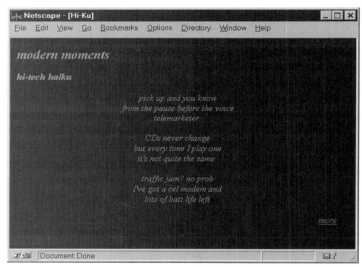

TIME SAVER

Even though you can specify millions of different colors, many computers are set to display only the 16 named colors. All others will be approximated by dithered patterns, which can make text look messy and difficult to read.

Also, you should be aware that different computers may display colors in different hues. I recently designed a page with a beautiful blue background for a company I work for—only to find out later that the president of the company saw it on his computer as a lovely purple background!

13

> The moral of the story: Stick to the named colors and don't waste time mucking with hexadecimal color codes, unless you have precise control over the computer displays of your intended audience.

Though the colors you specify in the <BODY> tag apply to all text on the page, you can also change the color of a particular word or section of text using the <FONT> tag. This is discussed in Chapter 6, "Font Control and Special Characters."

TIME SAVER

> You can set the color of an individual link to a different color than the rest by putting a <FONT> tag with a COLOR attribute *after* the <A HREF>. (Also include a </FONT> tag before the </A> tag.)
>
> Microsoft Internet Explorer 3.0, however, will always display all links with the colors set in the <BODY> tag.

Background Image Tiles

Background tiles are all the rage on the Web these days. They let you specify an image file to be used as a wallpaper tile behind all text and images in a document. You put the image filename after BACKGROUND= in the <BODY> tag like this:

```
<BODY BACKGROUND="image.gif">
```

For example, the tile.gif file referred to by the <BODY> tag in Figure 13.5 is an image of one small tile. As you can see in Figure 13.6, most Web browsers will repeat the image like a floor tile, behind any text and images on the page.

Figure 13.5.

You can specify a background image to tile behind a page in the BACKGROUND *attribute of the* <BODY> *tag.*

```
<HTML><HEAD><TITLE>The Tile Room</TITLE></HEAD>
<BODY BACKGROUND="tile.gif" TEXT="red">
<IMG SRC="stall.gif" ALIGN="right">
<H1>Background tiles, text colors,
and transparent graphics
help you set that certain special
<I>ambiance</I> to make each page
like "a room of your own."</H1>
</BODY></HTML>
```

13

Figure 13.6.

The tile.gif *file (specified in Figure 13.5) is automatically repeated to cover the entire page.*

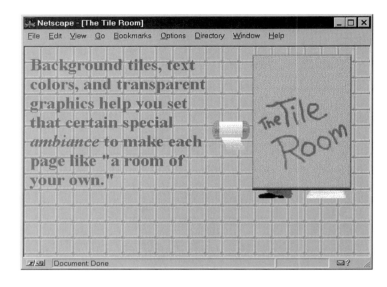

CAUTION

Tiled background images should be implemented with great care in order to avoid distracting from the main content of the page itself. The text in Figure 13.6, for example, would be difficult to read if I hadn't made it all a big <H1> heading. Many pages on the Web are almost impossible to read due to overdone backgrounds.

So before you include your company logo or baby pictures as wallpaper behind your Web pages, stop and think. If you had an important message to send someone on a piece of paper, would you write it over the top of the letterhead logo or on the blank part of the page? Backgrounds should be like fine papers: attractive, yet unobtrusive.

Transparent Images

The astute observer of Figure 13.6 (that's you) will notice that the background tiles show through portions of the rectangular image. You'll often want to use partially transparent images to make graphics look good over any background color or background image tile.

Figure 13.7 shows the image from Figure 13.6, as it looked in Paint Shop Pro when I created it. (Figure 13.7 also shows the single tile used for the background in Figure 13.6.)

13

Figure 13.7.

When I saved this image in Paint Shop Pro, I made the background color transparent.

To make part of an image transparent, the image must have 256 or fewer colors and you must save it in the GIF file format. (JPEG images can't be transparent.) Most graphics programs that support the GIF format allow you to specify one color to be transparent.

To Do:

To save a transparent GIF in Paint Shop Pro, follow these steps:

1. Select Colors | Decrease Color Depth | 256 Colors or Colors | Decrease Color Depth | 16 Colors, and check the Optimized and Nearest color boxes (as recommended in Chapter 10, "Creating Web Page Images").

2. Choose the eyedropper tool.

3. Right-click the color you want to make transparent.

4. Select File | Save As…

5. Choose the GIF-CompuServe image format and Version 89a-Noninterlaced or Version 89a-Interlaced Sub type. (See Chapter 10 for more about interlaced versus noninterlaced images.)

6. Click the Options button.

7. Choose Set the transparency value to the background color as shown in Figure 13.8 and click OK.

8. Enter a name for the file, then click OK to save it.

13

Figure 13.8.

Paint Shop Pro's GIF File Preferences dialog box lets you choose which palette color will become transparent.

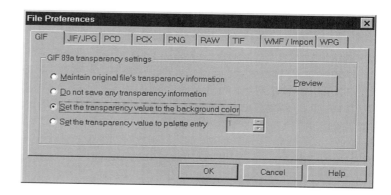

TIME SAVER

For a masked preview of which part of the image will be transparent, click on the Preview button shown in Figure 13.8. This will temporarily replace the transparent color with the current foreground color.

To emphasize the transparent color permanently, select Colors | Edit Palette and change the transparent palette color to some outrageous fluorescent green or another highly visible hue. If some areas aren't transparent that should be, use the color replacer tool to change their color.

Creating Your Own Backgrounds

Any GIF or JPEG image can be used as a background tile. But pages look best when the top edge of a background tile matches seamlessly with the bottom edge and the left edge matches up with the right.

If you're clever and have some time to spend on it, you can make any image into a seamless tile by meticulously cutting and pasting, while touching up the edges. You'll find the exact steps for doing this in my book, *Creating Your Own Web Page Graphics*, by Que Publishing.

Paint Shop Pro provides a much easier way to automatically make any texture into a seamless tile. You simply use the rectangular selection tool to choose the area you want to make into a tile, and then select Image | Special Effects | Create Seamless Pattern. Paint Shop Pro crops the image and uses a sophisticated automatic procedure to overlay and blur together opposite sides of the image.

13

In Figure 13.9 I did this with part of an image of the palm of my hand, taken with an inexpensive digital camera. The resulting tile, shown as the background of a Web page in Figure 13.10, tiles seamlessly but has the flesh tone and texture of skin.

You'll find similar features in other graphics programs, including Photoshop (use Filter | Other | Offset with Wrap turned on), Kai's Power Tools, and the Macintosh programs Mordant and Tilery.

Figure 13.9.

Paint Shop Pro can automatically take any region of an image and make it into a background pattern that can be easily made into tiles.

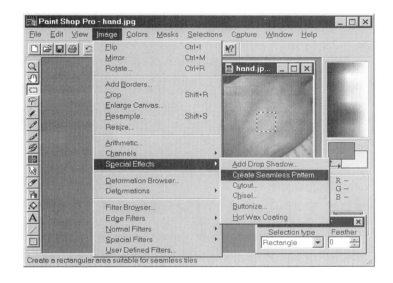

Figure 13.10.

The results of Figure 13.9 used as a background image for a Web page.

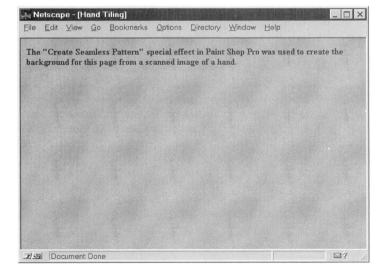

To Do:

Here are some tips for making your own background tiles with Paint Shop Pro.

☐ If you have a scanner or digital camera, try using some textures from around the house or office, such as the top of a wooden desk, leaves of houseplants, or clothing.

☐ When you select an area to make into a tile, try to choose part of the image that is fairly uniform in brightness from side to side. Otherwise, the tile may not look seamless even after you use the Create Seamless Pattern option.

☐ You must also use a big enough image so that you can leave at least the width and height of the tile on either side of your selection. If you don't, when you select Create Seamless Pattern you'll get a message saying `Your selection is too close to the edge to complete this operation`.

☐ You can also make some almost-automatic textures with the paper texture feature in the paintbrush style palette in Paint Shop Pro. Selecting Image | Special Filters | Add Noise followed by Image | Normal Filters | Blur and Colors | Colorize can make great paper textures, too.

Finding Good Backgrounds

If you just cannot seem to get the pattern you want, there are hundreds of sites on the Internet that offer public domain background images that you are free to use, or inexpensive professionally designed backgrounds. A good starting place is Gini Schmitz' Textures and Backgrounds Wonderland at:

`http://www.geocities.com/SiliconValley/Heights/1272/rainbow.html`

If you happen to see a background image on someone else's page that you wish you could use on your own page, it is a simple matter to click on the background with the right mouse button and select Save Background As to save a copy of it. Be careful, though, to ask the person who created the image if you can use it, because the image could very well be copyrighted or legally protected in some other way.

13

COFFEE BREAK

You'll see an unconventional use of background tiling at the newly wallpapered *24-Hour HTML Café*:

```
http://www.mcp.com/sams/books/235-8/cafe13.htm
```

(Can you figure out what I did and how I did it? If not, see Chapter 14, "Page Design and Layout," for some hints.)

You'll also find a selection of snazzy backgrounds you can use for your own pages at the Background Underground lounge:

```
http://www.mcp.com/sams/books/235-8/bgu/bgu.htm
```

While you're checking out the backgrounds, you'll get an animated appetizer hot from Chapter 12, "Creating Animated Graphics."

Summary

In this chapter, you learned how to set the background and text colors for a Web page. You also found out how to make a tiled background image appear behind a Web page, how to make foreground images partially transparent so the background shows through, and how to create seamless image tiles for use as backgrounds.

Table 13.1 summarizes the attributes of the <BODY> tag discussed in this chapter.

Table 13.1. Attributes of the <BODY> tag covered in Chapter 13.

Tag	Attribute	Function
<BODY>...</BODY>		Encloses the body (text and tags) of the HTML document.
	BACKGROUND="..."	The name or address of the image to tile on the page background.
	BGCOLOR="..."	The color of the page's background.
	TEXT="..."	The color of the page's text.
	LINK="..."	The color of unfollowed links.
	ALINK="..."	The color of activated links.
	VLINK="..."	The color of followed links.

13

Q&A

Q **Doesn't Netscape Navigator let people choose their own background and text color preferences?**

A Yes, and so does Microsoft Internet Explorer. Both programs allow users to override the colors you (as a Web page author) specify. So some may see your white-on-blue page as green-on-white, or their own favorite colors, instead. But very few people turn on the overriding document option, Always use my colors, so the colors specified in the <BODY> tag will usually be seen.

Q **I've heard that there are 231 "magic colors" that I should use to look good in Netscape Navigator. Is that true?**

A Here's the real story: There are 231 colors that will appear less "fuzzy" to people who operate their computers in a 256-color video mode (the other 25 colors are used for menus and stuff like that). So some Web page authors try to stick to those colors. However, true color or high color computer displays are increasingly common, and they show all colors with equal clarity. On the other hand, lots of people still use a 16-color video mode, which makes most of the 231 "magic" colors look fuzzy, too. I recommend sticking to the 16 named colors for text and using whatever colors you want for graphics.

Q **Can older versions of Web browsers see my custom colors and background tiles?**

A Some won't. Users of Mosaic will see only gray backgrounds. Early versions of Netscape Navigator (before 2.0) will display hexadecimal-coded colors, but won't recognize color names. However, everything will look right in Netscape Navigator 2.0 or higher and Microsoft Internet Explorer version 2.0 or higher.

Quiz

Questions

1. How would you give a Web page a black background and make all text, including links, bright green?

2. How would you make an image file named texture.jpg appear as a repeating tile behind the text and images on a Web page with white text and red links that turn blue after being followed?

13

3. If `elephant.jpg` is a JPEG image of an elephant standing in front of a solid white backdrop, how do you make the backdrop transparent so only the elephant shows on a Web page?

4. Which menu choice in Paint Shop Pro automatically creates a background tile from part of any image?

Answers

1. Put the following at the beginning of the Web page:

```
<BODY BGCOLOR="black"
TEXT="lime" LINK="lime" VLINK="lime" ALINK="black">
```

Or the following would do the same thing:

```
<BODY BGCOLOR="#000000"
TEXT="#00FF00" LINK="#00FF00" VLINK="#00FF00" ALINK="#000000">
```

2.
```
<BODY BACKGROUND="texture.jpg"
TEXT="white" LINK="red" VLINK="blue" ALINK="black">
```

3. Open the image in Paint Shop Pro, then use Colors | Decrease Color Depth | 256 Colors to pick the best 256 colors for the image. Right-click on the white area, and use File | Save As to save it in the GIF 89a format. Click the Options button to make the background color transparent before you save.

4. Image | Special Effects | Create Seamless Pattern. See the Paint Shop Pro documentation if you need a little more help using it than this chapter provided.

Activities

☐ Try getting creative with some background tiles that *don't* use Create Seamless Pattern. You'll discover some sneaky tricks in Chapter 14 for making background tiles that don't look like background tiles, but I bet you can figure out some interesting ones on your own right now. (Hint: What if you made a background tile 2,000 pixels wide and 10 pixels tall?)

☐ If you have some photos of objects for a Web-based catalog, consider taking the time to paint a transparent color carefully around the edges of them. (Sometimes the magic wand tool can help automate this process.) You can also use Paint Shop Pro's Image | Special Effects | Add Drop Shadow feature to add a slight shadow behind or beneath each object, so they appear to stand out from the background.

13

Hour 14

Page Design and Layout

You've learned in earlier chapters how to create Web pages with text and images on them. This chapter goes a step further by showing you some HTML tricks to control the spaces *between* your text and images. These tricks are essential for making your pages attractive and easy to read. This chapter also provides practical advice to help you design attractive and highly readable pages, even if you're not a professional graphics designer.

To Do:

The techniques covered in this chapter are intended to help you make pages you've already created better and faster. So select some of the most important or impressive pages that you've made to date, and try to see whether you can make them look even better.

- ☐ Choose pages with some graphics on them, because almost all the tricks in this chapter involve images.
- ☐ If you have a page that you think might especially benefit from a creative layout or unique background, start with that one.
- ☐ You may have some text and images that you haven't gotten around to putting on a Web page yet. If so, this chapter can help those new pages become your best yet.
- ☐ Copy the pages you select into their own directory folder, and play with new design possibilities for them as you read through this chapter.

Web Page Design

So far, this book has focused mostly on the exact mechanics of Web page creation. But before getting into the nitty-gritty of spacing and layout tricks, you should take a moment now to step back and think about the overall visual design of your Web pages. Now that you know basic HTML, you need to learn how to apply it wisely.

Every aspect of a Web page should reflect the goals that led you to create the page in the first place. Not only should the text and graphics themselves communicate your message, but the way you fit those elements together can itself make an enormous impact on readers' perceptions of you or your company.

Table 14.1 is a checklist to help you think about the key design elements of a Web page. You should aim for most of your pages to meet the recommendations in this table, though some individual pages will undoubtedly need to "break the rules."

Table 14.1. Key elements of Web page design.

Things to consider	Suggested guidelines
Text Content	Between 100 and 500 words per page
Text Breaks	A headline, rule, or image every 40 to 100 words (except in long articles or stories)
Page Length	Two to four screens (at 640×480 resolution)
File Size	No more than 50KB per page, including images (animated GIFs can be up to 100KB per page)
Speed	First screen of text and key images appear in under 5 seconds over a 14.4Kbps modem

14

Things to consider	Suggested guidelines
Colors	Two to four thematic colors dominant
Fonts	No more than three fonts (in graphics and text)
Blank Space	Background should show on at least 75 percent of page
Contrast	No color in background should be close to text color
Tone and Style	All text and graphics should be consistent in mood and theme
Overall Impact	Page as a whole should appear balanced and attractive

Most of the tips in Table 14.1 are common to any page design, on paper or electronic. But some of them are particularly tricky to control on Web pages.

The next section of this chapter presents some HTML commands for handling the blank space and overall visual impact of your pages. Then this chapter wraps up with some techniques for meeting the speed requirements of today's Web, even when you use relatively large images.

Image Spacing and Borders

Figures 14.1 through 14.3 show the HTML text, images, and final appearance of a well-designed Web page. It meets all the criteria outlined in Table 14.1 (with the exception of some tongue-in-cheek inconsistency in the tone of the text).

Notice the generous amount of space between images and paragraphs in Figure 14.3. Web browsers tend to crowd everything together, but you can easily add space three different ways:

- [ ] Use small, totally transparent images to leave room between other things. The spacer.gif file (shown in Figure 14.2 and referred to in Figure 14.1) creates 20 pixels of blank space between each of the main parts of this page.

- [ ] When you wrap text around an image using <IMG ALIGN="right"> or <IMG ALIGN="left">, you can skip down past the bottom of that image at any time with <BR CLEAR="right"> or <BR CLEAR="left">. If you have images on both the right and left, you can type <BR CLEAR="all"> to go past both of them.

- [ ] You can add extra space on the left and right sides of any image with <IMG HSPACE>. To add space on the top and bottom sides, use <IMG VSPACE>. For example, each image in Figure 14.3 has 20 pixels of blank space to the left and right of it, and 5 pixels above and below it. This is because each <IMG> tag in Figure 14.1 includes the attributes HSPACE=20 VSPACE=5.

The <IMG> tags in Figure 14.1 also include a BORDER=10 attribute, which enlarges the rectangular border around the images. The border is normally 1 pixel thick for any image inside an <A> link, but BORDER=10 makes it 10 pixels thick.

14

The most popular use of the BORDER attribute is to make the image border disappear completely by typing BORDER=0. This is especially handy with transparent images, which often look funny with a rectangle around them.

The color of the border will be the same as the color of any text links. In this page, images that link to pages someone hasn't visited yet will have maroon borders. Images that link to a recently visited page will have green borders.

JUST A MINUTE

If you include a BORDER attribute in an <IMG> that isn't between <A> and </A> link tags, Netscape Navigator will draw the border using the regular body text color. However, Microsoft Internet Explorer will never draw a border around an image that isn't a link, even if you include a <BORDER> tag.

Because of this difference between the two major Web browsers, you should only use <BORDER> with link images.

Figure 14.1.

This page uses several techniques for adding blank space between images and text.

```
<HTML><HEAD><TITLE>The Decoration Museum</TITLE></HEAD>
<BODY BACKGROUND="wainscot.gif"
 TEXT="green" LINK="maroon" VLINK="green" ALINK="white">
<DIV ALIGN="center"><IMG SRC="musee.gif"></DIV><BR>
<IMG SRC="spacer.gif"><BR><IMG SRC="spacer.gif"><BR>

<A HREF="classics.htm">
<IMG SRC="manhorse.gif" ALIGN="left"
 WIDTH=150 HEIGHT=120 BORDER=10 HSPACE=20 VSPACE=5>
<H2>Ornaments of Classical Antiquity</H2></A>
The Greeks and Romans were pretty handy with chisels,
and slave labor was cheap. So they carved a lot of
stuff. Like this guy and his horse. <I>Et cetera.</I>
<BR CLEAR="left">
<IMG SRC="spacer.gif"><BR>

<A HREF="fleur.htm">
<IMG SRC="fleuron.gif" ALIGN="right"
 WIDTH=120 HEIGHT=102 border=10 HSPACE=20 VSPACE=5>
<H2>Decorative Fleurons of the Renaissance</H2></A>
The French, Italians, and people around there are big
on flowers. And so when the Renaissance hit Europe, they
went wild painting and carving flowers on
<I>tout la monde.</I>
<BR CLEAR="right">
<IMG SRC="spacer.gif"><BR>

<A HREF="celts.htm">
<IMG SRC="celtic.gif" ALIGN="left"
 WIDTH=140 HEIGHT=125 BORDER=10 HSPACE=20 VSPACE=5>
<H2>Ancient Celtic Designs</H2></A>
Worshipping oak trees, casting pentacles, and making
those really cool interlocking 3D swirly things on tiles.
That's what those crazy celts were into, in
<I>auld lang syne.</I>
<BR CLEAR="left">
<IMG SRC="spacer.gif"><BR>

<DIV ALIGN="center">
<HR SIZE=10 WIDTH=70% COLOR="green"><P>
<A HREF="../examples.htm">Old Art: Gotta Love It.</A>
</DIV>
</BODY></HTML>
```

14

Figure 14.2.

The six image files referred to in Figure 14.1. (Note that Paint Shop Pro uses cross-hatching to indicate that a window is bigger than the image it contains. For example, spacer.gif *is actually a very small solid white square.)*

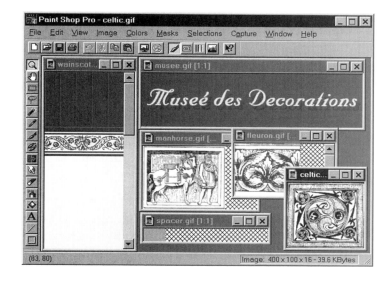

Figure 14.3.

Thanks to generous spacing and a carefully premeditated layout, the HTML in Figure 14.1 looks great as a Web page.

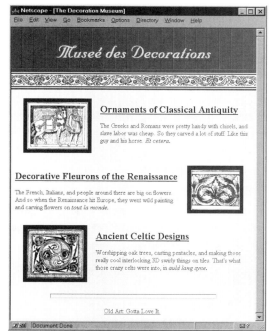

14

The Old Background Banner Trick

One of the most prominent tricks employed in Figure 14.3 is the use of a 1,000-pixel high background image (named `wainscot.gif`). Because the entire page is unlikely to turn out more than 1,000 pixels high, the background only appears to repeat in the horizontal direction. And since the bottom part of the image is all the same color, it looks like the background is only a banner at the top of the page.

Unlike a foreground image used as a banner, however, this wainscotting will automatically size itself to go from "wall to wall" of any sized window. It is also a smaller image file, because only one repetition of the pattern needs to be stored.

JUST A MINUTE

"Hang on," you say. "143×1000 is 143,000 pixels! Won't that make an enormous image file and take forever to download?" The answer is no; large areas of uniform color take up virtually no space at all when compressed in the GIF file format. (`Wainscot.gif` is only a 3KB file.)

If you use this trick to make background banners on your own Web pages, you should probably make them at least 2,000 pixels high. As Figure 14.4 demonstrates, the page can actually become longer than 1,000 pixels when someone uses Microsoft Internet Explorer's largest font size setting. Note that the wainscotting shows up again at the very bottom of the page.

By using a very wide background that repeats vertically, you can easily make a repeating banner that runs down the left side of a page, too. If you don't want text to obscure the banner, put a very large, totally transparent image at the beginning of the HTML page with `<IMG ALIGN="left">`.

Figures 14.5 through 14.7 show the HTML, graphics, and resulting Web pages to implement a left-side banner.

Note that I made the other graphics all right-justified, both for aesthetic reasons and so that I could avoid using `<BR CLEAR="left">`, which would skip all the way to the bottom of the left-justified banner graphic.

TIME SAVER

If you use a left-aligned transparent banner, be sure to add enough blank space around the actual foreground image to fill the area on the page you want to cover. The "Museé des Decorations" graphic in Figures 14.6 and 14.7, for example, is 150×1000 pixels.

Because almost nobody views Web pages in a window larger than 1600×1200 pixels, vertically tiled background banners can safely be 2,000 pixels wide.

14

Figure 14.4.

The 1,000-pixel high background begins to repeat when extremely large fonts are used in a small window.

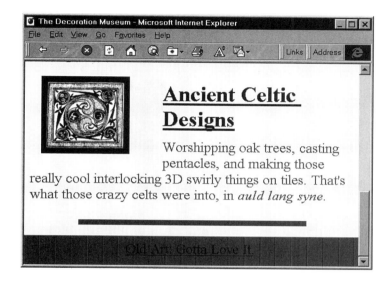

Figure 14.5.

With a few strategic changes, you could put the top banner in Figure 14.1 to the left side.

```
<HTML><HEAD><TITLE>The Decoration Museum</TITLE></HEAD>
<BODY BACKGROUND="wainsco2.gif"
 TEXT="green" LINK="maroon" VLINK="green" ALINK="white">
<IMG SRC="musee2.gif" ALIGN="left">

<A HREF="classics.htm">
<IMG SRC="manhorse.gif" ALIGN="right"
 WIDTH=150 HEIGHT=120 BORDER=10 HSPACE=20 VSPACE=5>
<H2>Ornaments of Classical Antiquity</H2></A>
The Greeks and Romans were pretty handy with chisels,
and slave labor was cheap. So they carved a lot of
stuff. Like this guy and his horse. <I>Et cetera.</I>
<BR CLEAR="right">
<IMG SRC="spacer.gif"><BR>

<A HREF="fleur.htm">
<IMG SRC="fleuron.gif" ALIGN="right"
 WIDTH=120 HEIGHT=102 border=10 HSPACE=20 VSPACE=5>
<H2>Decorative Fleurons of the Renaissance</H2></A>
The French, Italians, and people around there are big
on flowers. And so when the Renaissance hit Europe, they
went wild painting and carving flowers on
<I>tout la monde.</I>
<BR CLEAR="right">
<IMG SRC="spacer.gif"><BR>

<A HREF="celts.htm">
<IMG SRC="celtic.gif" ALIGN="right"
 WIDTH=140 HEIGHT=125 BORDER=10 HSPACE=20 VSPACE=5>
<H2>Ancient Celtic Designs</H2></A>
Worshipping oak trees, casting pentacles, and making
those really cool interlocking 3D swirly things on tiles.
That's what those crazy celts were into, in
<I>auld lang syne.</I>
<BR CLEAR="right">
<IMG SRC="spacer.gif"><BR>

<DIV ALIGN="center">
<HR SIZE=10 WIDTH=70% COLOR="green"><P>
<A HREF="../examples.htm">Old Art: Gotta Love It.</A>
</DIV>
</BODY></HTML>
```

14

Figure 14.6.

The rotated graphics for a left-side banner. (Notice how I changed the direction of the light source and shadowing, too.)

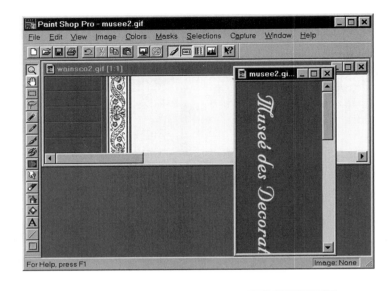

Figure 14.7.

The HTML from Figure 14.5 and the banner from Figure 14.6, as they appear in Netscape Navigator.

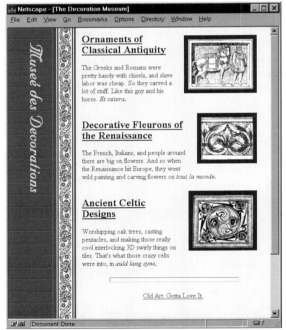

14

Customizing Horizontal Rules

There's one more page layout trick used in the "Museé des Decorations" page: a customized horizontal rule. If you look carefully, you'll see that Netscape Navigator renders it differently in Figure 14.3 than Microsoft Internet Explorer does in Figure 14.4.

The following <HR> tag uses some special attributes to control exactly how the horizontal rule looks:

```
<HR SIZE=10 WIDTH=70% COLOR="green">
```

The vertical size of the rule is set with the SIZE attribute. The number value in this attribute should be equal to the height in pixels that you want the line to be. <HR SIZE=1> will be a single-pixel "hairline" rule, while <HR SIZE=300> will be a big, fat rectangle across the page.

Normally, horizontal rules span the width of the window. You can override this, however, with the WIDTH attribute, which allows you to specify the size of the line either as a relative percentage or as a precise pixel value. <HR WIDTH=250> draws a 250-pixel-wide line, whereas <HR WIDTH=50%> draws a line halfway across the window, no matter what size the window happens to be.

The SIZE and WIDTH attributes together turn the <HR> attribute into a useful tool for drawing any size rectangle you choose.

It's the COLOR attribute that causes some disagreement between Netscape Navigator and Microsoft Internet Explorer. Navigator ignores it completely, and renders the rule as a transparent three-dimensional indentation. Internet Explorer, however, obediently colors the rule solid green. Feel free to specify a COLOR for any rule you draw, but keep in mind that only Internet Explorer users will see it.

TIME SAVER

Horizontal rules are normally centered, but you can use the ALIGN="left" or ALIGN="right" in the <HR> tag, too. Horizontal rules are also affected by <DIV ALIGN="right"> and <DIV ALIGN="left">.

COFFEE BREAK

The spacing and layout tricks in this chapter provide that certain extra something to the ever-expanding *24-Hour HTML Café*:

http://www.mcp.com/sams/books/235-8/cafe14.htm

I've also added some links from that page to especially well-designed sites to inspire your own efforts.

14

Summary

This chapter provided some guidelines for designing attractive, highly readable Web pages. It also explained how to create and control blank space on your pages, put borders around images, and draw customized rectangles and rules. You saw how to use backgrounds to create banners across the top or left edge of a page.

Table 14.2 summarizes the tags and attributes discussed in this chapter.

Table 14.2. HTML tags and attributes covered in Chapter 14.

Tag	Attribute	Function
<IMG>		Inserts an inline image into the document.
	SRC="..."	The address of the image.
	ALIGN="..."	Determines the alignment of the given image (see Chapter 9, "Putting Images on a Web Page").
	VSPACE="..."	The space between the image and the text above or below it.
	HSPACE="..."	The space between the image and the text to its left or right.
	WIDTH="..."	The width, in pixels, of the image. If WIDTH is not the actual width, the image is scaled to fit.
	HEIGHT="..."	The height, in pixels, of the image. If HEIGHT is not the actual height, the image is scaled to fit.
	BORDER="..."0	Draws a border of the specified value in pixels to be drawn around the image. In case the images are also links, BORDER changes the size of the default link border.
 		A line break.
	CLEAR="..."	Causes the text to stop flowing around any images. Possible values are RIGHT, LEFT, ALL.
<HR>		A horizontal rule line.
	SIZE="..."	The thickness of the rule, in pixels.
	WIDTH="..."	The width of the rule, in pixels or as a percentage of the document width.
	ALIGN="..."	How the rule line will be aligned on the page. Possible values are LEFT, RIGHT, and CENTER.
	COLOR="..."	Color of the horizontal rule (Microsoft Internet Explorer only).

Q&A

Q I'd like to know exactly how wide the margins of a page are so I can line up my background and foreground images the way I want.

A Unfortunately, different browsers (and even the same browser on different types of computers) leave different amounts of space along the top and left side of a page, so you can't precisely line up foreground graphics with background images. Generally, you can expect the top and left margins to be 8 to 12 pixels.

Microsoft Internet Explorer actually allows you to specify the exact margin size with MARGINHEIGHT and MARGINWIDTH in the <BODY> tag. Netscape has promised to provide the ability to control margins and image placement more precisely in Navigator version 4.0.

Q I've seen pages on the Web with multiple columns of text, wide margins, and other types of nice layouts you didn't discuss. How were those pages made?

A Probably with the HTML table tags, which are discussed in Chapter 16, "Advanced Layout with Tables."

Quiz

Questions

1. How would you wrap text around the right side of an image, leaving 40 pixels of space between the image and the text?

2. How could you insert exactly 80 pixels of blank space between two paragraphs of text?

3. Write the HTML to draw a 20- by 20-pixel square in the center of a page, shaded as if it were slightly indented into the background but hollow in the middle.

4. If you have a circular button that links to another page, how do you prevent a rectangle from appearing around it?

Answers

1. `<IMG SRC="myimage.gif" HSPACE=40 VSPACE=40 ALIGN="left">Text goes here.`

2. Create a small image that is all one color, and save it as `nothing.gif` with that color transparent. Then put the following tag between the two paragraphs of text:

   `<IMG SRC="nothing.gif" WIDTH=1 HEIGHT=80>`

3. `<HR SIZE=20 WIDTH=20>`

4. Use the `BORDER=0` attribute, like this:

   `<A HREF="another_page.htm"><IMG SRC="circle.gif" BORDER=0></A>`

Activities

☐ Try creating a page with the wildest layout you can manage with the HTML tags you've learned so far. If you're resourceful, you should be able to create a staggered diagonal line of images, or place short sentences of text almost anywhere on the page.

☐ Make a very large background—so big that people will see only one "tile" and you don't have to worry about it being seamless. Most Web browsers will display all foreground content (in front of the `BGCOLOR` you specify in the `<BODY>` tag) while the background image loads. So go ahead and play around with the creative possibilities that large backdrops open up.

14

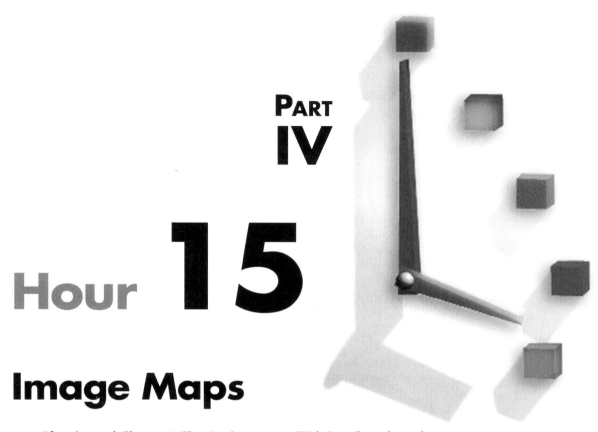

Hour 15

Image Maps

If you've read Chapter 9, "Putting Images on a Web Page," you know how to make an image link to another document. (If you don't quite recall how to do it right now, it looks like this: `<A HREF="gohere.htm"><IMG SRC="image.gif"> </A>`.)

You can also subdivide an image into regions that link to different documents, depending on where someone clicks. This is called an *image map*, and any image can be made into an image map. A Web site with medical information might show an image of the human body and bring up different pages of advice for each body part. Or a map of the world could allow people to click on any country for regional information. Many people use image maps to create a "navigation bar" that integrates icons for each page on their Web site into one cohesive image map.

Netscape Navigator and Microsoft Internet Explorer allow you to choose between two different methods for implementing image maps. Nowadays, all your image maps should be done using the latest method, which is called a client-side image map. You may also want to make them work the old-fashioned server-side way for users of older browser programs. I explain both kinds of image maps in this chapter.

NEW TERM An *image map* is an image on a Web page that leads to two or more different links, depending on which part of the image someone clicks. Modern Web browsers use *client-side image maps,* but you can also create *server-side image maps* for compatibility with old browsers.

Mapping Regions Within an Image

To make any type of image map, you'll need to figure out the numerical pixel coordinates of each region within the image that you want to be a clickable link. An easy way to do this is to open the image with Paint Shop Pro and watch the coordinates at the bottom of the screen as you use the rectangle selection tool to select a rectangular region of the image (see Figure 15.1). When the mouse button is down, the coordinates at the bottom of the screen show both the top-left and bottom-right corners of the rectangle, instead of just a single x,y position as shown here.

TIME SAVER There are fancy programs that let you highlight a rectangle with your mouse and automatically spew out image map coordinates into a file, but they are rather cumbersome to use. You'll save the most time by ignoring the "time saver" programs and just locating the pixel coordinates in Paint Shop Pro or your favorite general-purpose graphics program.

Figure 15.1.

Paint Shop Pro can easily tell you the coordinates for image map regions without mucking about with special image-mapping utilities.

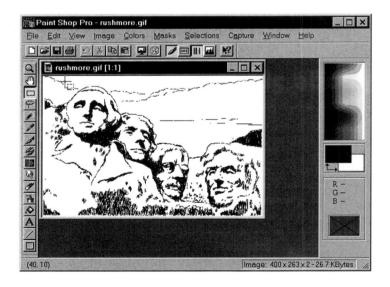

15

You could use the image in Figure 15.1 as an image map, linking to four Web pages about the presidents immortalized on Mount Rushmore. To do so, first jot down the pixel coordinates of the top-left and bottom-right corners of each rectangular region shown in Figure 15.2. (Just write the coordinates on a piece of paper for now. You'll see exactly how to put them into an HTML file momentarily.)

These coordinates are:

> George Washington (region 1): 40,10 to 130,130
> Thomas Jefferson (region 2): 130,60 to 200,170
> Teddy Roosevelt (region 3): 201,120 to 270,240
> Abraham Lincoln (region 4): 280,120 to 380,250

Figure 15.2.
You don't actually have to draw anything that looks like this. I just made it to show you which regions in Figure 15.1 will become clickable links.

To Do:

You'll remember how to make image maps better if you get an image of your own and turn it into an image map as you read the following explanation.

- [ ] For starters, choose a fairly large image that is visually divided into roughly rectangular regions.
- [ ] If you don't have a suitable image handy, use Paint Shop Pro (or your favorite graphics program) to make one. One easy and useful idea is to put a word or icon for each of your important pages together into a button bar or signpost.

Client-Side Image Maps

Once you have the coordinates written down, you're ready to create an HTML image map. Just after the <BODY> tag in your Web page, put

```
<MAP NAME="heads">
```

(You can use whatever name you want if "heads" seems too disrespectful of our late great leaders.)

Now you need to type an <AREA> tag for each region of the image. Figure 15.3 shows how you would define the four regions of the Mount Rushmore image.

Figure 15.3.

The <MAP> and <AREA> tags define the regions of an image map.

```
<HTML><HEAD><TITLE>Mount Rushmore</TITLE></HEAD>
<BODY BGCOLOR="white" TEXT="black" LINK="black" VLINK="black">
<MAP NAME="heads">
<AREA SHAPE="RECT" COORDS="40,10,130,130" HREF="george.htm">
<AREA SHAPE="RECT" COORDS="131,60,200,170" HREF="thomas.htm">
<AREA SHAPE="RECT" COORDS="201,120,270,240" HREF="teddy.htm">
<AREA SHAPE="RECT" COORDS="280,120,380,250" HREF="abraham.htm">
</MAP>
<DIV ALIGN="center">
<H1>The Immortal Presidents</H1>
<IMG SRC="rushmore.gif" WIDTH=400 HEIGHT=263 USEMAP="#heads">
<P><A HREF="george.htm">Washington</A> |
<A HREF="thomas.htm">Jefferson</A> |
<A HREF="teddy.htm">Roosevelt</A> |
<A HREF="abraham.htm">Lincoln</A>
</DIV>
</BODY></HTML>
```

Each <AREA> tag in Figure 15.3 has three attributes:

☐ SHAPE="RECT" indicates that the region is rectangular. You'll see how to create regions with other shapes later in this chapter.

☐ COORDS="40,10,130,130" gives the top-left and bottom-right corner coordinates for the rectangular region.

☐ HREF="george.htm" specifies the page that clicking on the region will link to. You can use any address or filename that you would use in an ordinary <A HREF> link tag.

After the <AREA> tags, you are finished defining the image map, so you insert a closing </MAP> tag.

To place the actual image map on the page, you use an ordinary <IMG> tag, and add a USEMAP attribute:

```
<IMG SRC="rushmore.gif" USEMAP="#heads">
```

15

Use the name you put in the <MAP> tag (and don't forget the # symbol). In Figure 15.3, I also included WIDTH and HEIGHT attributes, as you should for any image on a Web page.

JUST A MINUTE

It is also possible to put the map definition in a separate file by including that file's name in the USEMAP attribute, like this:

```
<IMG SRC="/thisthat.gif" USEMAP="maps.htm#thisthat">
```

For instance, if you used an image map on every page in your Web site, you could just put the <MAP> and <AREA> tags for it on one page instead of repeating it on every single page where the image map appeared.

Figure 15.4 shows the image map in action. Notice that Netscape Navigator displays the link address for whatever region the mouse is moving over at the bottom of the window, just as it does for "normal" links. If someone clicked where the mouse cursor (the little hand) is shown in Figure 15.4, the page named george.htm would come up.

Figure 15.4.

The image map defined in Figure 15.3 as it appears on the Web page.

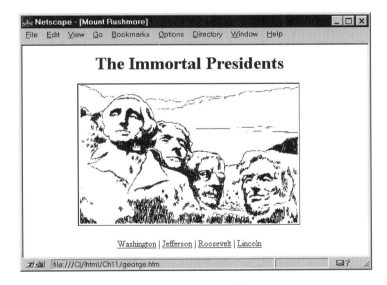

TIME SAVER

Notice that I included text links on this page that go to the same pages as the image map links. This allows people who have older Web browsers—or who don't want to wait for the image to finish loading—to access those pages.

Image Maps with Non-rectangular Regions

Some images don't lend themselves to being broken up into neat rectangular regions. The image in Figure 15.5, for example, would make a great image map—but the regions you would want to click on couldn't be defined just by specifying the top-left and bottom-right corners.

Figure 15.5.

To divide this image into regions, you need more shapes than just upright rectangles.

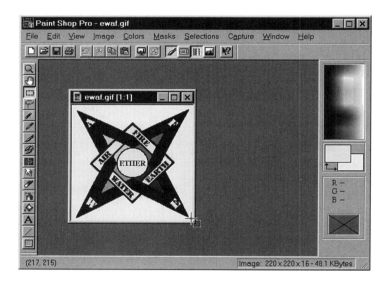

Fortunately, HTML image maps let you create polygonal regions with any number of corners. You can also define circular regions, which would be handy for the "ETHER" region in Figure 15.5.

I've sketched the clickable regions for this image map in Figure 15.6.

Figure 15.7 shows the HTML to define the actual image map, and Figure 15.8 shows the resulting Web page. To make polygonal regions, use SHAPE="poly" in the <AREA> tag, and put each of the corner points in the COORDS attribute. For circular regions, use SHAPE="circle" and put the center point and radius (in pixels) in the COORDS attribute.

15

Figure 15.6.

Triangular and circular regions would work much better than rectangular ones for the image in Figure 15.5.

Figure 15.7.

A page defining the image map regions shown in Figure 15.6.

```
<HTML><HEAD><TITLE>The Medieval Elements</TITLE></HEAD>
<BODY BACKGROUND="gradient.jpg">
<MAP NAME="elements">
<AREA SHAPE="poly" COORDS="217,215, 185,84, 109,159"
 HREF="earth.htm">
<AREA SHAPE="poly" COORDS="5,218, 139,185, 64,108"
 HREF="water.htm">
<AREA SHAPE="poly" COORDS="5,7, 33,141, 112,61"
 HREF="air.htm">
<AREA SHAPE="poly" COORDS="216,5, 86,39, 161,109"
 HREF="fire.htm">
<AREA SHAPE="circle" COORDS="111,111,30"
 HREF="ether.htm">
</MAP>
<A HREF="nomaps.htm">
<IMG SRC="ewaf.gif" WIDTH=220 HEIGHT=220
 BORDER=0 ALIGN="right" USEMAP="#elements" ISMAP></A>
<H2>The Medieval Elements</H2>
Scientific knowledge has progressed far beyond
the four "elements" of earth, water, air, and fire as an
explanation of objective physical phenomena <P>
However, many people still view these four qualities
as essential elements of our subjective inner experience
of the world. Click on one of the elements to the right
to read more about it.
</BODY></HTML>
```

Figure 15.8.

This is how the image map in Figure 15.7 appears to a reader about to click on the "AIR" link.

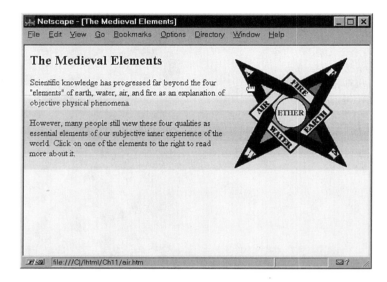

Instead of including text links on the page in Figures 15.7 and 15.8, I used a tricky little attribute of the <IMG> tag called ISMAP. If you put ISMAP in an image tag, you can also put an <A HREF> link around the image. That link will only work for older browsers that don't support client-side image maps. The nomaps.htm file I linked to might lead to a page of text links, or simply a page saying Sorry, your browser is too old and feeble to handle the client-side image map on my awesome Web page (not necessarily in so many words).

COFFEE BREAK

You can often avoid even the minimal hassle involved in creating an image map by breaking up the map into separate images and simply placing them next to each other on a Web page.

For an example, go to the page at

http://www.mcp.com/sams/books/235-8/cwg/welcome.htm

The three graphical links at the bottom of that page look like an image map, but they're actually just three regular old images with an <A HREF> tag around each of them.

If you try this yourself, be careful not to put a space or line break between the <IMG> tags, or the images won't meet at the edges.

Wherever you can avoid image maps, do so; individual images are easier to maintain, and you can often use the pieces again in creative and useful ways. (Click on the links at the above address to see what I mean.)

15

> I've prepared a little quiz to help you learn to tell when image maps are
> necessary and when they aren't. Check it out by clicking on the Pop Quiz
> icon in the new image map at
>
> ```
> http://www.mcp.com/sams/books/235-8/cafe15.htm
> ```

Server-Side Image Maps

The old-fashioned way to create an image map is to let the server computer where the Web
page resides do all the work. Most Web authors don't bother with server-side image maps
anymore, because it's easier and just as effective to provide text links for people using older
browsers. But there are still an awful lot of people out there using pre–1995 Web browsers,
and it isn't really *that* hard to make your image maps work for them. You can read the
following explanation of what's involved and decide for yourself whether it's worth your time
to provide server-side image maps.

When the user clicks an image that has been mapped this way, the browser program just sends
the x,y coordinates of the mouse pointer's location to a special script on the server. Usually,
this script is located in some subdirectory of cgi-bin on the server, and the HTML to
implement the image map is just a normal anchor link.

```
<A HREF="/cgi-bin/imagemap/thisthat"><IMG SRC="thisthat.gif" ISMAP></A>
```

Simple. But when you install a Web page including such a link, you need to tell the image
map script which parts of the image should be associated with which link addresses. This is
normally done in a *map file*. Each line in the map file is simply the word rect followed by
a URL address and two sets of x,y coordinates representing the top-left corner and the
bottom-right corner of a region of the image. Some server scripts also support non-
rectangular regions with the word poly and circle (or round).

The first line in a map file begins with the word default followed by the URL address that
should be used if the user happens to click outside any rectangular region defined by a rect
line. A map file named thisthat.map might look like this:

```
default /top/this.htm
rect /top/this.htm 0,0,102,99
rect /top/that.htm 103,0,205,99
```

The final step in setting up a server-side image map is telling the image map script which
map file to use for which image by adding a line to a system file named imagemap.conf. This
file will already exist and includes entries for every image map defined on the server. You
simply add a line with the name used in the HREF attribute of the <A> tag, a colon, and then

the actual location and name of the associated map file. For example, the previous reference is HREF="/cgi-bin/imagemap/thisthat", and the preceding map file is named thisthat.map. If this map file was in a directory named /mapfiles, the line in imagemap.conf would read

```
thisthat : /mapfiles/thisthat.map
```

All this isn't nearly as difficult as it may sound if you've never set up an image map before, but it can be a hassle, especially if your pages reside on somebody else's server and you don't have the rights to modify system files such as imagemap.conf yourself. What's worse, server-side image maps don't work at all on Web pages located on your hard drive, a CD-ROM, or most local networks.

There are also some variations in the exact syntax for image map implementation, depending on the software installed on your server. So if you move your pages to a different server, the image maps may not work anymore. Yuck.

Fortunately, the latest versions of all the major browsers support the client-side image maps discussed earlier in this chapter, where the association of links with specific regions in an image is handled by the browser itself instead of a server script. This means that you can include image maps in your HTML files without imposing an additional burden on your Internet service provider's server, and you can be more certain that they will be processed correctly and dependably.

Combined Client/Server Image Maps

There is a way for you to provide client-side image maps that automatically switch to server-side image maps if the user's browser doesn't support client-side maps. With a single line of code, you can allow an image map to be interpreted either by the end user's software or by the server by including the ISMAP attribute in the <IMG> tag, then including both a USEMAP= attribute and cgi-bin/imagemap reference.

```
<MAP "#thisthat">
<AREA SHAPE="rect" COORDS="0,0,102,99" HREF="this.htm">
<AREA SHAPE="rect" COORDS="103,0,205,99" HREF="that.htm"></MAP>
<A HREF="/cgi-bin/imagemap/thisthat">
<IMG SRC="thisthat.gif" USEMAP="#thisthat" ISMAP></A>
```

Here, as with any unrecognized tag, browsers that don't support client-side image maps will simply ignore the <USEMAP> and <ISMAP> tags and treat the preceding code like an old-fashioned server-side image map.

15

Summary

This chapter explained how to create *image maps*—links that lead to more than one place, depending on where you click on an image. You saw how to define rectangular and circular link regions within an image, as well as irregularly shaped polygonal regions. You also learned to provide an alternate link just for people using older browsers that don't support the current image map standard. Finally, you got a quick rundown on providing server-side image maps on most types of Web servers—just in case you want to provide the best possible experience for users of outdated browsers.

Table 15.1 is a summary of the tags and attributes covered in this chapter.

Table 15.1. HTML tags and attributes covered in Chapter 15.

Tag	Attribute	Function
`<IMG>`		Inserts an image into the document.
	`ISMAP`	This image is a clickable image map.
	`SRC="..."`	The URL of the image.
	`USEMAP="..."`	The name of an image map specification for client-side image mapping. Used with `<MAP>` and `<AREA>`.
`<MAP>...</MAP>`		A client-side image map, referenced by `<IMG USEMAP="...">`. Includes one or more `<AREA>` tags.
`<AREA>`		Defines a clickable link within a client-side image map.
	`SHAPE="..."`	The shape of the clickable area. Currently, `rect`, `poly`, and `circle` (or `round`) are the valid options.
	`COORDS="..."`	The left, top, right, and bottom coordinates of the clickable region within an image.
	`HREF="..."`	The URL that should be loaded when the area is clicked.

Q&A

Q **I'd like to know exactly which browsers support client-side image maps, and which ones support server-side image maps.**

A All browsers that display graphics support server-side image maps. All versions of Netscape Navigator and Microsoft Internet Explorer with version numbers 2.0 or higher also support client-side image maps. Any other Web browser produced after 1995 probably supports client-side image maps, too.

Q **My image maps with polygonal and circular regions don't seem to work right in Netscape 2.0. Why?**

A Netscape Navigator version 2.0 and Microsoft Internet Explorer version 2.0 only support rectangular regions in client-side image maps. Only people using version 3.0 or later of these browsers will be able to click on non-rectangular regions.

Q **I don't have Paint Shop Pro and my graphics software doesn't tell me x,y coordinates. How do I figure out the coordinates for my image maps?**

A Here's a sneaky way to do it using Netscape Navigator. Put the image on a page with the ISMAP attribute and an `<A>` tag around it, like this:

```
<A HREF="nowhere"><IMG SRC="myimage.gif" ISMAP></A>
```

When you view that page with Navigator, move the mouse over the image. You will see the coordinates in the message box at the bottom of the window.

Quiz

Questions

1. You have a 200×200-pixel image named `quarters.gif` for your Web page. When someone clicks in the top-left quarter of the image, you want them to get a page named `toplft.htm`. When they click on the top-right quarter, they should get `toprgt.htm`. Clicking on the bottom left should bring up `btmlft.htm`, and the bottom right should lead to `btmrgt.htm`. Write the HTML to implement this as a client-side image map.

2. If you wanted people using older browsers that don't support client-side image maps to get a page named `oldies.htm` when they click on any part of the image map, how would you modify the HTML you wrote for Question 1?

3. How could you implement the effect described in Question 1 without using image maps at all?

15

Answers

1. ```
<MAP NAME="quartersmap">
<AREA SHAPE="rect" COORDS="0,0,99,99" HREF="toplft.htm">
<AREA SHAPE="rect" COORDS="100,0,199,99" HREF="toprgt.htm">
<AREA SHAPE="rect" COORDS="0,100,99,199" HREF="btmlft.htm">
<AREA SHAPE="rect" COORDS="100,100,199,199" HREF="btmrgt.htm">
</MAP>
<IMG SRC="quarters.gif" WIDTH=200 HEIGHT=200
 USEMAP="#quartersmap">
```

2. Replace the <IMG> tag above with

   ```
<A HREF="oldies.htm">
<IMG SRC="quarters.gif WIDTH=200 HEIGHT=200 ISMAP
 USEMAP="#quartersmap"></A>
```

3. Use a graphics program such as Paint Shop Pro to chop the image into quarters, and save them as separate images named toplft.gif, toprgt.gif, btmlft.gif, and btmrgt.gif. Then type

   ```
<A HREF="toplft.htm"><IMG SRC="toplft.gif"
WIDTH=100 HEIGHT=100 BORDER=0></A><A
HREF="toprgt.htm"><IMG SRC="toprgt.gif"
WIDTH=100 HEIGHT=100 BORDER=0></A><BR>
<A HREF="btmlft.htm"><IMG SRC="btmlft.gif"
WIDTH=100 HEIGHT=100 BORDER=0></A><A
HREF="btmrgt.htm"><IMG SRC="btmrgt.gif"
WIDTH=100 HEIGHT=100 BORDER=0></A>
```

   (Be careful to break the lines of the HTML *inside* the tags as shown above, to avoid introducing any spaces between the images.)

Activities

☐ If you have some pages containing short lists of links, see if you can cook up an interesting image map to use instead.

☐ Image maps are usually more engaging and attractive than a row of repetitive-looking icons or buttons. Can you come up with a visual metaphor related to your site that would make it easier—and maybe more fun—for people to navigate through your pages? (Thinking along these lines is a good preparation for the issues you'll be tackling in Part VI, "Building a Web Site," by the way.)
```

Hour **16**

Advanced Layout with Tables

One of the most powerful tools for creative Web page design is the *table,* which allows you to arrange text and images into multiple columns and rows. This chapter shows you how to build HTML tables and how to control the spacing, layout, and appearance of the tables you create.

A *table* is an orderly arrangement of text and/or graphics into vertical *columns* and horizontal *rows*.

To Do:

As you read this chapter, think about how arranging text into tables could benefit your Web pages. Here are some specific ideas to keep in mind:

- [ ] Of course, the most obvious application of tables is to organize tabular information, such as a multi-column list of names and numbers.
- [ ] If you want more complex relationships between text and graphics than `<IMG ALIGN="left">` or `<IMG ALIGN="right">` can provide, tables can do it.
- [ ] Tables can be used to draw borders around text, or around several graphics images.
- [ ] Whenever you need multiple columns of text, tables are the answer.

For each of your pages that meets one of these criteria, try adding a table modeled after the examples in this chapter. The "Activities" section at the end of this chapter offers a couple of detailed suggestions along these lines, as well.

Creating a Simple Table

To make tables, you have to start with a `<TABLE>` tag. Of course, you end your tables with the `</TABLE>` tag. If you want the table to have a border, use a `BORDER` attribute to specify the width of the border in pixels. A border size of 0 (or leaving the `BORDER` attribute out entirely) will make the border invisible, which is often handy when you are using a table as a page layout tool.

There are a number of optional attributes you can specify in the `<TABLE>` tag, but these are discussed after you get the basics under your belt.

With the `<TABLE>` tag in place, the next thing you need is the `<TR>` tag. `<TR>` creates a table row, which contains one or more *cells* of information. To create these individual cells, you use the `<TD>` tag. `<TD>` stands for table data; you place the table information within the `<TD>` and `</TD>` tags.

 A *cell* is a rectangular region which can contain any text, images, and HTML tags. Each row in a table is made up of at least one cell.

You can create as many cells as you want, but each row in a table should have the same number of columns as the other rows. The example in Figures 16.1 and 16.2 shows a simple table using only these three tags.

Figure 16.1.

The <TABLE>, <TR>, and <TD> tags are all you need to create simple tables.

```
<HTML><HEAD><TITLE>A Simple Table</TITLE></HEAD>
<BODY>
<TABLE BORDER=1>
<TR>
<TD>Any  table cell can contain text...</TD>
<TD><IMG SRC="graphics.gif"><BR>
    <IMG SRC="table1.gif"></TD>
<TD>...or both text and graphics.<P>
    <IMG SRC="table2.gif"></TD>
</TR>
</TABLE>
</BODY></HTML>
```

Figure 16.2.

The HTML table in Figure 16.1 has a single row with three cells.

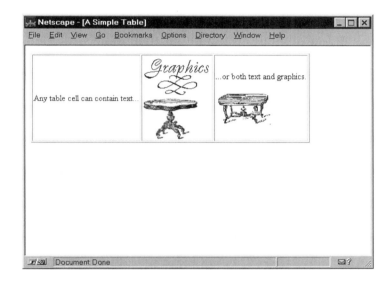

You can place virtually any other HTML element into a table cell. However, tags used in one cell don't carry over to other cells, and tags from outside the table don't apply within the table. For example, if you wrote

```
<FONT SIZE=5>
<TABLE><TR>
 <TD><FONT SIZE=6>Hello</TD>
 <TD>There</FONT></TD>
</TR></TABLE>
</FONT>
```

The word "There" would be normal-sized because neither the <FONT> tag outside the table nor the <FONT> tag from the previous cell affects it. To make both the words "Hello" and "There" larger than normal, you would need to type:

```
<TABLE><TR>
 <TD><FONT SIZE=6>Hello</FONT></TD>
 <TD><FONT SIZE=6>There</FONT></TD>
</TR></TABLE>
```

Table Size

Ordinarily, the size of a table and the size of its individual cells automatically expand to fit the data you place into it. However, you can choose to control the exact size of the entire table by putting WIDTH and/or HEIGHT attributes in the <TABLE> tag. You can also control the size of each cell by putting WIDTH and HEIGHT attributes in the individual <TD> tags. The WIDTH and HEIGHT can be specified as either pixels or percentages. For example, the following HTML makes a table 500 pixels wide and 400 pixels high:

```
<TABLE WIDTH=500 HEIGHT=400>
```

To make the first cell of the table 20 percent of the total table width, and the second cell 80 percent of the table width, you would type:

```
<TABLE><TR><TD WIDTH=20%>Skinny cell</TD>
<TD WIDTH=80%>Fat cell</TD>
```

Alignment and Spanning

By default, anything you place inside a table cell is aligned to the left and vertically centered. You can align the contents of table cells both horizontally and vertically with the ALIGN and VALIGN attributes.

You can apply these attributes to either <TR> or <TD> tags. Alignment attributes assigned to <TR> tags apply to all cells in that row. Depending on the size of your table, you can save yourself a considerable amount of time and effort by applying these attributes at the <TR> level and not in each individual <TD> tag. The HTML code in Figure 16.3 uses VALIGN="top" to bring the text to the top of each cell and VALIGN="bottom" to bring the table images to the bottom of their cells. Figure 16.4 shows the result.

At the top of Figure 16.4, a single cell spans three columns. This is accomplished with the COLSPAN=3 attribute in the <TD> tag for that cell. As you might guess, you can also use the ROWSPAN attribute to create a cell that spans more than one row. (You'll see ROWSPAN in Figures 16.5 and 16.7, later in this chapter.)

16

TIME SAVER

As you know, HTML ignores extra spaces between words and tags. However, you might find your HTML tables easier to read (and less prone to time-wasting errors) if you use spaces to indent <TD> tags a bit, as I did in Figure 16.3.

Figure 16.3.

Use ALIGN *and* VALIGN *to control the alignment of any row or individual cell.*

16

```
<HTML>
<HEAD><TITLE>Tabula Rasa</TITLE></HEAD>
<BODY BGCOLOR="white">
<TABLE BORDER=2 CELLPADDING=10>
<TR>
    <TD></TD>
    <TD COLSPAN=3 BACKGROUND="scratch2.gif">
    <IMG SRC="tabula.gif" ALIGN="left">
    <DIV ALIGN="center">
    <FONT COLOR="maroon">
    <H1>Tabula Rasa, Inc.</H1>
    <B>Antique tables for the modern home</B>
    </FONT></DIV>
    </TD>
</TR>
<TR VALIGN="top">
    <TD></TD>
    <TD><I>Product</I></TD>
    <TD><I>Description</I></TD>
    <TD><I>Price</I></TD>
</TR>
<TR VALIGN="top">
    <TD HEIGHT=110 VALIGN="bottom">
    <IMG SRC="table1.gif"></TD>
    <TD><H2>Tabula Suprema</H2></TD>
    <TD>A classic ornamental dining table
        to take you back to a more refined age.</TD>
    <TD><H2>$795</H2></TD>
</TR>
<TR  VALIGN="top">
    <TD HEIGHT=110 VALIGN="bottom">
    <IMG SRC="table2.gif"></TD>
    <TD><H2>Tabula Allegro</H2></TD>
    <TD>Sophistication underneath, with ample room
        for bounty on top. Gather the family!</TD>
    <TD><H2>$675</H2></TD>
</TR>
<TR VALIGN="top">
    <TD HEIGHT=110 VALIGN="bottom">
    <IMG SRC="table3.gif"></TD>
    <TD><H2>Tabula El-Cheapo</H2></TD>
    <TD>Imminently practical, with folding ends
        and tasteful ornamentation.</TD>
    <TD><H2>$295</H2></TD>
</TR>
</TABLE>
</BODY></HTML>
```

TIME SAVER

Keeping the structure of rows and columns organized in your mind can be the most difficult part of creating complex tables, especially because the tiniest error can throw the whole thing into disarray. You'll save yourself time and frustration by sketching out your tables on graph paper before you start writing the HTML to implement them.

Figure 16.4.

The COLSPAN *attribute in Figure 16.3 allows the top cell to span multiple columns.*

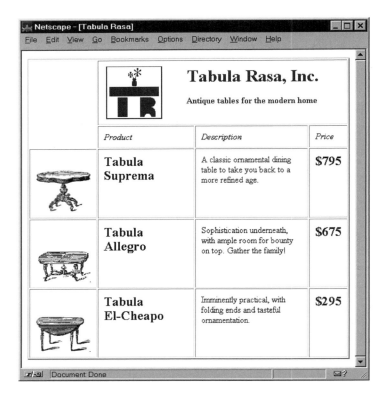

Backgrounds and Spacing

You can give an entire table—and each individual row or cell in a table—its own background, distinct from any background you might use on the Web page itself. You do this by placing a BGCOLOR or BACKGROUND attribute in the <TABLE>, <TR>, or <TD> tags exactly as you would in the <BODY> tag (see Chapter 13, "Backgrounds and Color Control"). To give an entire table a yellow background, for example, you would use <TABLE BGCOLOR="yellow">.

JUST A MINUTE

Only users of Netscape Navigator and Microsoft Internet Explorer versions 3.0 or higher will see table background colors, and only Microsoft Internet Explorer currently supports table background images.

16

You can also control the space around the borders of a table with the CELLPADDING and CELLSPACING attributes. The CELLSPACING attribute sets the amount of space (in pixels) between table borders and between table cells themselves. The CELLPADDING attribute sets the amount of space around the edges of information in the cells. Setting the CELLPADDING value to zero causes all the information in the table to align as closely as possible to the table borders, possibly even touching the borders. CELLPADDING and CELLSPACING give you good overall control of the table's appearance.

You can see the effect of background color and spacing attributes in Figures 16.5 and 16.6. This table uses a 1-pixel-wide border, with 10 pixels of cell padding inside the cells and 5 pixels between the cells.

16

Figure 16.5.

This table uses background colors for individual cells, as well as cell padding and spacing controls.

```
<HTML>
<HEAD><TITLE>Tabula Rasa</TITLE></HEAD>
<BODY BGCOLOR="white">

<TABLE BORDER=1 CELLPADDING=10 CELLSPACING=5>
<TR VALIGN="top">
    <TD BGCOLOR="#FFB080"><I>Product</I></TD>
    <TD BGCOLOR="#FFB080"><I>Description</I></TD>
    <TD BGCOLOR="#FFB080"><I>Price</I></TD>
</TR>
<TR  VALIGN="top">
    <TD HEIGHT=110 VALIGN="bottom"><IMG SRC="table1.gif"></TD>
    <TD BGCOLOR="#FFFF80"><H2>Tabula Suprema</H2></TD>
    <TD BGCOLOR="#FFFF80"><H2>$795</H2></TD>
</TR>
<TR  VALIGN="top">
    <TD HEIGHT=110 VALIGN="bottom"><IMG SRC="table2.gif"></TD>
    <TD BGCOLOR="#FFFF80"><H2>Tabula Allegro</H2></TD>
    <TD BGCOLOR="#FFFF80"><H2>$675</H2></TD>
</TR>
<TR VALIGN="top">
    <TD HEIGHT=110 VALIGN="bottom"><IMG SRC="table3.gif"></TD>
    <TD BGCOLOR="#FFFF80"><H2>Tabula El-Cheapo</H2></TD>
    <TD BGCOLOR="#FFFF80"><H2>$295</H2></TD>
</TR>
</TABLE>

</BODY></HTML>
```

Figure 16.6.

Compare the spacing and overall aesthetics of this table (from the HTML in Figure 16.5) to the "plain" table in Figure 16.4.

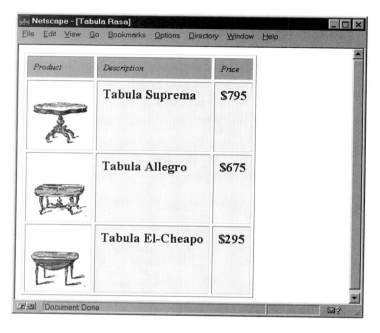

Nested Tables

You can place an entire table within a table cell, and that separate table can possess any and all the qualities of any table you might want to create.

For example, the table in Figures 16.7 and 16.8 has no borders, but in its bottom-left cell, I included the entire table from Figure 16.6, which does have borders. Nested tables open up a vast universe of possibilities for creative Web page layout.

COFFEE BREAK

The boring, conventional way to use tables is for tabular arrangements of text and numbers. But the real fun begins when you make the borders of your tables invisible, and use them as guides for arranging graphics and columns of text any which way you please. For an example, take a look at:

http://www.mcp.com/sams/books/235-8/look.htm

While I worked on building this table, I left the borders visible so I could make sure everything was placed the way I wanted. Then, before incorporating this table into the final Web page, I changed to BORDER=0 to make the lines invisible.

16

This page also links to a site called *LOOK*, which uses nontraditional layouts—and everything else we can pull out of the bag— to be eye-catching and distinctive (albeit without any actual informative content). Your real-world site will probably be a bit more tame than the *LOOK* site, but of course some of you will start getting even crazier ideas.

You can also see how I incorporated some simple tables into the *24-Hour HTML Café* site to enhance its aesthetics and functionality:

```
http://www.mcp.com/sams/books/235-8/cafe16.htm
```

16

Figure 16.7.

The actual source for this HTML file contains all the text from the <TABLE> tag to the </TABLE> tag in Figure 16.5.

```
<HTML>
<HEAD><TITLE>Tabula Rasa</TITLE></HEAD>
<BODY BGCOLOR="white">
<TABLE>
<TR><TD>
        <IMG SRC="tabula.gif" ALIGN="left">
        <DIV ALIGN="center">
        <FONT COLOR="maroon">
        <H1>Tabula Rasa, Inc.</H1>
        <B>Antique tables<BR>for the modern home</B>
        </FONT></DIV>
    </TD>
    <TD ROWSPAN=2>
At Tabula Rasa, our mission is to locate and restore the
most beautiful tables in the world and sell them to you.
If you put one of our tables in your dining room, then you
can eat on it. Or if you don't want to get it dirty, you
could just put a vase with some flowers on it and eat in
front of the TV. In any case, guests and relatives are sure
to comment on your refined taste and obscene wealth
when they see your new antique table,
and you sure can't beat that feeling.<P>
So enough chit-chat. The bottom line is: You buy a table,
or we have our boys pay a little visit to your house once
or twice a week for the rest of your life. And trust me,
these guys are not vacuum salesmen. So hand over the credit
card and let's get this over with. You'll be glad you did.
We guarantee it.<P> <I>Tabula Rasa is a wholly owned
subsidiary of Cosa Nostra Furnishings Inc.</I>
</TD></TR>
<TR><TD>
        ...the table from Figure 16.5 goes here...

</TD></TR></TABLE>
</BODY></HTML>
```

Figure 16.8.

*Nesting one table inside
another lets you use
different borders and
spacing in different parts
of your layout.*

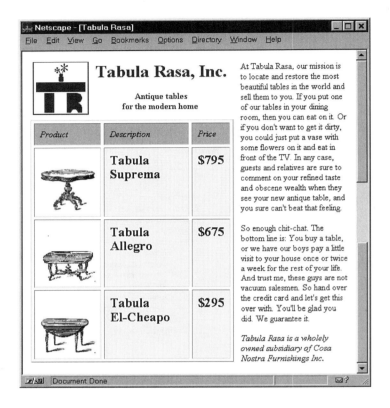

Summary

In this chapter, you learned to arrange text and images into organized arrangements or rows and columns, called *tables*. You learned the three basic tags for creating tables, and many optional attributes for controlling the alignment, spacing, and appearance of tables. You also saw that tables can be nested within one another for an even wider variety of layout options.

Table 16.1 summarizes the tags and attributes covered in this chapter.

Table 16.1. HTML tags and attributes covered in Chapter 16.

Tag	Attribute	Function
`<TABLE>...</TABLE>`		Creates a table that can contain any number of rows (`<TR>` tags).
	`BORDER="..."`	Indicates the width in pixels of the table borders. (`BORDER=0`, or omitting the `BORDER` attribute, makes borders invisible.)

16

Tag	Attribute	Function
	CELLSPACING="..."	The amount of space between the cells in the table.
	CELLPADDING="..."	The amount of space between the edges of the cell and its contents.
	WIDTH="..."	The width of the table on the page, in either exact pixel values or as a percentage of page width.
	BGCOLOR="..."	Background color of all cells in the table that do not contain their own BACKGROUND or BGCOLOR attribute.
	BACKGROUND="..."	Background image to tile within all cells in the table that do not contain their own BACKGROUND or BGCOLOR attribute (Microsoft Internet Explorer 3.0 only).
<TR>...</TR>		Defines a table row, containing one or more cells (<TD> tags).
	ALIGN="..."	The horizontal alignment of the contents of the cells within this row. Possible values are LEFT, RIGHT, and CENTER.
	VALIGN="..."	The vertical alignment of the contents of the cells within this row. Possible values are TOP, MIDDLE, and BOTTOM.
	BGCOLOR="..."	Background color of all cells in the row that do not contain their own BACKGROUND or BGCOLOR attributes.
	BACKGROUND="..."	Background image to tile within all cells in the row that do not contain their own BACKGROUND or BGCOLOR attributes (Microsoft Internet Explorer 3.0 only).
<TD>...</TD>		Defines a table data cell.
	ALIGN="..."	The horizontal alignment of the contents of the cell. Possible values are LEFT, RIGHT, and CENTER.
	VALIGN="..."	The vertical alignment of the contents of the cell. Possible values are TOP, MIDDLE, and BOTTOM.

continues

Table 16.1. continued

Tag	Attribute	Function
	ROWSPAN="..."	The number of rows this cell will span.
	COLSPAN="..."	The number of columns this cell will span.
	WIDTH="..."	The width of this column of cells, in exact pixel values or as a percentage of the table width.
	BGCOLOR="..."	Background color of the cell.
	BACKGROUND="..."	Background image to tile within the cell (Microsoft Internet Explorer 3.0 only).

Q&A

Q I made a big table, and when I load the page nothing appears for a long time. Why the wait?

A Because the Web browser has to figure out the size of everything in the table before it can display any part of it, complex tables can take a while to appear on the screen. You can speed things up a bit by always including WIDTH and HEIGHT tags for every graphics image within a table. Using WIDTH attributes in the <TABLE> and <TD> tags also helps.

Q I've noticed that a lot of pages on the Web have tables in which one cell will change while other cells stay the same. How do they do that?

A Those sites are using *frames*, not tables. Frames are similar to tables except that each frame contains a separate HTML page and can be updated independently of the others. The new "floating frames" can actually be put inside a table, so they can look just like a regular table even though the HTML to create them is quite different. You'll find out how to make frames in Chapter 17, "Interactive Layout with Frames."

Q I read in another book that there are four table tags, but you didn't mention the <TH> tag in this book. Why not?

A In addition to <TABLE>, <TR>, and <TD>, there is a fourth tag, <TH>. It is used exactly like <TD>, but is meant to imply that the cell is part of the heading of the table. Because there is no visible difference between <TD> and <TH> cells, many Web page authors don't bother using <TH>. Considering how much you're learning at once here, I didn't think you needed an extra tag to memorize!

For the record, I also left out another "basic" table tag called <CAPTION>. All it does is center some text over the top of the table, which you can easily do with the <DIV ALIGN="center"> tag you're already familiar with.

16

Q The Microsoft Web site says there's a whole new table standard, and that they're the only ones that support it. Is that true?

A The proposed HTML 3.*x* standard introduces several new table tags, which are supported (in their current, unofficial form) by Internet Explorer 3.0. The primary practical uses of these extensions are to exert greater control over where borders are placed in and around a table, and to prepare the ground for some advanced features that Internet Explorer does not yet offer, such as tables with their own scrollbars. Keep your eye on the Microsoft and Netscape Web sites (`http://www.microsoft.com` and `http://home.netscape.com`) for details about these new table tags.

But don't worry; the new standard will *not* make any of the table tags covered in this chapter obsolete. They will all continue to work just as they do now.

Quiz

Questions

1. You want a Web page with two columns of text side-by-side. How do you create it?

2. You think the columns you created for Question 1 look too close together. How do you add 30 pixels of space between them?

3. Write the HTML to create the table shown below:

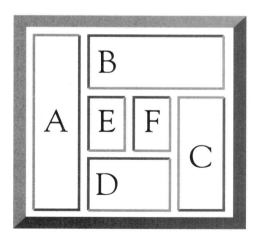

4. Write the HTML to create the nested tables shown below:

Answers

1. With the following table:

```
<TABLE><TR><TD ALIGN="top">
...First column of text goes here...
</TD><TD ALIGN="top">
...Second column of text goes here...
</TD></TR></TABLE>
```

2. Add CELLSPACING=30 to the <TABLE> tag. (Or you could use CELLPADDING=15 to add 15 pixels of space inside the edge of each column.)

3.
```
<TABLE BORDER=5>
<TR>
 <TD ROWSPAN=3>A</TD>
 <TD COLSPAN=3>B</TD>
</TR>
<TR>
 <TD>E</TD>
 <TD>F</TD>
 <TD ROWSPAN=2>C</TD>
</TR>
<TR>
 <TD COLSPAN=2>D</TD>
</TR>
</TABLE>
```

16

4. ```
<TABLE><TR>
<TD>A</TD>
<TD>
<TABLE BORDER=1>
<TR><TD>B</TD></TR>
<TR><TD>C</TD></TR>
</TABLE>
</TD>
<TD>D</TD>
</TR></TABLE>
```

# Activities

☐ You can use a simple one-celled table with a border to draw a rectangle around any section of text on a Web page. By nesting that single-cell table in another two-column table, you can put a "sidebar" of text to the left or right side of your Web page. Outlined sections of text and sidebars are very common on printed paper pages, so you'll probably find uses for them on your Web pages, too.

☐ Do you have any pages where different visitors might be interested in different information? Use a table to present two or three columns of text, each with its own heading (and perhaps its own graphic). Then something of interest to everyone will be visible at the top of the page when it first appears.
```

PART V

Interactive Web Pages

Hour

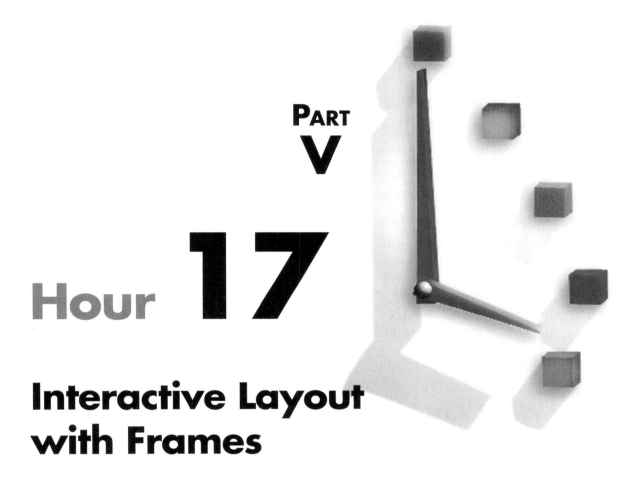

Hour 17

Interactive Layout with Frames

One major limitation of HTML in the old days was that you could see only one page at a time. *Frames* overcome this limitation by dividing the browser window into multiple HTML documents. Like tables, frames allow you to arrange text and graphics into rows and columns of text and graphics.

However, unlike a table cell, any frame can contain links that change the contents of other frames (or itself). For example, one frame could display an unchanging table of contents while the other frames change based on which links the reader follows.

JUST A MINUTE

Frames are only supported by Netscape Navigator version 2.0 or higher and Microsoft Internet Explorer version 3.0 or higher. You'll see how to provide alternative content for other browsers in the "Supporting Frameless Browsers" section near the end of this chapter.

To Do:

Frames are basically a way of arranging and presenting several Web pages at once. You'll be able to learn the material in this chapter faster if you have a few interrelated Web pages all ready before you continue.

☐ If you have an index page or table of contents for your Web site, copy it to a separate directory folder so you can experiment with it without changing the original. Copy a few of the pages that the index links to as well.

☐ As you read this chapter, try modifying the sample frames I present to incorporate your own Web pages.

What Are Frames?

At first glance, Figure 17.1 may look like an ordinary Web page, but it is actually three separate Web pages all displayed in the same Netscape Navigator window. Each of these pages is displayed in its own *frame*, separated by horizontal bars.

A *frame* is a rectangular region within the browser window that displays a Web page, alongside other pages in other frames.

The main advantage of using frames becomes apparent when a reader clicks on one of the links in the bottom frame of Figure 17.1. The top and bottom frames will not change at all, but a new page will be loaded and displayed in the middle frame, as in Figure 17.2.

17

Figure 17.1.

Frames allow more than one Web page to be displayed at once.

Figure 17.2.

Clicking on "See Us Make It" in Figure 17.1 brings up a new middle page, but leaves the top and bottom frames the same.

Creating a Frameset Document

How did I make the site in Figures 17.1 and 17.2? First, I created the contents of each frame as an ordinary HTML page. These pages (listed in Figures 17.4 through 17.7) don't contain any tags that you haven't already seen in other chapters.

To put them all together, I used a special kind of page called a *frameset document.*

A frameset document actually has no content. It only tells the browser which pages to load, and how to arrange them in the browser window. Figure 17.3 shows the frameset document for the Sandiwood Farm site in Figures 17.1 and 17.2.

Figure 17.3.

If you load this frameset document in Netscape Navigator, you'll see the site in Figure 17.1.

```
<HTML>
<HEAD><TITLE>Maple Syrup from Sandiwood Farm</TITLE></HEAD>
<FRAMESET ROWS="80,*,80">
<FRAME SRC="banner.htm" SCROLLING=NO
 MARGINHEIGHT=4 MARGINWIDTH=4>
<FRAME SRC="main.htm" NAME="main">
<FRAME SRC="bottom.htm" SCROLLING=NO
 MARGINHEIGHT=4 MARGINWIDTH=4>
</FRAMESET>
</HTML>
```

In Figure 17.3, instead of a <BODY> tag, there is a <FRAMESET> tag. No tags that would normally be contained in a <BODY> tag can be within the <FRAMESET> tag. The <FRAMESET> tag in Figure 17.3 includes a ROWS attribute, meaning that the frames should be arranged on top of each other like the horizontal rows of a table. If you want your frames to be side-by-side, use a COLS attribute instead of ROWS.

You must specify the sizes of the ROWS or COLS, either as precise pixel values or as percentages of the total size of the browser window. You can also use an asterisk (*) to indicate that a frame should fill whatever space is available in the window. If more than one frame has an * value, the remaining space will be allotted equally between them.

In Figure 17.3, <FRAMESET ROWS="80,*,80"> means to split the window vertically into three frames. The top and bottom frames will be exactly 80 pixels tall, and the middle frame will take up all the remaining space in the window. The top frame contains the document banner.htm, and the bottom frame contains bottom.htm.

TIME SAVER

Because you can't predict the size of the window that someone will view your Web page in, it is usually safest to use percentages rather than exact pixel values to dictate the size of the rows and columns. For example, to make a left frame 20 percent of the width of the browser window with a right frame taking up the remaining 80 percent, you would type

<FRAMESET COLS="20%,80%">

17

An exception to this rule would be when you want a frame to contain a single image of a certain size; then you would specify that size in pixels and add a few pixels for the frame borders. This is the case in Figure 17.3, where the background images for the "boards" are exactly 80 pixels thick.

In any case, if you specify any frame size in pixels, there must also be at least one frame in the same frameset with a variable (*) width so that the document can be displayed in a window of any size.

The <FRAME> Tag

17

Within the <FRAMESET> and </FRAMESET> tags, you should have a <FRAME> tag indicating which HTML document to display in each frame. (If you have fewer <FRAME> tags than the number of frames defined in the <FRAMESET> tag, any remaining frames will be left blank.) You don't need to specify a closing </FRAME> tag.

Include a SRC attribute in each <FRAME> tag, with the address of the Web page to load in that frame. (You can insert the address of an image file instead of a Web page if you just want a frame with a single image in it.)

You can include any HTML page you want in a frame. For example, the middle frame of Figure 17.1 is listed in Figure 17.5. For smaller frames, however, it's a good idea to create documents specifically for the frames with the reduced display area for each frame in mind. The top frame in Figure 17.1, for instance, is listed in Figure 17.4. It is much shorter than most Web pages, because it was designed specifically to fit in a frame 80 pixels tall.

Figure 17.4.

This page was designed specifically to fit in the top frame of Figures 17.1 and 17.2.

```
<HTML>
<HEAD><TITLE>Maple Syrup from Sandiwood Farm</TITLE></HEAD>
<BODY BACKGROUND="hboard.jpg">
<IMG SRC="corner1.gif" ALIGN="left">
<IMG SRC="corner2.gif" ALIGN="right">
<DIV ALIGN="center">
<FONT FACE="Lucida Handwriting" SIZE=2 COLOR="maroon">
<B>The Schlosser Family<BR>
<IMG SRC="swfarm.gif" ALT="Sandiwood Farm"><BR>
Wolcott, Vermont, USA</B></FONT>
</DIV>
</BODY></HTML>
```

Figure 17.5.

This ordinary Web page appears in the middle frame in Figure 17.1.

```
<HTML>
<HEAD><TITLE>Maple Syrup from Sandiwood Farm</TITLE></HEAD>
<BODY BACKGROUND="paper.jpg"
 TEXT="maroon" VLINK="red" LINK="red" ALINK="black">
<IMG SRC="maple.gif" ALIGN="left" HSPACE=10>
<FONT FACE="Lucida Handwriting" SIZE=4>
<H1>Pure Maple Syrup</H1> <H2>A Vermont Tradition</H2>
Every spring, when the snow turns to the texture of
granulated sugar and the warm morning sun melts the frost
on the window panes, the sugar maples come out of their
long winter's sleep. The result is one of Nature's most
sumptous delights - fresh maple sap, boiled down to a thick,
rich syrup as sweet as springtime itself.<P>
<IMG SRC="foods.gif" ALIGN="right">
<H2>It's Not Just for Breakfast!</H2>
Every Vermonter knows that if you save your maple syrup just
for pancakes, you're depriving yourself of a vast variety of
luscious, mapley treats: cookies, muffins, breads, and
almost any baked goods will truly come to life with the
special flavor of fresh syrup. Use a touch of maple instead
of vanilla in whipped cream or ice cream. Drizzle it over
hams and other meats, or add it to spicy sauces and curries
(in India, a very similar syrup is made from the sap of local
trees). Try a little in seltzer water for a healthy and
exotic refresher! And of course, nothing compares to the
Native American delicacies of blueberries and syrup in the
summer, and maple-flavored squash in the fall.<P>
<IMG SRC="mapleaf.gif" ALIGN="left" HSPACE=6>
<H2>A Wholesome, Healthy Treat</H2>
Vermont maple syrup is healthier and lower in calories than
refined sugar, and is better for the planet since it involves
less industrial waste in its production. We invite you to
<A HREF="makeit.htm">see how our family produces syrup at
Sandiwood farm</A> the traditional way, and
<A HREF="order.htm">order some of our fresh syrup</A>
for your own kitchen and table.<P>
</BODY>
</HTML>
```

Linking Between Frames and Windows

The real fun begins when you give a frame a name with the <FRAME NAME> attribute. You can then make any link on the page change the contents of that frame using the <A TARGET> attribute. For example, Figure 17.3 includes the following tag:

```
<FRAME SRC="main.htm" NAME="main">
```

This displays the main.htm page in that frame when the page loads, and names the frame "main." (The frame name doesn't have to match the name of its contents. It just happens to in this example.)

In the bottom frame, listed in Figure 17.6, you will see the following link:

```
<A HREF="makeit.htm" TARGET="main">See us make it.</A>
```

When the user clicks this link, the makeit.htm is displayed in the frame named main (the middle frame). To accomplish this sort of interactivity before the invention of frames, you would have had to use complex programming or scripting languages. Now you can do it with a simple link!

If the TARGET="main" attribute hadn't been included, the makeit.htm page would be displayed in the current (bottom) frame instead.

17

Figure 17.6.

This is the bottom frame in Figure 17.1. Clicking on a link causes the contents of the middle frame to change.

```
<HTML>
<HEAD><TITLE>Maple Syrup from Sandiwood Farm</TITLE></HEAD>
<BODY BACKGROUND="hboard.jpg"
 TEXT="maroon" VLINK="red" LINK="red" ALINK="black">
<IMG SRC="corner3.gif" ALIGN="left">
<IMG SRC="corner4.gif" ALIGN="right">
<DIV ALIGN="center">
<FONT FACE="Lucida Handwriting" SIZE=4>
<A HREF="main.htm" TARGET="main">Pure Maple Syrup</A>
<IMG SRC="icon.gif" ALIGN="middle">
<A HREF="makeit.htm" TARGET="main">See Us Make It </A><BR>
<A HREF="order.htm" TARGET="main">Order Some!</A>
</DIV>
</BODY></HTML>
```

To save space, I haven't listed the makeit.htm page in a figure; it's just a regular Web page with no special frame-related features. You can see what the top of it looks like in Figure 17.2, and see this whole site online at

http://www.mcp.com/sams/books/235-8/ch17/syrup.htm

TIME SAVER

When you include the TARGET attribute in a link, you can use a few special frame names in addition to the names you have defined with FRAME NAME:

- ☐ _blank loads the link into a new, unnamed window.
- ☐ _self loads the link into the current frame, replacing the document now being displayed in this frame.
- ☐ _top loads the link into the entire browser window.
- ☐ _parent loads the link over the parent frame if the current frame is nested within other frames (This name is the same as _top unless the frames are nested more than one level deep).

Note that all other names beginning with an underscore (_) will be ignored.

Margins, Borders, and Scrolling

In addition to the NAME attribute, the <FRAME> tag can take the following special frame-related attributes:

- ☐ MARGINWIDTH: Left and right margins of the frame (in pixels)
- ☐ MARGINHEIGHT: Top and bottom margins of the frame (in pixels)
- ☐ SCROLLING: Display scrollbar for the frame? ("yes" or "no")
- ☐ NORESIZE: Don't allow this frame to be resized by the user

MARGINWIDTH and MARGINHEIGHT are pretty self-explanatory, but each of the other attributes is discussed in detail in the next few paragraphs.

Normally, any frame that isn't big enough to hold all of its contents will have its own scrollbar(s). The middle frames in Figures 17.1 and 17.2 are examples. If you don't want a particular frame to ever display scrollbars, you can put SCROLLING=NO in the frame tag. Conversely, SCROLLING=YES forces both horizontal and vertical scrollbars to appear, whether or not they are needed.

TIME SAVER

You might wonder why I included SCROLLING=NO for the top and bottom <FRAME> tags in Figure 17.3. I did so because the images in those frames don't quite fit within the 80 pixels I allowed, when you count the margin of the page, too. So Netscape Navigator displays scrollbars that only scroll down a few pixels, and have no real purpose. Rather than make the frame bigger (and take up valuable window real estate with empty margin space), I just turned off the scrollbars.

The only situation I can think of where you might want to use SCROLLING=YES is if some graphics won't line up right unless you can count on the scrollbars always being there. Chances are, you'll probably never need SCROLLING=YES.

People viewing your frames can ordinarily resize them by grabbing the frame border with the mouse and dragging it around. If you don't want anyone messing with the size of a frame, put NORESIZE in the <FRAME> tag.

JUST A MINUTE

Both Microsoft Internet Explorer and Netscape Navigator allow you to control the size of the frame borders, or eliminate the borders altogether.

Unfortunately, Microsoft and Netscape do not yet agree on how frame borders should be controlled, so you need to use two different sets of non-standard HTML tags. For Microsoft Internet Explorer, you can make the borders disappear by including FRAMEBORDERS=NO in the <FRAMESET> tag. This makes a frame document look just like a regular Web page, with no ugly lines breaking it up. The FRAMESPACING attribute also lets you specify the number of pixels between frames in a frameset.

For Netscape Navigator, use BORDER=0 in the <FRAMESET> tag to eliminate borders, or BORDER= followed by a number of pixels to change the size of the frame borders.

If you want borderless frames to show up in both Netscape Navigator and Microsoft Internet Explorer, type FRAMEBORDERS=NO BORDER=0 in your <FRAMESET> tag (see Figures 17.7 and 17.8).

17

Nested Frames

By nesting one <FRAMESET> within another, you can create rather complex frame layouts. For example, the document shown in Figure 17.7 and listed in Figure 17.8 has a total of five frames. A COLS frameset is used to split the middle frame of the ROWS frameset into three pieces.

The two side pieces contain the simple page in Figure 17.9, which is nothing but a background tile. The net effect is to surround the changing middle frame with a static wooden "picture frame."

Figure 17.7.

This window contains five frames. (In Microsoft Internet Explorer, there would be no white lines between them.)

Figure 17.8.

To create Figure 17.7, I used a <FRAMESET> within a <FRAMESET>.

```
<HTML>
<HEAD><TITLE>Maple Syrup from Sandiwood Farm</TITLE></HEAD>
<FRAMESET ROWS="80,*,80" FRAMEBORDER=NO BORDER=0>
<FRAME SRC="banner.htm"
  SCROLLING=NO MARGINHEIGHT=4 MARGINWIDTH=4>
<FRAMESET COLS="80,*,80" FRAMEBORDER=NO BORDER=0>
<FRAME SRC="side.htm">
<FRAME SRC="main.htm" NAME="main">
<FRAME SRC="side.htm">
</FRAMESET>
<FRAME SRC="bottom.htm"
  SCROLLING=NO MARGINHEIGHT=4 MARGINWIDTH=4>
</FRAMESET>

<NOFRAMES><BODY>
<H1>Sandiwood Farm</H1>
<H2>Pure Vermont Maple Syrup</H2>
Your Web browser doesn't support frames,
but you can still <A HREF="main.htm">
explore our Web pages the old-fashioned way.</A>
</BODY></NOFRAMES>
</HTML>
```

Figure 17.9.

This is the side.htm
*page, which is just a
background tile with no
foreground text or images
at all.*

```
<HTML>
<BODY BACKGROUND="vboard.jpg">
</BODY>
</HTML>
```

Supporting Frameless Browsers

After the framesets in Figure 17.8, I included a complete Web page between the <BODY> and </BODY> tags. Notice that this doesn't appear at all in Figure 17.7. All Web browsers that support frames will ignore anything between the <NOFRAME> and </NOFRAME> tags.

To users of older Web browsers that don't support frames, the page listed in Figure 17.8 looks like Figure 17.10.

Figure 17.10.

*This is what Figure 17.8
looks like when you view
it with Netscape Naviga-
tor version 1.2, which
doesn't support frames.*

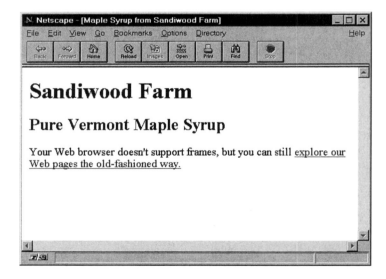

Because some browsers still do not support frames, it is probably wise to include alternative content with the <NOFRAME> tag. If nothing else, just include a note recommending that people get either Microsoft's or Netscape's browser to see the frames.

17

TIME SAVER

Some Web page publishers actually produce two versions of their site—one with frames, and one without. You can save yourself that hassle by simply including links between all the pages that will appear in your primary frame.

For example, all the pages that appear in the middle frame in this chapter's sample site are linked together with ordinary links (that don't use TARGET). You can get all the information from the site by starting at the main.htm page instead of the syrup.htm frameset document.

Summary

In this chapter, you learned how to display more than one page at a time by splitting the Web browser window into *frames*. You learned to use a *frameset document* to define the size and arrangement of the frames, as well as which Web page or image will be loaded into each frame. You saw how to create links that change the contents of any frame you choose, while leaving the other frames unchanged. You also discovered several optional settings that control the appearance of resizable borders and scrollbars in frames. Finally, you saw how to nest framesets to create complex frame layouts.

Table 17.1 summarizes the tags and attributes covered in this chapter.

Table 17.1. HTML tags and attributes covered in Chapter 17.

Tag	Attribute	Function
`<FRAMESET>...</FRAMESET>`		Divides the main window into a set of frames that can each display a separate document.
	`ROWS="..."`	Splits the window or frameset vertically into a number of rows specified by a number (such as 7), a percentage of the total window width (such as 25%), or as an asterisk (*) indicating that a frame should take up all the remaining space, or divide the space evenly between frames (if multiple * frames are specified).

continues

Table 17.1. continued

Tag	Attribute	Function
	COLS="..."	Works similar to ROWS, except that the window, or frameset, is split horizontally into columns.
	FRAMESPACING="..."	Space between frames, in pixels. (Microsoft Internet Explorer 3.0 only.)
	FRAMEBORDER="..."	Specifies whether or not to display a border for the frames. Options are YES and NO. (Microsoft Internet Explorer 3.0 only.)
	BORDER="..."	Size of the frame borders in pixels. (Netscape Navigator only.)
<FRAME>		Defines a single frame within a <FRAMESET>.
	SRC="..."	The URL of the document to be displayed in this frame.
	NAME="..."	A name to be used for targeting this frame with the TARGET attribute in <A HREF> links.
	MARGINWIDTH="..."	The amount of space (in pixels) to leave to the left and right side of a document within a frame.
	MARGINHEIGHT="..."	The amount of space (in pixels) to leave above and below a document within a frame.
	SCROLLING="..."	Determines whether or not a frame has scrollbars. Possible values are YES, NO, and AUTO.
	NORESIZE	Prevents the user from resizing this frame (and possibly adjacent frames) with the mouse.
<NOFRAME>...</NOFRAME>		Provides an alternative document body in <FRAMESET> documents for browsers that do not support frames (usually encloses <BODY>...</BODY>).

Q&A

Q Once I have some frames, how do I get rid of them and go back to a single page again?

A Link to the page you want to display, and include TARGET="_top" in the <A> tag. This page will take up the entire browser window and eliminate all frames (unless the page you load is a frameset document, too).

Q Can I display other people's Web pages from the Internet in one frame, and my own pages in another frame at the same time? What if those sites use frames, too?

A You can load any document from anywhere on the Internet (or an intranet) into a frame. If the document is a frameset, its frames will be sized to fit within the existing frame you load it into.

For example, you could put a hotlist of your favorite links in one frame, and have the pages that those links refer to appear in a separate frame. This makes it easy to provide links to other sites without risking that someone will get "lost" and never come back to your own site. Note, however, that if any link within that site has TARGET="_top", it will replace all your frames.

Q Can I make my pages appear in two separate browser windows instead of two frames within the same window?

A Yes. Just put TARGET="_blank" in any <A> link tag to open a new browser window for the page the link leads to. The contents of the current browser window won't change, though they probably will be hidden behind the new window when it appears.

Q Do I need to put a <TITLE> in all my frames? If I do, which title will be displayed at the top of the window?

A The title of the frameset document is the only one that will be displayed. But it's a good idea to give all your pages titles just in case somebody opens one by itself, outside any frame.

17

Quiz

Questions

1. Write the HTML to list the names Mickey, Minnie, Donald, Goofy, and Pluto in a frame taking up the left 25 percent of the browser window. Make it so that clicking on each name brings up a corresponding Web page in the right 75 percent of the browser window.
2. Write a frameset document to make the frame layout pictured below.

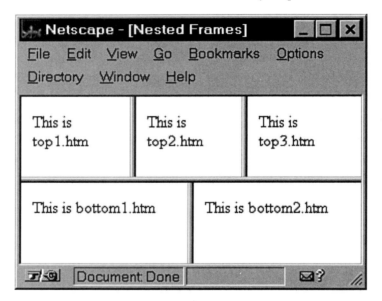

Answers

1. You need seven separate HTML documents. The first document is the frameset:
   ```
   <HTML><HEAD><TITLE>Our Friends</TITLE></HEAD>
   <FRAMESET COLS="25%,75%">
   <FRAME SRC="index.htm">
   <FRAME SRC="mickey.htm" NAME="mainframe">
   </FRAMESET>
   </HTML>
   ```

17

Next, you need the index.htm document for the left frame:

```
<HTML><HEAD><TITLE>Our Friends Index</TITLE></HEAD>
<BODY>
Pick a friend:<P>
<A HREF="mickey.htm" TARGET="mainframe">Mickey</A><P>
<A HREF="minnie.htm" TARGET="mainframe">Minnie</A><P>
<A HREF="donald.htm" TARGET="mainframe">Donald</A><P>
<A HREF="goofy.htm" TARGET="mainframe">Goofy</A><P>
<A HREF="pluto.htm" TARGET="mainframe">Pluto</A><P>
</BODY></HTML>
```

Finally, you need the five HTML pages named mickey.htm, minnie.htm, donald.htm, goofy.htm, and pluto.htm. These will contain the information about each friend.

2.
```
<HTML><HEAD><TITLE>Nested Frames</TITLE></HEAD>
<FRAMESET ROWS="*,*">
 <FRAMESET COLS="*,*,*">
 <FRAME SRC="top1.htm">
 <FRAME SRC="top2.htm">
 <FRAME SRC="top3.htm">
 </FRAMESET>
 <FRAMESET COLS="*,*">
 <FRAME SRC="bottom1.htm">
 <FRAME SRC="bottom2.htm">
 </FRAMESET>
</FRAMESET>
</HTML>
```

Activities

☐ In Chapter 22, "HTML Tags for Site Management," you'll find out how to make a page that loads another page automatically after a specified time interval. When you combine this trick with frames, you can create all sorts of interesting animated layout effects.

Hour 18

Creating HTML Forms

Up to this point, everything in this book has focused on getting information out to others. (E-mail links, introduced in Chapter 8, "Intra-Page and E-mail Links," are the one exception.) But HTML is a two-way street; you can use your Web pages to gather information *from* the people who read them as well.

Web forms allow you to receive feedback, orders, or other information from the readers of your Web pages. If you've ever used a Web search engine such as Lycos or Excite, you're familiar with HTML forms. Product order forms are also an extremely popular use of forms.

This chapter shows you how to create your own forms and the basics of how to handle form submissions.

 An HTML *form* is part of a Web page that includes areas where readers can enter information to be sent back to you, the publisher of the Web page.

How HTML Forms Work

Before you learn the HTML tags to make your own forms, you should understand how the information that someone fills out on a form makes its way back to you. You also need to have the person who runs your Web server computer set it up to process your forms.

Every form must include a button for the user to submit the form. When someone clicks on this button, all the information they have filled in is sent (in a standard format) to an Internet address that you will specify in the form itself. For that information to get to you, you have to put a special forms-processing program at that address.

Almost all Internet service provider companies that offer Web page hosting also provide pre-programmed scripts to their customers for processing forms. The most common thing that such a script would do is forward the information from the form to your e-mail address, though it might also save the information to a file on the Web server or format the form data to make it easier for you to read.

It's also possible to set things up so that much of the form information can be interpreted and processed automatically. For example, server software exists to authorize a credit card transaction automatically over the Internet, confirm an order to the customer's e-mail address, and enter the order directly into your company's in-house database for shipment. Obviously, setting up that sort of thing can get quite complex, and it's beyond the scope of this book to explain all the things you could do with form data once it has been submitted.

To Do:

Before you start building your first form, you should do the following:

- [ ] Ask your Internet service provider what they offer for form processing scripts and what exact address your forms should send their information to. In the next chapter, you'll see where and how to put that address into your forms.

- [ ] If you run your own Web server computer, the server software probably came with some basic form processing scripts. Consult your documentation to set them up properly and find out the address on your server where each is located.

 18

☐ If you have a choice of several forms-processing scripts, I recommend starting with the script to simply send the "raw" form data to your e-mail address. The example in this chapter uses such a script. You can experiment with fancier scripts later.

Once you have the address of your forms-processing script, you're ready for the rest of this chapter. As usual, I recommend that you create a form of your own as you read through my examples.

Creating a Form

Every form must begin with a `<FORM>` tag, which can be located anywhere in the body of the HTML document. The `<FORM>` tag normally has two attributes, METHOD and ACTION:

```
<FORM METHOD="post" ACTION="/cgi/generic">
```

Nowdays, the METHOD is almost always `"post"`, which means to send the form entry results as a document. (In some special situations, you may need to use METHOD=`"get"`, which submits the results as part of the URL header instead. For example, `"get"` is sometimes used when submitting queries to search engines from a Web form. If you're not yet an expert on forms, just use `"post"`, unless someone tells you to do otherwise.)

The ACTION attribute specifies the address of the program or script on the server computer that will process the information a user enters on a form. This is the address that your service provider or Web server manager should be able to give you, as mentioned in the previous "To Do" section. If you are a programmer, you can also write your own scripts in any language supported on the server.

The form in Figures 18.1 and 18.2 includes every type of input that you can currently use on HTML forms. Figure 18.3 is the same form, as it might look after someone fills it out. As you read through the rest of this chapter, refer to these figures for an example of each type of input element.

Figure 18.1.

All parts of a form must fall between the <FORM> and </FORM> tags.

```
<HTML><HEAD><TITLE>Get Me Rich Quick</TITLE></HEAD>
<BODY>
<H2>Get Me Rich Quick</H2>
<FORM METHOD="post" ACTION="/htbin/generic">

<INPUT TYPE="hidden" NAME="cant_see_me"
        VALUE="the user won't see this">
<PRE>Check this checkbox if you want to send me money: <INPUT
TYPE="checkbox" NAME="checkme" CHECKED>

Enter your credit card number in this text box: <INPUT
TYPE="text" NAME="cardnum" SIZE=20>
Expiration date: <INPUT TYPE="text" NAME="ext" SIZE=5>

Select the card type with these radio buttons:
<INPUT TYPE="radio" NAME="payment" VALUE="v" CHECKED> Visa
<INPUT TYPE="radio" NAME="payment" VALUE="m"> MasterCard
<INPUT TYPE="radio" NAME="payment" VALUE="d"> Discover

Choose the amount of your contribution from
this scrolling list: <SELECT
NAME="howmuch" SIZE=3>
  <OPTION SELECTED> $1,000,000
  <OPTION>$100,000
  <OPTION>$10,000
  <OPTION>$1,000
  <OPTION>$100
  <OPTION> Whatever</OPTION>
</SELECT>

Pick your reason from this pull-down list: <SELECT
NAME="why">
  <OPTION SELECTED> You deserve it
  <OPTION> I don't deserve it
  <OPTION> I'm rich
  <OPTION> I'm stupid
  <OPTION> I love you
  <OPTION> What the heck
</SELECT>

Enter any comments in this text area:<BR>
<TEXTAREA NAME="comments" rows=4 cols=40>
Gosh, this is a rare privilege.
Thanks and enjoy the dough.</TEXTAREA>
</PRE>
<INPUT TYPE=submit VALUE="     I Submit!      ">
<INPUT TYPE=reset  VALUE="Never Mind.">
</FORM>
</BODY></HTML>
```

18

Figure 18.2.

The form listed in Figure 18.1 uses every type of HTML form input element.

Netscape - [Get Me Rich Quick]

File Edit View Go Bookmarks Options Directory Window Help

Get Me Rich Quick

Check this checkbox if you want to send me money: ☑

Enter your credit card number in this text box:

Expiration date:

Select the card type with these radio buttons:
◉ Visa
○ MasterCard
○ Discover

Choose the amount of your contribution from
$1,000,000
$100,000
this scrolling list: $10,000

Pick your reason from this pull-down list: You deserve it ▼

Enter any comments in this text area:

Gosh, this is a rare privilege.
Thanks and enjoy the dough.

[I Submit!]   [Never Mind.]

Document: Done

18

TIME SAVER

Notice that most of the text in Figure 18.2 is monospaced. Monospaced text makes it easy to line up a form input box with the box above or below it and makes your forms look neater. To use monospaced text throughout a form, enclose the entire form between <PRE> and </PRE> tags. Using these tags also relieves you from having to put <BR> at the end of every line because the <PRE> tag puts a line break on the page at every line break in the HTML document.

Figure 18.3.

*Visitors to your Web site
fill out the form with
their mouse and/or
keyboard, and then click
on the I Submit! button.*

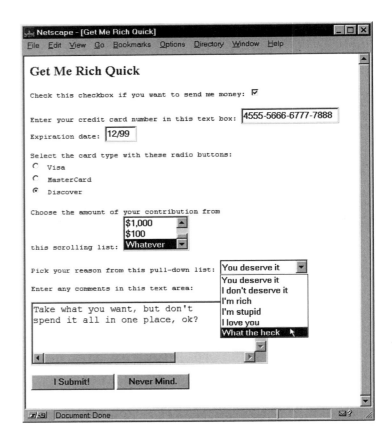

Text Input

To ask the user for a specific piece of information within a form, use the <INPUT> tag. This
tag must fall between the <FORM> and </FORM> tags, but it can be anywhere on the page in
relation to text, images, and other HTML tags. For example, to ask for someone's name you
could type the following:

```
What's your first name? <INPUT TYPE="text" SIZE=20 MAXLENGTH=30
NAME="firstname">
What's your last name? <INPUT TYPE="text" SIZE=20 MAXLENGTH=30 NAME="lastname">
```

The TYPE attribute indicates what type of form element to display, a simple one-line text entry
box in this case. (Each element type is discussed individually in the following sections.)

18

The SIZE attribute indicates approximately how many characters wide the text input box should be. If you are using a proportionally spaced font, the width of the input will vary depending on what the user enters. If the input is too long to fit in the box, most Web browsers will automatically scroll the text to the left.

MAXLENGTH determines the number of characters the user is allowed to type into the text box. If someone tries to type beyond the specified length, the extra characters won't appear. You may specify a length that is longer, shorter, or the same as the physical size of the text box. SIZE and MAXLENGTH are only used for TYPE="text" because other input types (check boxes, radio buttons, and so on) have a fixed size.

TIME SAVER

> If you want the user to enter text without it being displayed on the screen, you can use <INPUT TYPE="password"> instead of <INPUT TYPE="text">. Asterisks (***) are then displayed in place of the text the user types. The SIZE, MAXLENGTH, and NAME attributes work exactly the same way for TYPE="password" as for TYPE="text".

Identifying Each Piece of Form Data

18

No matter what type an input element is, you must give a name to the data it gathers. You can use any name you like for each input item, as long as each one on the form is different. When the form is sent to the server script, each data item is identified by name.

For example, if the user entered Jane and Doe in the text box previously defined under the "Text Input" section, the server script would receive a document including the following:

```
firstname='Jane'
lastname='Doe'
```

If the script mails the raw data from the form submission to you directly, you would see these two lines in an e-mail message from the server. The script might also be set up to format the input into a more readable format before reporting it to you.

Figure 18.4 is a sample e-mail message from the form in Figure 18.3. Notice that each data element is identified by the name given to it in Figure 18.1. Your server script might present the data in a different format than that shown in Figure 18.4, but it should include all the same information.

Figure 18.4.

*Clicking on the I Submit!
button in Figure 18.3
causes this information to
be sent to a server script.
(The script may then
be e-mailed to you.)*

```
From: nobody@shore.net
Date: Mon, 9 Dec 1996 22:15:29 -0500 (EST)
To: dicko@shore.net
Subject: Web page form

cant_see_me='the user won'\''t see this'
checkme='on'
cardnum='4555-5666-6777-7888'
ext='12/98'
payment='d'
howmuch='Whatever'
why='What the heck'
comments='Take what you want, but don'\''t
spend it all in one place, ok?'
```

Check Boxes

The simplest input type is a check box, which appears as a small square the user can select or deselect by clicking. A check box doesn't take any attributes other than NAME:

```
<INPUT TYPE="checkbox" NAME="baby" VALUE="yes"> Baby Grand Piano
<INPUT TYPE="checkbox" NAME="upright"> Upright Piano
```

Selected check boxes appear in the form result sent to the server script as follows:

```
baby='yes'
```

Blank (deselected) check boxes do not appear in the form output result at all. If you don't specify a VALUE attribute, the default VALUE of "on" is used.

TIME SAVER

You can use more than one check box with the same name, but different values, as in the following code:

```
<INPUT TYPE="checkbox" NAME="pet" VALUE="dog"> Dog
<INPUT TYPE="checkbox" NAME="pet" VALUE="cat"> Cat
<INPUT TYPE="checkbox" NAME="pet" VALUE="iguana"> Iguana
```

If the user checked both cat and iguana, the submission result would include the following:

```
pet='cat'
pet='iguana'
```

Radio Buttons

Radio buttons, where only one choice can be selected at a time, are almost as simple to implement as check boxes. Just use TYPE="radio" and give each of the options its own INPUT tag, as in the following code:

```
<INPUT TYPE="radio" NAME="card" VALUE="v" CHECKED> Visa
<INPUT TYPE="radio" NAME="card" VALUE="m"> MasterCard
```

The VALUE can be any name or code you choose. If you include the CHECKED attribute, that button will be selected by default. (No more than one button with the same name can be checked.)

If the user selected MasterCard from the preceding radio button set, the following would be included in the form submission to the server script:

```
card='m'
```

If the user didn't change the default CHECKED selection, card='v' would be sent instead.

Selection Lists

Both scrolling lists and pull-down pick lists are created with the <SELECT> tag. This tag is used together with the <OPTION> tag:

```
<SELECT NAME="extras" SIZE=3 MULTIPLE>
<OPTION SELECTED> Electric windows
<OPTION> AM/FM Radio
<OPTION> Turbocharger
</SELECT>
```

No HTML tags other than <OPTION> should appear between the <SELECT> and </SELECT> tags.

Unlike the text input type, the SIZE attribute here determines how many items show at once on the selection list. If SIZE=2 had been used in the preceding code, only the first two options would be visible, and a scrollbar would appear next to the list so the user could scroll down to see the third option.

Including the MULTIPLE attribute allows users to select more than one option at a time, and the SELECTED attribute makes an option selected by default. The actual text accompanying selected options is returned when the form is submitted. If the user selected Electric windows and Turbocharger, for instance, the form results would include the following lines:

```
extras='Electric windows'
extras='Turbocharger'
```

18

TIME SAVER

If you leave out the SIZE attribute or specify SIZE=1, the list will create a pull-down pick list. Pick lists cannot allow multiple choices; they are logically equivalent to a group of radio buttons. For example, another way to choose between credit card types would be:

```
<SELECT NAME="card">
<OPTION> Visa
<OPTION> MasterCard
</SELECT>
```

Text Areas

The <INPUT TYPE="text"> attribute mentioned earlier only allows the user to enter a single line of text. When you want to allow multiple lines of text in a single input item, use the <TEXTAREA> and </TEXTAREA> tags instead. Any text you include between these two tags will be displayed as the default entry. Here's an example:

```
<TEXTAREA NAME="comments" ROWS=4 COLS=20>
Please send more information.
</TEXTAREA>
```

As you probably guessed, the ROWS and COLS attributes control the number of rows and columns of text that fit in the input box. Text area boxes do have a scrollbar, however, so the user can enter more text than fits in the display area.

JUST A MINUTE

Some older browsers do not support the placement of default text within the text area. In these browsers, the text may appear outside the text input box.

Submit!

Every form must include a button that submits the form data to the server. You can put any label you like on this button with the VALUE attribute:

```
<INPUT TYPE="submit" VALUE="Place My Order Now!">
```

A gray button will be sized to fit the label you put in the VALUE attribute. When the user clicks the button, all data items on the form are sent to the program or script specified in the FORM ACTION attribute.

18

Normally, this program or script generates some sort of reply page and sends it back to be displayed for the user. If no such page is generated, the form remains visible, however.

You may also optionally include a button that clears all entries on the form so users can start over again if they change their minds or make mistakes. Use this line:

```
<INPUT TYPE="reset" VALUE="Clear This Form and Start Over">
```

Creating a Custom Submit Button

You can combine forms with all the HTML bells and whistles you've learned in this book, including backgrounds, graphics, text colors, tables, and frames. When you do so, however, the standard submit and reset buttons may start looking a little bland.

Fortunately, there is an easy way to substitute your own graphics for those buttons. To use an image of your choice for a submit button, type:

```
<INPUT TYPE="image" SRC="button.gif" NAME="buttonxy">
```

The image named button.gif will appear on the page, and the form will be submitted whenever someone clicks on that image. You can also include any attributes normally used with the <IMG> tag, such as BORDER or ALIGN.

JUST A MINUTE

When the form data is sent to the server, the exact pixel coordinates of the click will be included as a data item with the name you specify in <INPUT NAME>. For example, the line in the previous paragraph might send

```
buttonxy="12,40"
```

Normally, you should ignore this information, but some server scripts use it to make the button into an image map.

There is no specific form type for a graphical reset button, but you can achieve the same effect by putting an image link to the current page, like this:

```
<A HREF="thispage.htm"><IMG SRC="cancel.gif"></A>
```

TIME SAVER

You can make a button that cancels the form and proceeds to another page (ignoring all information the user has entered so far) simply by linking to that other page. For example:

```
<A HREF="nodice.htm">Click here to cancel.</A>
```

18

Figures 18.5 and 18.6 show a jazzed-up version of the "Get Me Rich Quick" form which uses customized submit and reset buttons.

Figure 18.5.

The last <INPUT> tag on this page creates a custom graphical submit button. The <IMG> tag after it resets the form.

```
<HTML><HEAD><TITLE>Get Me Rich Quick</TITLE></HEAD>
<BODY BACKGROUND="moneybk.gif" TEXT="red">
<DIV ALIGN="center">
<IMG SRC="getrich.gif" ALT="Get Me Rich Quick">
<P>
<FORM METHOD="post" ACTION="/htbin/generic">
<INPUT TYPE="hidden" SIZE=32 NAME="mail_to" VALUE="dicko">
Check here if you want to send me money:
<INPUT TYPE="checkbox" NAME="checkme" CHECKED><P>

<TABLE BORDER=2 CELLPADDING=20>
<TR><TD>
   Credit card number<BR>
   <INPUT TYPE="text" NAME="cardnum" SIZE=20><P>
   Exp. Date <INPUT TYPE="text" NAME="ext" SIZE=5>
</TD><TD>
   <INPUT TYPE="radio" NAME="payment" VALUE="v" CHECKED>
   Visa<P>
   <INPUT TYPE="radio" NAME="payment" VALUE="m"> MasterCard<P>
   <INPUT TYPE="radio" NAME="payment" VALUE="d"> Discover
</TD></TR>
<TR><TD>
   Amount of your contribution<P>
   <SELECT NAME="howmuch" SIZE=3>
     <OPTION SELECTED> $1,000,000
     <OPTION>$100,000
     <OPTION>$10,000
     <OPTION>$1,000
     <OPTION>$100
     <OPTION> Whatever</OPTION>
   </SELECT>
</TD><TD>
   Justification:
   <SELECT NAME="why">
     <OPTION SELECTED> You deserve it
     <OPTION> I don't deserve it
     <OPTION> I'm rich
     <OPTION> I'm stupid
     <OPTION> I love you
     <OPTION> What the heck
   </SELECT>
</TD></TR>
</TABLE>
<P>
<INPUT TYPE="image" SRC="takeit.gif" NAME="submitted"
 BORDER=0 ALIGN="top">
<A HREF="getrich2.htm">
<IMG SRC="forget.gif" BORDER=0 ALIGN="top"></A>
</FORM>
</DIV>
</BODY></HTML>
```

18

Figure 18.6.

The HTML in Figure 18.5 combines graphics, tables, and form input elements on this Web page.

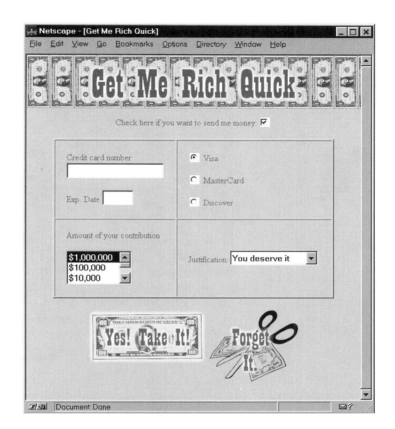

Including Hidden Data

If you want to send certain data items to the server script that processes a form, but you don't want the user to see them, you can use the INPUT TYPE="hidden" attribute. This attribute has no effect on the display at all; it just adds any name and value you specify to the form results when they are submitted.

You might use this attribute to tell a script where to e-mail the form results. For example, Figure 18.5 includes the following input element:

```
<INPUT TYPE="hidden" NAME="mail_to" VALUE="dicko">
```

which adds the following line to the form output:

```
mail_to='dicko'
```

For this attribute to have any effect, someone must create a script or program to read this line and do something about it. My Internet service provider's form script uses this hidden value to determine where to e-mail the form data. (My account name with them is dicko.)

Most scripts require at least one or two hidden input elements. Consult the person who wrote or provided you with the script for details. You can also use hidden items to indicate which of the many similar forms a particular result came from.

COFFEE BREAK

The most common mistake many companies make when putting a first order form on the Internet is the same one all too often made on paper order forms: leaving out a key piece of information. To save yourself the embarrassment of an incomplete order form, you might want to start with the sample form at

http://www.mcp.com/sams/books/235-8/ch18/order.htm

This is just your basic, run-of-the-mill product order form with credit card information, name, address, and so forth. Use it as a starting template and then add your own products, graphics, and unique information. Don't forget to change the <FORM ACTION> to the address of your own server script!

You can also use form selection lists as menus to navigate around your site. For an example, go to the *24-Hour HTML Café* at

http://www.mcp.com/sams/books/235-8/cafe18.htm

Summary

This chapter demonstrated how to create HTML forms, which allow readers of your Web pages to enter specific information and send it back to you.

You also found that you need to set up a script or program to process form data before you actually create a form. Your Internet service provider or server software vendor can help you do this.

Table 18.1 summarizes the HTML tags and attributes covered in this chapter.

Table 18.1. HTML tags and attributes covered in Chapter 18.

Tag	Attribute	Function
`<FORM>...</FORM>`		Indicates an input form.
	`ACTION="..."`	The address of the script to process this form input.
	`METHOD="..."`	How the form input will be sent to the server. Normally set to POST, rather than GET.
`<INPUT>`		An input element for a form.
	`TYPE="..."`	The type for this input widget. Possible values are CHECKBOX, HIDDEN, RADIO, RESET, SUBMIT, TEXT, or IMAGE.
	`NAME="..."`	The name of this item, as passed to the script.
	`VALUE="..."`	For a text or hidden item, the default value; for a check box or radio button, the value to be submitted with the form; for reset or submit buttons, the label for the button itself.
	`SRC="..."`	The source file for an image.
	`CHECKED`	For check boxes and radio buttons, indicates that this item is checked.
	`SIZE="..."`	The width, in characters, of a text input region.
	`MAXLENGTH="..."`	The maximum number of characters that can be entered into a text region.
	`ALIGN="..."`	For images in forms, determines how the text and image will align (same as with the `<IMG>` tag).

continues

18

Table 18.1. continued

Tag	Attribute	Function
`<TEXTAREA>...</TEXTAREA>`		Indicates a multiline text entry form element. Default text can be included.
	`NAME="..."`	The name to be passed to the script.
	`ROWS="..."`	The number of rows this text area displays.
	`COLS="..."`	The number of columns (characters) this text area displays.
`<SELECT>...</SELECT>`		Creates a menu or scrolling list of possible items.
	`NAME="..."`	The name that is passed to the script.
	`SIZE="..."`	The number of elements to display. If `SIZE` is indicated, the selection becomes a scrolling list. If no `SIZE` is given, the selection is a pop-up menu.
	`MULTIPLE`	Allows multiple selections from the list.
`<OPTION>`		Indicates a possible item within a `<SELECT>` element.
	`SELECTED`	With this attribute included, the `<OPTION>` will be selected by default in the list.
	`VALUE="..."`	The value to submit if this `<OPTION>` is selected when the form is submitted.

Q&A

Q I've heard that it's dangerous to send credit card numbers over the Internet. Can't thieves intercept form data on its way to me?

A It is possible to intercept form data (and any Web pages or e-mail) as it travels through the Internet. If you ask for credit card numbers or other sensitive

18

information on your forms, you should ask the company who runs your Web server about "secure" forms processing. There are several reliable technologies for eliminating the risk of high-tech eavesdroppers, but it may cost you quite a bit to implement the security measures.

To put the amount of risk in perspective, remember that it is *much* more difficult to intercept information traveling through the Internet than it is to look over someone's shoulder in a restaurant or retail store. Unless you service hundreds of credit card transactions per day, it will probably never be worth it to a would-be thief to bother tapping in to your forms data. Of the billions of dollars lost to credit card fraud each year, so far exactly zero has been from "unsecure" Internet transactions.

Q Can I put forms on a CD-ROM, or do they have to be on the Internet?

A You can put a form anywhere you can put a Web page. If it's on a disk or CD-ROM instead of a Web server, it can be filled out by people whether or not they are connected to the Internet. Of course, they must be connected to the Internet (or your local intranet) when they click on the submit button, or the information won't get to you.

Quiz

18

Questions

1. What do you need to get from the people who administer your Web server computer before you can put a form on the Internet?

2. Write the HTML to create a "guestbook" form that asks someone for his name, sex, age, and e-mail address.

3. If you had created an image named `sign-in.gif`, how would you use it as the submit button for the guestbook in Question 2?

Answers

1. The Internet address of a script or program which is set up specifically to process form data.

2.
```
<HTML><HEAD><TITLE>My Guestbook</TITLE></HEAD>
<BODY>
<H1>My Guestbook: Please Sign In</H1>
<FORM METHOD="post" ACTION="/cgi/generic">
```

```
Your name: <INPUT TYPE="text" NAME="name" SIZE=20><P>
Your sex:
<INPUT TYPE="radio" NAME="sex" VALUE="male"> male
<INPUT TYPE="radio" NAME="sex" VALUE="female"> female<P>
Your age: <INPUT TYPE="text" NAME="age" SIZE=4><P>
Your e-mail address:
<INPUT TYPE="text" NAME="email" SIZE=30><P>
<INPUT TYPE="submit" VALUE="Sign In">
<INPUT TYPE="reset" VALUE="Erase">
</FORM>
</BODY></HTML>
```

3. Replace `<INPUT TYPE="submit" VALUE="Sign In">` with

   `<INPUT TYPE="image" SRC="sign-in.gif" NAME="signxy">`

Activities

☐ You should make a form using all of the different types of input elements and selection lists to make sure you understand how each of them works.

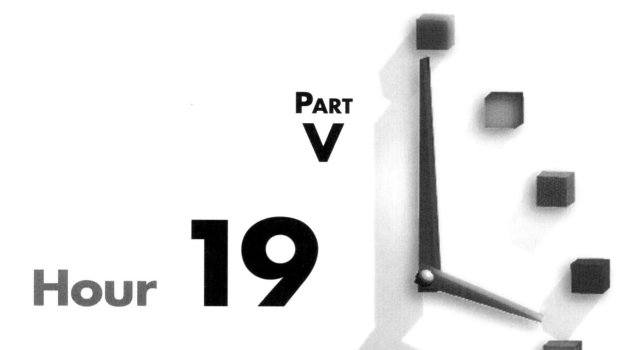

Hour 19

Embedding Multimedia in Web Pages

Multimedia is a popular buzzword for sound, motion video, and interactive animation. This chapter shows you how to include audiovisual and interactive media in your Web pages.

The first thing you should be aware of is that computer multimedia is still in its youth, and Internet multimedia is barely in its infancy. The infant technology's rapid pace of growth creates three obstacles for anyone who wants to include audiovisual material in a Web page:

- [ ] There are many incompatible multimedia file formats to choose from, and none have emerged as a clear "industry standard" yet.
- [ ] Most people do not have fast enough Internet connections to receive high-quality audiovisual data without a long wait.
- [ ] Each new Web browser version that comes out uses different HTML tags to include multimedia in Web pages.

The moral of the story: Whatever you do today to implement a multimedia Web site, plan on changing it before too long.

The good news is that you can sidestep all three of these obstacles to some extent today, and they are all likely to become even easier to overcome in the near future. This chapter will show you how to put multimedia on your Web pages for maximum compatibility with current Web browsers, and then introduce you to the new standard way that Web page multimedia will be handled in future Web browsers.

JUST A MINUTE

The Microsoft ActiveX controls and Java applets discussed in Chapter 20, "Scripting, Applets, and ActiveX," can be used with many of the same types of media files discussed in this chapter. Be sure to read Chapter 20 before you make any final decisions about how you will incorporate multimedia into your Web site.

To Do:

Before you see how to place multimedia on your Web pages in any way, you need to have some multimedia content to start with.

Creating multimedia of any kind is a challenging and complicated task. If you're planning to create your own content from scratch, you'll need far more than this book to become the next crackerjack multimedia developer. Once you've got some content, however, this chapter will show you how to place your new creations into your Web pages.

For those of us who are artistically challenged, a number of alternative ways to obtain useful multimedia assets are available. Aside from the obvious (hire an artist), here are a few suggestions:

- ☐ The Web itself is chock-full of useful content of all media types, and stock media clearinghouses of all shapes and sizes now exist online. See the hotlist at the *24-Hour HTML Café* (`http://www.mcp.com/sams/books/235-8/hotlist.htm`) for links to some of the best stock media sources on the Web.

- ☐ Don't feel like spending any money? Much of the material on the Internet is free. Of course, it's still a good idea to double-check with the accredited author or current owner of the content; you don't want to get sued for copyright infringement. In addition, various offices of the U.S. government generate content which, by law, belongs to all Americans. (Any NASA footage found online, for instance, is free for you to use.)

- ☐ Check out the online forums and Usenet newsgroups that cater to the interests of videographers. As clearly as possible, describe your site and what you want to do with it. Chances are you'll find a few up-and-coming artists who'd be more than happy to let thousands of people peruse their work online.

19

Putting Video on a Web Page

The following sections show you how to add some audio and video to a Web page in four different ways:

☐ The "old way" for maximum compatibility with all Web browsers

☐ The "Microsoft way" that works best with Microsoft Internet Explorer 2.0 and 3.0

☐ The "Netscape way" that's best for Netscape Navigator 2.0 and 3.0

☐ The "new way" that will work with future versions of all Web browsers, including those from Microsoft and Netscape.

For the examples in this chapter, I created a Web page allowing hungry Web surfers a chance to preview the daily menu for a (fictitious) seafood restaurant. A picture of a lobster was modified to create a short video. We then recorded and mixed a voice-over with some music in the background. All this was done with readily available software and hardware costing less than $200 (not counting the computer).

JUST A MINUTE

In this chapter's sample page, I use Windows AVI video and WAV sound files. For better compatibility with non-Windows computers, you could use Apple's QuickTime audio/video format or any other video format supported by today's Web browsers. The procedures shown in this chapter for incorporating the files into your Web pages are the same, no matter which file format you choose.

19

Multimedia the Old-fashioned Way

The simplest and most reliable option for incorporating a video or audio file into your Web site is to simply link it in with <A HREF>, exactly as you would link to another HTML file. (See Chapter 3, "Linking to Other Web Pages," for coverage of the <A> tag.)

For example, the following line could be used to offer an AVI video of a Maine lobster:

```
<A HREF="lobstah.avi">Play the lobster video.</A>
```

When someone clicks on the words "Play the lobster video," the lobstah.avi video file will be transferred to their computer. Whichever *helper application* or *plug-in* the user has installed will automatically start as soon as the file has finished downloading.

JUST A MINUTE

In case you're not familiar with *helper applications* (or *helper apps* for short), they are the external programs that a Web browser calls upon to display any type of file that it can't handle on its own. You can see what helper apps your browser is set up to use by selecting Options | General Preferences | Helpers in Netscape Navigator 3.0 or selecting View | Options | Programs | File Types in Microsoft Internet Explorer 3.0.

Plug-ins are a special sort of helper application that is specifically designed for tight integration with Netscape Navigator. You'll read more about plug-ins under the "Multimedia the Netscape Way" section later in this chapter.

Embedding Video the Microsoft Way

In Chapter 9, "Putting Images on a Web Page," you learned to use the `<IMG>` tag. Microsoft Internet Explorer 3.0 also allows you to include AVI videos in a Web page with `<IMG>`.

The HTML code to include the video can be as simple as

```
<IMG DYNSRC="lobstah.avi" WIDTH=160 HEIGHT=120>
```

The DYNSRC stands for *dynamic source*, and tells Explorer that this is a motion video file instead of just a still SRC image. If you include both SRC and DYNSRC attributes in an IMG tag, then older browsers that don't support DYNSRC will simply display the SRC image instead.

Two more new attributes can be used along with DYNSRC in an IMG tag, too. CONTROLS displays a set of controls beneath the video clip. LOOP=INFINITE makes the video automatically repeat forever, while LOOP=*n* plays the video *n* times and then stops (for example, LOOP=3 would play three times). Naturally, you can also use any of the standard IMG attributes, such as ALIGN, BORDER, and so on.

JUST A MINUTE

As of version 3.0, Netscape Navigator does not yet support the DYNSRC attribute. You'll see how to handle embedded video for Netscape later in this chapter.

Figures 19.1 and 19.2 include an AVI video clip embedded in a Web page using `<IMG DYNSRC>`. You can see the video by viewing this page with Microsoft Internet Explorer 3.0 at `http://www.mcp.com/sams/books/235-8/ch19/lobstah.htm`.

19

Figure 19.1.

This page includes embedded video and audio that will be played only by Microsoft Internet Explorer.

```
<HTML>
<HEAD><TITLE>The DownEast Restaurant</TITLE></HEAD>
<BODY BACKGROUND="wicker.jpg">
<DIV ALIGN="center">

<BGSOUND SRC="lobstah8.wav">
<A HREF="lobstah.avi">
  <IMG SRC="lobstah.jpg" DYNSRC="lobstah2.avi" LOOP=INFINITE
    WIDTH=160 HEIGHT=120 ALIGN="left" BORDER=0>
</A>

<FONT COLOR="red"><H1>The DownEast Restaurant</H1>
<H3>Portland, Maine</H3>
<H2><I>"Come DownEast, 'n have a Feast"</I></H2></FONT>
<BR CLEAR="all">
</DIV>
<HR><B>~Today's Catch~</B><P>
Fresh lobstah (a three-poundah!), <B>$14.95</B><P>
Scrod and potatahs, baked in buttah, <B>$10.95</B><P>
Heaping plattah of steamed clams,
fresh outtah th' mud, <B>$12.95</B><P>
<HR><B>Come on ovah! The food's wicked good!</B>
</BODY></HTML>
```

Figure 19.2.

The page listed in Figure 19.1. (The lobster looks like an ordinary image when printed in this book, but it's a short video.)

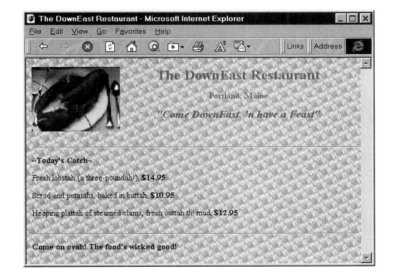

19

To make the lobster video in the DownEast Restaurant sample page available to users who don't have Internet Explorer 3.0, I enclosed the <IMG> tag with an <A HREF> link, and included the words "CLICK ME!" in the SRC image, as you can see in Figure 19.3.

Figure 19.4 shows what happens when a Netscape Navigator 3.0 user clicks on the image. The first frame of the AVI video appears, and users can click on it to play the video (or right-click for a menu of playback options, as seen in Figure 19.4). Users of other browsers see whatever AVI viewer their software was configured to use, or they may be given the chance to save the AVI file to disk if no viewer is available.

Figure 19.3.

Users of Netscape (and other browsers) see a still image, which they can click for the AVI video. This is the same page as seen with Explorer 3.0 in Figure 19.2.

Figure 19.4.

Clicking on the image in Figure 19.3 lets users play the video using whatever AVI-compatible plug-in or helper app they have installed.

Note that DYNSRC begins playing video clips as soon as they begin downloading, but users whose browsers don't support DYNSRC have to wait until the video is completely done downloading before they begin to see it.

Microsoft Background Sounds

Video files embedded with <IMG DYNSRC> can include soundtracks, but Microsoft Internet Explorer also lets you specify a background sound for a page like this:

```
<BGSOUND SRC="lobstah.wav">
```

The background sound may or may not synchronize exactly with video content on the page, but when synchronization isn't important to you, BGSOUND can offer several advantages. Not only does the background sound usually start playing sooner than video, but you can include more than one video on the page, and use BGSOUND to provide a master soundtrack for all of them.

Multimedia the Netscape Way

While Microsoft opted to add the DYNSRC attribute to the old familiar <IMG> tag, Netscape chose instead to introduce an entirely new tag called <EMBED>.

The <EMBED> tag enables you to place *any* type of file directly into your Web page. In order for the media to appear on the Web page, however, every user must have a *plug-in* that recognizes the incoming data type and knows what to do with it. A plug-in is like a helper application that is fused into Navigator itself; it adds a new set of display capabilities directly into the browser.

The plug-ins that come bundled with Netscape Navigator 3.0 can handle most common media types, including WAV, AU, MPEG, MID, EPS, VRML, and many more. Many other plug-ins are also available from other companies to handle almost any type of media file.

19

TIME SAVER

Netscape maintains a Web page that lists all registered plug-ins and plug-in developers. To check out the current assortment, head to this page:

`http://home.netscape.com/comprod/products/navigator/version_2.0/plugins/index.html`

The Plug-ins Development Kit, available for free from Netscape, allows developers to create new plug-ins for their own products and data types (for more information, see Netscape's Web site at `http://home.netscape.com/`).

The following line of HTML would embed a video clip named `lobstah.avi` at the current position on the page, as long as visitors to the page have an AVI-compatible plug-in or helper app.

```
<EMBED SRC="lobstah.avi">
```

Notice that, like the `<IMG>` tag, `<EMBED>` requires a `SRC` attribute to indicate the address of the embedded media file. Also like `<IMG>`, the `<EMBED>` tag can take `ALIGN`, `WIDTH`, and `HEIGHT` attributes. The `SRC`, `WIDTH`, `HEIGHT`, and `ALIGN` attributes are interpreted by the browser just as they would be for a still image. However, the actual display of the video is handled by whichever plug-in or helper app each user may have installed.

The `<EMBED>` tag also enables you to set any number of optional parameters, which are specific to the plug-in or player program. For instance, the page in Figure 19.5 includes the following:

```
<EMBED SRC="lobstah.avi" WIDTH=160 HEIGHT=120 ALIGN="left"
 AUTOPLAY="true" LOOP="true" ONCURSOR="play">
```

`AUTOPLAY`, `LOOP`, and `ONCURSOR` are not standard attributes of the `<EMBED>` tag, so the browser simply hands them over to the plug-in program to interpret. `AUTOPLAY="true"` and `LOOP="true"` are specific to the Netscape Navigator 3.0 LiveVideo plug-in (they tell it to automatically play the video as soon as it loads, and to play it over again each time it finishes).

If a user happens to have the CoolFusion AVI viewer plug-in (from Iterated Systems, Inc. at `http://www.iterated.com`), CoolFusion will interpret the `ONCURSOR="play"` command to mean that whenever the user passes the mouse cursor over the video, it should restart. If a user has a different AVI plug-in, or no plug-in at all for handling AVI files, this attribute will do nothing at all. (Refer to the Web pages of each plug-in developer for information on the commands that their plug-in will accept as attributes in the `<EMBED>` tag.)

19

Figure 19.5.

The <EMBED> tag embeds multimedia files directly into a Web page in Netscape Navigator.

```
<HTML>
<HEAD><TITLE>The DownEast Restaurant</TITLE></HEAD>
<BODY BACKGROUND="wicker.jpg">
<DIV ALIGN="center">

<BGSOUND SRC="lobstah8.wav">
<EMBED SRC="lobstah2.avi" WIDTH=160 HEIGHT=120 ALIGN="left"
 AUTOPLAY="true" LOOP="true" ONCURSOR="play">
<NOEMBED>
  <A HREF="lobstah.avi">
    <IMG SRC="lobstah.jpg" DYNSRC="lobstah2.avi" LOOP=INFINITE
      WIDTH=160 HEIGHT=120 ALIGN="left" BORDER=0>
  </A>
</NOEMBED>

<FONT COLOR="red"><H1>The DownEast Restaurant</H1>
<H3>Portland, Maine</H3>
<H2><I>"Come DownEast, 'n have a Feast"</I></H2></FONT>
<BR CLEAR="all">
</DIV>
<HR><B>~Today's Catch~</B><P>
Fresh lobstah (a three-poundah!),  <B>$14.95</B><P>
Scrod and potatahs, baked in buttah,  <B>$10.95</B><P>
Heaping plattah of steamed clams,
fresh outtah th' mud,  <B>$12.95</B><P>
<HR><B>Come on ovah! The food's wicked good!</B>
</BODY></HTML>
```

Figure 19.6.

With the appropriate Navigator plug-in installed, AVI files appear on the Web page just as if AVI support were built in to Netscape Navigator.

JUST A MINUTE

Netscape Navigator 2.0 did not include a plug-in to view AVI files, so users had to install a third-party plug-in, such as CoolFusion, before they could view video clips. But the Navigator version 3.0 comes precon-figured with a plug-in for AVI files, so most new users of Netscape will be able to see embedded videos without installing any additional software.

If a suitable plug-in can't be found for an <EMBED> tag, the Windows 95 versions of both Netscape Navigator 3.0 and Microsoft Internet Explorer 3.0 may embed an OLE-compliant application to play the media file. For example, Figure 19.7 shows the same page as Figure 19.6 viewed with Microsoft Internet Explorer 3.0. The Windows Media Player application is embedded directly in the Web page.

Figure 19.7.

Microsoft Internet Explorer 3.0 may embed a separate helper application to play a media file in an <EMBED> *tag.*

Basically, when Navigator and Explorer encounter an <EMBED> tag, they try their hardest to find some way to embed the media file directly in the Web page. As a Web page author, you can't predict what plug-in or helper application will be selected, but you can at least put some instructions on the Web page telling your audience where to download a suitable player.

JUST A MINUTE

Embedded helper apps only work in Windows 95 and Windows NT. They will not function for Macintosh or UNIX users.

Also, you should not confuse this use of Windows object linking and embedding (OLE) with the ActiveX controls discussed in the next chapter—even though they do rely on the same underlying OLE technology.

You can use <EMBED> with any type of audio, video, or interactive multimedia files as long as your audience has the correct player software installed.

Unfortunately, you as a Web page author have no control over or knowledge of which file types and applications people who visit your pages will have configured on their computers, or even how many visitors will be using a Microsoft Windows operating system. So the exotic uses of <EMBED> are probably best left to corporate intranets or other situations where the page publisher has some control over the intended audience's computer setup.

Trying to Please Everybody

Because Netscape knew that its browser would be the first (and perhaps only) browser to support the <EMBED> tag, they provided an easy way to include alternate content for other browsers. Immediately following an <EMBED> tag, you can specify any amount of HTML code for other browsers, between the <NOEMBED> and </NOEMBED> tags. For example, Figure 19.5 contains the following code:

```
<BGSOUND SRC="lobstah8.wav">
<EMBED SRC="lobstah.avi" WIDTH=160 HEIGHT=120 ALIGN="left"
 AUTOPLAY="true" LOOP="true" ONCURSOR="play">
<NOEMBED>
<A HREF="lobstah.avi">
 <IMG SRC="lobstah.jpg" DYNSRC="lobstah2.avi" LOOP=INFINITE
  WIDTH=160 HEIGHT=120 ALIGN="left" BORDER=0>
 </A>
</NOEMBED>
```

Here's how this will work in various browsers:

☐ Netscape Navigator 3.0 sees only the EMBED tag and ignores everything between <NOEMBED> and </NOEMBED>. It ignores the Microsoft-specific <BGSOUND> tag. (If the Netscape LiveMedia plug-in is installed, it interprets AUTOPLAY and LOOP as discussed earlier. If the CoolFusion plug-in is installed, it interprets the ONCURSOR command.)

19

- [ ] In Netscape Navigator 2.0, if no AVI-compatible plug-in is installed, users may see an unsightly puzzle-piece icon and a message saying Plug-in Not Loaded. If they click on the Get the Plug-in button, they will be taken to a page on Netscape Corporation's Web site explaining how to get and install plug-ins and helper apps.

- [ ] Microsoft Internet Explorer 3.0 looks in the Windows file type registry for a player for the <EMBED> tag. If it can't find one, it plays the video specified in <IMG DYNSRC> with its internal video player. It also plays the sound in the <BGSOUND> tag.

- [ ] Microsoft Internet Explorer 2.0 sees the <BGSOUND> and IMG tags. It plays the lobstah8.wav sound file in the background and displays the lobstah.jpg image. I added the words "CLICK ME!" to this image so that users with an AVI helper app can click on the image to play the lobstah.avi video clip specified in the A HREF attribute.

- [ ] Most other browsers see only the IMG SRC attribute and display the lobstah.jpg still image. If they have an AVI-compatible helper application installed, they can click on the image to see the video play in a separate window.

- [ ] Netscape Navigator version 1.2 is actually a special problem case because it recognizes the <EMBED> tag, but not the <NOEMBED> tag. It displays *both* the image specified in IMG SRC *and* an embedded OLE display or, more often, a broken image icon resulting from a failed attempt to display the <EMBED> tag. Clicking on the "CLICK ME!" image will still launch an AVI helper app if one is available.

To thicken the plot, some people who already have the software they need to view your EMBED media files may see a message announcing boldly "Warning: There is a possible security hazard here," which appears in Figure 19.8. What this message really means is that the user has a helper app available on his system that can display the media file, and Netscape Navigator (version 2.0 or 3.0) is about to run it. The alarmist tone of the message is very unfortunate, because the likelihood of having any security risk is actually no greater than any other time a helper app is invoked or a page is displayed.

Some novice users are sure to become convinced that they must click Cancel or risk having the monitor blow up, but what you really want them to do is click Continue, so they can watch a totally harmless video clip.

Unfortunately, there's really nothing you can do as a Web page author to control whether this message appears, or any of the configuration options discussed in the next few pages. However, you should still be aware of what users may see so you can intelligently choose if and when to use the <EMBED> tag, and what sort of caveats to offer along with your embedded media.

19

Figure 19.8.

This alarmist message may appear in Netscape Navigator before users can see your innocent media files.

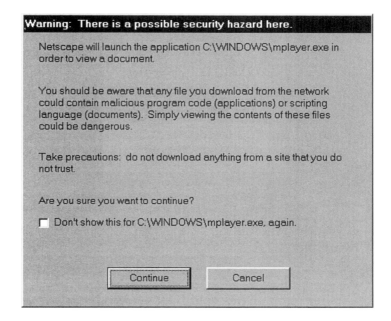

Multimedia the New Way

Both Microsoft's `<IMG DYNSRC>` and Netscape's `<EMBED>` tag have come under fire for a number of reasons, both technical and political. At present, it looks nearly certain that they will be made obsolete very soon by a new tag called `<OBJECT>`, which has the blessing of Netscape, Microsoft, and the official World Wide Web Consortium (W3C) standards-setting committee. The `<OBJECT>` tag will do everything Netscape wants the `<EMBED>` tag to do, plus a lot more.

You can read more about the `<OBJECT>` tag, including an example of its use, under "ActiveX Controls" in Chapter 20, "Scripting, Applets, and ActiveX." The exact usage of `<OBJECT>` is still under revision by the standards committee, so you should also keep an eye on the W3C pages at `http://www.w3.org/pub/WWW/` for more information.

Summary

In this chapter, you've seen how to embed video and sound into a Web page. But remember that the `<EMBED>` tag (and its successor, the `<OBJECT>` tag) can be used to include a vast array of media types besides just Windows AVI and WAV files. Some of these media types are alternative audio and video formats that aim to achieve greater compression, quality, or compatibility than the Windows standard formats. Others, such as Shockwave and QuickTime VR, add a variety of interactive features that old-fashioned audiovisual media types lack.

Table 19.1 summarizes the tags discussed in this chapter.

Table 19.1. HTML tags and attributes covered in Chapter 19.

Tag	Attribute	Function
`<IMG>`		Normally inserts an image, but Microsoft Internet Explorer 3.0 also supports the inclusion of AVI video with the following attributes. (All `<IMG>` attributes covered in Chapter 9 can also be used with DYNSRC video.)
	`SRC="..."`	The URL of the image to be shown by browsers that can't show video.
	`DYNSRC="..."`	The address of a video clip in the Windows AVI format (dynamic source).
	`CONTROLS`	Used to display a set of video playback controls.
	`LOOP="..."`	The number of times a video clip will loop. (-1 or INFINITE means to loop indefinitely.)
	`START="..."`	When a DYNSRC video clip should start playing. Valid options are FILEOPEN (play when a page is displayed) or MOUSEOVER (play when a mouse cursor passes over the video clip).
`<BGSOUND>`		Plays a sound file as soon as the page is displayed (in Microsoft Internet Explorer version 2.0 or higher only).
	`SRC="..."`	The URL of the WAV, AU, or MIDI sound file to embed.
	`LOOP="..."`	The number of times a video clip will loop. (-1 or INFINITE means to loop indefinitely.)
`<EMBED>`		Embeds a file to be read or displayed by a Netscape plug-in application.
	`SRC="..."`	The URL of the file to embed.

Tag	Attribute	Function
	WIDTH="..."	The width of the embedded object in pixels.
	HEIGHT="..."	The height of the embedded object in pixels.
	ALIGN="..."	Determines the alignment of the media window. Values are the same as for the <IMG> tag.
	VSPACE="..."	The space between the media and the text above or below it.
	HSPACE="..."	The space between the media and the text to its left or right.
	BORDER="..."	Draws a border of the specified size in pixels around the media.
<NOEMBED>...</NOEMBED>		Alternate text or images to be shown to users who do not have a plug-in installed or are using browsers that don't recognize the <EMBED> tag.
<OBJECT>		Inserts images, videos, Java applets, ActiveX controls, or other objects into a document.

(Note: The <OBJECT> tag was under revision when this book went to press. Check http://www.w3.org for current standard usage.)

19

JUST A MINUTE

In addition to the <EMBED> attributes listed in Table 19.1, you can designate applet-specific attributes to be interpreted by the plug-in which displays the embedded object.

Q&A

Q I hear a lot about "streaming" video and audio. What does that mean?

A In the past, video and audio files took minutes and sometimes hours to retrieve through most modems, which severely limited the inclusion of video and audio on Web pages. The goal that everyone is moving toward is *streaming* video or audio, which will play while the data is being received. This is to say that you will not have to completely download the clip before you can start to watch it.

Streaming playback is now widely supported for Windows AVI video and WAV audio files through Microsoft Internet Explorer 3.0's built-in features and Netscape Navigator 2.0 and 3.0 plug-ins. The examples in this chapter use these media types to demonstrate both streaming and the old-fashioned download-and-play methods of delivering audiovisual media.

Q How do I choose between video formats such as QuickTime, Windows AVI, and MPEG? Is there any significant difference between them?

A QuickTime is the most popular format among Macintosh users, though QuickTime players are available for Windows 3.1 and Windows 95 as well. Similarly, AVI is the format of choice for Windows users, but you can get AVI players for the Macintosh. However, both QuickTime and AVI are almost certain to be eclipsed by MPEG as the online video standard of choice within the next couple of years. MPEG-1 is best for Internet transmission because it is far more compact than MPEG-2. Unfortunately, few people have MPEG-compatible players installed now.

So how do you choose? If your audience is mostly Windows users, pick AVI. If it includes a significant number of Mac users, pick QuickTime. In either case, plan to switch to MPEG eventually.

Q When I say I want multimedia on my Web pages, everybody tells me to get Shockwave. What is it, and do I need it?

A Macromedia Director is by far the most popular multimedia development platform, both for CD-ROMs and on the Internet. The online player for Director files is called Shockwave, and you should certainly take a look at it if you're serious about creating your own Web page multimedia. See Macromedia's site at http:// www.macromedia.com for more information.

(There are also many other excellent multimedia development tools available—too many to list in this chapter!)

Quiz

Questions

1. What's the simplest way to let the widest possible audience see a video on your Web site?

2. Write the HTML to insert a video clip named thevideo.avi that will be seen only by users of Microsoft Internet Explorer 3.0. Users of other browsers should see an

image named `standin.gif` instead. While you're at it, make the video automatically play when the page loads and repeat as long as the page is showing.

3. Write the HTML to embed a video file named `myvideo.avi` into a Web page so that both Netscape Navigator 3.0 and Microsoft Internet Explorer 3.0 users will be able to see it, and users of other browsers would see an image linking to it.

4. What tag will soon replace both `<IMG DYNSRC>` and `<EMBED>`, and work with future versions of all major Web browsers?

Answers

1. Just link to it, like this:

```
<A HREF="myvideo.avi">My Video</A>
```

2.
```
<IMG DYNSRC="thevideo.avi" SRC="standin.gif"
START="fileopen" LOOP="infinite">
```

3. Use the following HTML:

```
<EMBED SRC="myvideo.avi">
<NOEMBED>
<A HREF="myvideo.avi"><IMG SRC="theimage.gif"></A>
</NOEMBED>
```

4. `<OBJECT>`

Activities

19

☐ If you include multimedia elements that require special players, you might need a special page to help people understand and set up what they need to make the most of your site. A link to that page should be prominently located near the top of your home page, steering newcomers aside just long enough to give them a clue.

☐ The techniques and tags covered in this chapter for embedding media also work with Virtual Reality Modeling Language (VRML) files. To find out how you can use VRML to put interactive three-dimensional scenes and objects in your Web pages, check out the VRML home page at

```
http://home.netscape.com/eng/live3d/howto/vrml_primer_index.html
```

Hour 20

Scripting, Applets, and ActiveX

Congratulations. You've got HTML under your belt, and you're ready to graduate from the school of Web publishing and enter the real world of Web development. The World Wide Web of the past was simply a way to present information, and browsing wasn't too different from sitting in a lecture hall, watching a blackboard, or staring at an overhead projector screen. But today's Web surfer is looking for interactive, animated sites that change with each viewer and each viewing.

To achieve that level of interactivity, this chapter introduces a number of ways you can go beyond passive text and graphics into the dynamic world of modern Web site development.

It would take a book many times the length of this one to teach you all the scripting and programming languages that can be used to create interactive programs for the Web. However, you can easily learn the HTML to incorporate prewritten programs into your Web pages.

To Do:

Reading this chapter will give you enough information to decide what types of programs or scripts might be best for your Web site. If you decide to take the leap into actually using some (or even creating your own) on your pages, you should look to the following resources:

☐ You'll find a list of online sources for prewritten scripts and reusable program components in the *24-Hour HTML Café* hotlist page at http://www.mcp.com/sams/books/235-8/hotlist.htm

☐ If you want to write your own interactive programming for Web pages, I recommend *Web Page Publishing Unleashed, Professional Reference Edition*, by Sams.net Publishing. You'll also find some online tutorials in the hotlist mentioned here.

The Old Way

Until very recently, there were only two ways to enhance the functionality of a Web browser. You could write and place programs on the Web server computer to manipulate documents as they were sent out, or you could write and install programs on the user's computer to manipulate or display documents as they were received.

You can still do both of these things, and they may still be the most powerful and flexible means of enhancing Web pages. Unfortunately, both involve a high level of expertise in traditional programming languages (such as C++) and knowledge of Internet transfer protocols and operating system architecture. If you're not fortunate enough to already be an experienced UNIX or Windows programmer, as well as something of a Net guru, you're not going to start cranking out cool Web applications tomorrow (or the next day, or the next…).

On the server side, simplified scripting languages like Perl can flatten the learning curve quite a bit. Many people who don't consider themselves real programmers can hack out a Common Gateway Interface (CGI) script to process Web forms or feed animations to a Web page without too many false starts. With visual programming tools such as Visual Basic, you can learn to produce a respectable client-side helper application fairly quickly as well.

But there is an easier way, and because this chapter is intended to take you on the fast track to Web development, I have to recommend that you avoid the old ways until you run into something that you just can't accomplish any other way.

Plug-in Power

Before dashing into the inside lane, though, I do need to tell you about one very new way to enhance the Web that is not any easier than the old ways. It is, however, even more powerful

20

when used well. I'm referring to Netscape Navigator plug-ins, which are custom applications designed especially to extend Netscape's capabilities. The Live3D, LiveAudio, and LiveVideo capabilities that are built in to Netscape Navigator 3.0 are actually accomplished through plug-ins, for example.

You're probably familiar with some of the more popular plug-ins, such as Shockwave and Acrobat. Because these programs (which are usually written in C++) have direct access to both the client computer's operating system and Netscape's data stream, they are usually faster, more user-friendly, and more efficient than any other program you can create. They can draw directly to the Netscape window, making their output seem as though it were embedded into a Web page, or they can process invisibly in the background.

All this power comes at a price, however. The user must manually download and install your plug-in, and you must write a completely separate plug-in for every operating system you want to support. And woe betide you if your plug-in is distributed with a bug in it. Because plug-ins run at the machine level, they can easily crash Netscape and/or the user's computer if they malfunction.

Therefore, developing plug-ins is not for the faint of heart. Yet the lure of power has seduced many a programmer before, and if you can call yourself a "programmer" without blushing, you too may find it well worth the effort. All in all, writing and debugging a plug-in is still considerably less daunting than developing a full-blown business application.

Internet Programming for the Rest of Us

Suppose you just want your Web order form to add up totals automatically when customers check off which products they want. This is not rocket science. Implementing it shouldn't be either. You don't want to learn UNIX or C++ or the Windows 95 Applications Programming Interface. You don't want to compile and install half a dozen extra files on your Web server, or ask the user to download your handy-dandy calculator application. You just want to add up some numbers. Or maybe you just want to change a graphic depending on the user's preferences, or the day of the week, or whatever. Or maybe you want to tell a random joke every time somebody logs on to your home page. Until now, there really was no simple way to do these simple things.

JavaScript gives you a way. OK, so it's still programming. But it's the kind of programming you can learn in an afternoon, or in an hour if you've fooled around with BASIC or Excel macros before. It's programming for the rest of us. JavaScripts go right into the HTML of your Web pages, wherever you want something intelligent to happen. For example, the code to add up an order form might look like Figure 20.1.

20

Figure 20.1.

JavaScript allows you to include simple programming directly in an HTML document.

```html
<HTML>
<HEAD>
<SCRIPT LANGUAGE="JavaScript">
  function CalculateTotal(Qty,Amt)
    { document.forms[0].total.value = (0+Qty.value)*Amt }
</SCRIPT>
</HEAD>
<BODY>
<H1>Widget Order Form</H1>
Indicate the quantity you wish to order.
The total for your order will be calculated automatically.
<FORM METHOD="POST" NAME="order_form" ACTION="cgi/generic">
Send me
<INPUT NAME="qty" SIZE=3 ONBLUR="CalculateTotal(this,25)">
widgets at $25 each = TOTAL: <INPUT  NAME="total" SIZE=7>
<INPUT  NAME="purchase" TYPE="BUTTON"  VALUE="Order Now">
</FORM>
<SCRIPT LANGUAGE="JavaScript">
        document.forms[0].qty.value="0"
        document.forms[0].total.value="0"
</SCRIPT>
</BODY></HTML>
```

Though the code in Figure 20.1 is unrealistically simple for any real company's order form (most companies would like at least the address and phone number of the person placing the order), it is a completely functional JavaScript-enhanced Web page. Figure 20.2 demonstrates what the form would look like after a user entered the number 3 in the left box. The number 75 in the right box is computed automatically.

Figure 20.2.

The JavaScript in Figure 20.1 produces this form, which adds up the total based on the number of widgets you enter.

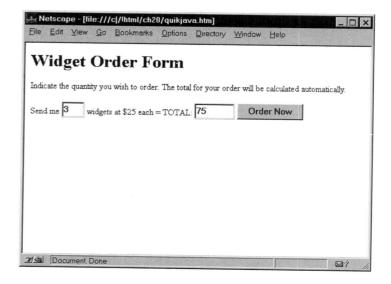

20

Even if you don't immediately understand the exact syntax of each JavaScript statement, it should be obvious that it is much easier to learn than any other way to accomplish the same thing. Most programmers could probably customize and expand the page in Figure 20.1 quite a bit without knowing anything whatsoever about JavaScript. What's more, this page works on any server and any JavaScript-enabled browser on any operating system.

Even if you don't do programming at all, you may find a JavaScript that can be incorporated into a Web page of your own with little or no modification. Use Figure 20.1 as a guide for placing the JavaScript elements where they should go; generally, functions go in the `<HEAD>` area, preceded by `<SCRIPT LANGUAGE="JavaScript">`, and followed by `</SCRIPT>`. The parts of the script that actually carry out the actions when the page is loaded go in the `<BODY>` part of the page, but still need to be set aside with the `<SCRIPT>` tag. Sections of script that respond to specific form entries go in the `<INPUT>` tag, with special attributes such as `ONCURSOR`.

TIME SAVER

> For maximum compatibility with older Web browsers, you can put the old comment tag `<!-` just after the `<SCRIPT>` tag, and put `->` just before `</SCRIPT>`. This will hide the script from any browser too old to recognize the `<SCRIPT>` tag.

You can also put JavaScript into a separate file by putting the name of that file in a `SRC` attribute within the `<SCRIPT>` tag, like this:

```
<SCRIPT LANGUAGE="JavaScript" SRC="bingo.htm"></SCRIPT>
```

This is especially handy when you are using a script that someone else wrote and you don't want it cluttering up your HTML. Some parts of the script, such as JavaScript attributes of form `<INPUT>` tags, may still have to go in your HTML document, however.

JUST A MINUTE

> Note that Netscape and Microsoft have slightly different—and often incompatible—implementations of JavaScript (Microsoft officially calls theirs Jscript). The Web sites at `http://home.netscape.com` and `http://www.microsoft.com` are the best place to find out about the exact differences.
>
> You'll also find links to JavaScript learning resources at `http://www.mcp.com/sams/books/235-8/hotlist.htm`.

20

Strong Java

JavaScript does have its drawbacks and limitations. For any high-volume data or image-processing work, it would be too slow. Complex applications of any kind are poorly suited for inclusion in HTML pages. There are only so many lines of code you want to wade through to see the Web page itself.

When you outgrow JavaScript, does that mean you'll need to return to server-side scripting or applications programming? No. JavaScript is just the baby sister of a more robust and powerful language called Java. Like JavaScript, Java is especially designed for the Web. And like JavaScript scripts, Java programs install and run automatically whenever a Web page is loaded. However, unlike JavaScript, Java programs are compiled into a more compact and efficient form (called bytecodes) and stored in a separate file from the Web pages that may call them.

Java also includes a complete graphics drawing library, security features, strong type checking, and other professional-level programming amenities that serious developers need. The biggest limiting factor with Java mini-applications (called *applets*) is that they must be small enough so that downloading them won't delay the display of a Web page by an intolerable amount. Fortunately, Java applets are extremely compact in their compiled form and are often considerably smaller than the images on a typical Web page.

Best of all, the syntax of Java is nearly identical to JavaScript, so you can cut your teeth on JavaScript and easily move to Java when you need or want to.

You'll find many ready-to-use Java applets on the Web, and Figure 20.3 shows how to include one in a Web page. The following HTML inserts a Java applet named RnbText.class (which must be placed in the same directory as the Web page) with the <APPLET> tag. This applet makes some text wiggle like a wave while rainbow colors flow through it, as shown in Figure 20.4.

```
<APPLET CODE="RnbText.class" WIDTH=580 HEIGHT=50>
<PARAM NAME="text"
 VALUE="H a w a ii's C o m p u t e r N e w s">
</APPLET>
```

The WIDTH and HEIGHT attributes do just what you'd expect them to—specify the dimensions of the region on the Web page that will contain the applet's output. The <PARAM> tag is used to supply any information that the specific applet needs to do its thing. The NAME identifies what information you're supplying to the applet, and VALUE is the actual information itself. In this example, the applet is designed to display some text, so you have to tell it what text to display.

20

Every applet will require different settings for the NAME and VALUE attributes, and most applets require more than one <PARAM> tag to set all their options. Whoever created the applet will tell you (usually in some kind of readme.txt or other documentation file) what NAME attributes you need to include, and what sort of information to put in the VALUE attributes for each NAME.

Note that in Figure 20.3, the same applet is used twice on the page. This is quite efficient, because it will only need to be downloaded once, and the Web browser will then create two copies of it automatically. Figure 20.4 shows a still snapshot of the resulting animated Web page.

Figure 20.3.

Java applets are pre-written programs that you place on your Web page with the <APPLET> tag.

```
<HTML>
<HEAD><TITLE>Hawaiian Hard Drive</TITLE></HEAD>
<BODY BACKGROUND="hhd.jpg">
<DIV ALIGN="center">
<IMG SRC="hhd2.gif" ALT="Hawaiian Hard Drive"><BR>
<APPLET CODE="RnbText.class" WIDTH=580 HEIGHT=50>
<PARAM NAME="text"
 VALUE="H a w a ii's  C o m p u t e r  N e w s">
</APPLET>
<P></DIV>
<FONT SIZE=4>The mission of the Hawaiian Hard Drive
newspaper and Web site are to inform a broad range of
computer users and the general general public of the
latest trends in the computer market. Through our writers
and advertisers, you'll find out about software, hardware,
applications  and other areas of interest.<P>
<DIV ALIGN="center">
<HR SIZE=10>
<APPLET CODE="RnbText.class" WIDTH=230 HEIGHT=50>
<PARAM NAME="text" VALUE="F e a t u r e s">
</APPLET>
<P><B><A HREF="webpages.htm">Making Your Own Web Page</A><BR>
<A HREF="virus.htm">A Computer Virus Primer</A><BR>
<A HREF="copyrite.htm">Software Copyright Protection</A><BR>
<P>
</FONT>
<HR SIZE=10>
<A HREF="mailto:PDeptula@aol.com">PDeptula@aol.com</A>
</ADDRESS><P>
All stories are copyright, 1995-1996 by their authors.<BR>
The Java Applet on this page was designed by
<A HREF="http://www.crl.com/~integris">
Integris Network Services</A>.<P>
</DIV>
</BODY></HTML>
```

20

JUST A MINUTE

In the near future, the standard tag for inserting a Java applet on a Web page will change from <APPLET> to <OBJECT>. You'll read more about that change in Chapter 24, "Preparing for the Future of HTML."

Figure 20.4.

The <APPLET> *tags in Figure 20.3 insert a program to draw wiggly, colorful animated text on the page.*

ActiveX Controls

For quite some time, Microsoft Windows has included a feature called object linking and embedding (OLE), which allows all or part of one program to be embedded in a document that you are working on with another program. For example, you can use OLE to put a spreadsheet in a word processing document.

When the Internet explosion rocked the world in the mid-90's, Microsoft adapted their OLE technology to work with HTML pages online and renamed it ActiveX. Everybody likes to invent their own jargon, so ActiveX programs are called *controls* rather than applets.

Though ActiveX is touted as the main competitor of Java, it actually isn't a specific programming language. It's a standard for making programs written in any language conform to the same protocols, so that neither you, the Web page author, nor the people who view your pages need to be aware of what language the control was written in. It just works, whether the programmer used VisualBasic, VBScript (a simplified version of VisualBasic), C++, or even Java.

It's not surprising that support for the Microsoft ActiveX protocol is built into Microsoft Internet Explorer 3.0. For users of Netscape Navigator 2.0 and 3.0 to be able to see ActiveX controls, they need to download and install a plug-in from Ncompass Labs (`http://www.ncompasslabs.com`).

Version 4.0 of Netscape Navigator hasn't been released as of this date, but Netscape is promising that it will have some limited support for ActiveX built-in.

Note, however, that ActiveX controls will still only work on Windows and Macintosh computers. Also, ActiveX controls must be separately compiled for each different operating system.

Because ActiveX is the newest of the technologies discussed in this chapter, you must use the new `<OBJECT>` tag to insert it into a page.

As Figure 20.5 shows, an ActiveX `<OBJECT>` tag looks rather bizarre. Here's the relevant HTML from that page:

```
<OBJECT CLASSID="CLSID:812AE312-8B8E-11CF-93C8-00AA00C08FDF"
 ID="cntrl">
<PARAM NAME="ALXPATH" REF VALUE="cntrl.alx">
</OBJECT>
```

The bizarre part is the `CLASSID` attribute, which must include a unique identifier for the specific ActiveX control you are including. If you use an automated program such as Microsoft's ActiveX Control Pad to create your ActiveX pages, it will figure out this magic number for you. Otherwise, you'll need to consult the documentation that came with the ActiveX control to find the correct `CLASSID`.

As if the long string of gibberish in `CLASSID` wasn't enough, the `ID` attribute must include another unique identifier, but this time you get to make it up. You can use any label you want for `ID`, as long as you don't use the same label for another ActiveX control in the same document. (`ID` is used for identifying the control in any scripts you might add to the page.)

If you are something of a whiz with Windows, you can look in the Windows class registry for the `CLSID` in `HKEY_CLASSES_ROOT`. If the previous sentence makes no sense to you, you'll need to rely on the person who wrote the ActiveX control (or an automated Web page authoring tool) to tell you the correct `CLASSID`.

20

The `<PARAM>` tags work the same with `<OBJECT>` as discussed earlier in this chapter with the `<APPLET>` tag. It provides settings and options specific to the particular ActiveX control you are placing on the Web page, with `NAME` identifying the type of information, and `VALUE` giving the information itself. In the example from Figure 20.5, the REF attribute indicates that the <PARAM> tag is specifying the location of the ActiveX control itself. No other <PARAM> parameters are needed by this particular control.

Notice that nothing in the HTML itself gives any clue as to what the ActiveX control on that page actually looks like or does. Only when you view the page, as in Figure 20.6, do you see that it is a nifty little program to mix custom colors by combining red, green, and blue brightness settings.

Figure 20.5.

The <OBJECT> tag on this page embeds an ActiveX control.

```
<HTML>
<HEAD><TITLE>Colour Calculator</TITLE></HEAD>
<BODY>
<A HREF="mailto:kencox@user.rose.com">kencox@user.rose.com</A>
<DIV ALIGN="center">
<BODY TOPMARGIN="4" BGCOLOR="white">
<OBJECT CLASSID="CLSID:812AE312-8B8E-11CF-93C8-00AA00C08FDF"
 ID="cntrl">
<PARAM NAME="ALXPATH" REF VALUE="cntrl.alx">
</OBJECT>
</DIV>
</BODY></HTML>
```

Figure 20.6.

The ActiveX control on this page is a program for mixing custom colors, though you wouldn't know it by looking at the HTML in Figure 20.5.

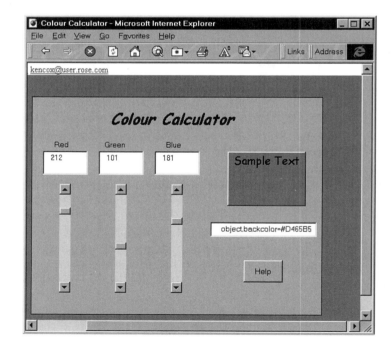

Neither Figure 20.5 nor Figure 20.6 reveal what language the person who created the ActiveX control used to write it. If you opened the `cntrl.alx` file itself, you'd see that Ken Cox used a version of VisualBasic specifically designed for Web page use, called VBScript. I'll spare you the rather lengthy source code listing here, but you can find this and other controls by Ken Cox at

`http://www.rose.com/~kencox/index.html`

COFFEE BREAK

This and the previous chapter have introduced a whirlwind of different options for adding cutting-edge multimedia and programming to your Web site. For an example of how to use multimedia and interactive elements with discretion (and, in some cases, "gee-whiz" abandon), meet the latest incarnation of the *24-Hour HTML Café* at

`http://www.mcp.com/sams/books/235-8/cafe20.htm`

You may find it difficult to distinguish the custom programming from the more traditional animation and HTML tricks, which is exactly as it should be in a well-balanced, integrated site. Always try to leave your audience free to experience the *content* of the site, rather than trying to awe them with your high-tech prowess.

(Okay, okay, so there's just a little too much high-tech prowess visible at the HTML Café. That's okay in a site that's trying to teach HTML, but try to show a little more restraint than I did, and stick to only one or two types of interactive media!)

Summary

This chapter has given you a brief outline of the three types of interactive programming that are easiest to add to your Web site: JavaScript, Java applets, and ActiveX controls. It also discussed the difference between these technologies and more traditional server-side scripting and Netscape plug-ins.

You didn't get enough technical stuff in this short chapter to write your own programs and scripts, but you did learn the basic HTML to insert prewritten ones into your Web pages.

Table 20.1 summarizes the tags covered in this chapter.

20

Table 20.1. HTML tags and attributes covered in Chapter 20.

Tag	Attribute	Function
<!— ... —>		The old way to create comments. Can also be used to hide JavaScript from browsers that do not support it.
<SCRIPT>		An interpreted script program.
	LANGUAGE="..."	Currently only JAVASCRIPT is supported by Netscape. Both JAVASCRIPT and VBSCRIPT are supported by Microsoft.
	SRC="..."	Specifies the URL of a file that includes the script program.
<APPLET>		Inserts a self-running Java applet.
	CLASS="..."	The name of the applet.
	SRC="..."	The URL of the directory where the compiled applet can be found (should end in a slash / as in "http://mysite/myapplets/"). Do not include the actual applet name, which is specified with the CLASS attribute.
	ALIGN="..."	Indicates how the applet should be aligned with any text that follows it. Current values are TOP, MIDDLE, and BOTTOM.
	WIDTH="..."	The width of the applet output area in pixels.
	HEIGHT="..."	The height of the applet output area in pixels.
<PARAM>		Program-specific parameters. (Always occurs within <APPLET> or <OBJECT> tags.)
	NAME="..."	The type of information being given to the applet or ActiveX control.
	VALUE="..."	The actual information to be given to the applet or ActiveX control.
<OBJECT>		Inserts images, videos, Java applets, or ActiveX OLE controls into a document (see Chapter 24).

JUST A MINUTE

In addition to the standard <APPLET> attributes in Table 20.1, you can specify applet-specific attributes to be interpreted by the Java applet itself.

20

Q&A

Q So just what exactly is the difference between "scripting" and "programming," anyway?

A Usually, the word "scripting" is used for programming in relatively simple computer languages that are integrated directly into an application (or into HTML pages). However, the line between scripting and "real programming" is pretty fuzzy.

Q I've used Visual Basic before, and I heard I could use it in Web pages. Is that true?

A Yes, but only if you want to limit the audience for your pages to users of Microsoft Internet Explorer version 3.0 or higher. Microsoft has implemented LANGUAGE= "VBScript" as one of the language options in the <SCRIPT> tag, but so far the rest of the world is sticking to JavaScript. Visit the Microsoft Web site (http://www. microsoft.com) for details about the differences between VBScript and Visual Basic.

Q I've heard about ActiveX scripting and ActiveX documents. How are these different from ActiveX controls?

A In Microsoft-speak, "ActiveX Scripting" means VBScript or JavaScript linking into a page as an ActiveX control. ActiveX documents are HTML pages that use an ActiveX control to view a word processing document or spreadsheet within a Web page. (Career tip: If you want a job at Microsoft, consider listing your first name as "ActiveX" on the application form. They like that.)

Q Most of the Java applets I find on the Internet have two files, one ending with .java and one ending with .class. Which one do I put on my Web page, and what do I do with the other one?

A Put the file ending with .class on your Web page with the <APPLET> tag. The .java file is the actual Java source code, provided in case you are a Java programmer and you want to change it. You don't need the .java file to use the applet.

20

Quiz

Questions

1. What tag is used to distinguish JavaScript or VBScript from the rest of a Web page?
2. Suppose you found a cool Java game on the Internet and the documentation with it says it's free for anyone to use. It says you need to give the applet two parameters:

the "speed" should be between 1 and 100, and the "skill" should be between 1 and 5. The applet itself is named `roadkill.class`. Write the HTML to display it in a 400×200-pixel area in the middle of a Web page.

3. From the Microsoft Internet Explorer Web site (`http://www.microsoft.com/ie/`), you can download the `IELABEL.OCX` control, which displays some text in any orientation you choose. Write the HTML to insert the ActiveX control in a Web page, given the following information:

The class ID is:

☐ `clsid:{99B42120-6EC7-11CF-A6C7-00AA00A47DD2}`

Confine the display area to 300×300 pixels.

☐ Specify the following parameter values:

Caption: "New and Exciting!"

Angle: 45

FontName: Arial Black

FontSize: 18

Answers

1. `<SCRIPT>`

2.
```
<APPLET CODE="roadkill.class" WIDTH=400 HEIGHT=200>
<PARAM NAME="speed" VALUE=50>
<PARAM NAME="skill" VALUE=2>
</APPLET>
```

3.
```
<OBJECT CLASSID="clsid:{99B42120-6EC7-11CF-A6C7-00AA00A47DD2}" ID="label"
WIDTH=300 HEIGHT=300>
<PARAM NAME="caption" VALUE="New and Exciting!">
<PARAM NAME="angle" VALUE="45">
<PARAM NAME="fontname" VALUE="Arial Black">
<PARAM NAME="fontsize" VALUE="18">
</OBJECT>
```

Activities

☐ Two of the most common uses of programming elements in a Web page are order forms that add up their own totals and marquees that scroll text across part of the page to draw attention to it. I've created a simple sample page to demonstrate both

20

of these using Java and JavaScript. If you've had even a smattering of programming experience, you'll probably find it easy to modify my page to add up your own order form totals. The page is at

`http://www.mcp.com/sams/books/235-8/ch20/carparts.htm`

You can also use the Marquee Java applet on the page for your own pages. The file name is `marquee.class`, and how to use it should be clear from the sample page.

You'll find many more reusable scripts and applets by exploring the `http://www.mcp.com/sams/books/235-8/hotlist.htm` JavaScript and Java links.

20

PART
VI

Building a
Web Site

Hour

Hour 21

Organizing Multiple Pages

The first twenty chapters of this book led you through the design and creation of your own Web pages and the graphics to put on them. Now it's time to stop thinking about individual *Web pages* and start thinking about your *Web site* as a whole.

This chapter shows you how to organize and present multiple Web pages so that people will be able to navigate among them without confusion. It also discusses ways to communicate the unique message of your Web site effectively, ways to organize the files on your Web site, and ways to make your Web site memorable enough to visit again and again.

To Do:

By this point in the book, you should have enough knowledge of HTML to produce most of your Web site. You have probably made a number of pages already, and perhaps even published them online.

As you read this chapter, think about how your pages are organized now and how you can improve that organization. Don't be surprised if you decide to do a "redesign" that involves changing almost all of your pages—the results are likely to be well worth the effort!

Organizing a Simple Site

For many companies and individuals, building and organizing an attractive and effective Web site doesn't need to be a complex task. The Web page shown in Figure 21.1, for example, does its job quietly with a single graphics image and two short lists of links.

The goal of the home page in Figure 21.1, like the goal of many Web sites today, is simply to make the organization "visible" on the Internet. Many people today immediately turn to the World Wide Web when they want to find out about an organization, or find out whether a particular type of organization exists at all. A simple home page should state enough information so that someone can tell whether they want to find out more. It should then provide both traditional address and telephone contact information and an electronic mail address.

The beauty of the Web is that a simple, short list like the "Materials currently available online from the GMWS" in Figure 21.1 can lead to a surprising wealth of information. Clicking on the first link on that list brings up the page in Figure 21.2, which in turns leads to a dozen more articles.

Having seen all the fancy graphics and layout tricks in Part III, "Web Page Graphics", you may be tempted to forget that a good old-fashioned outline is often the most clear and efficient way to organize a Web site. If you aren't selling visually oriented products or trying to prove that you're an "artist," a list like the one in Figure 21.2 may be the best way to guide people through a relatively small Web site.

21

Figure 21.1.

This home page establishes a presence on the Internet with a minimum of fuss.

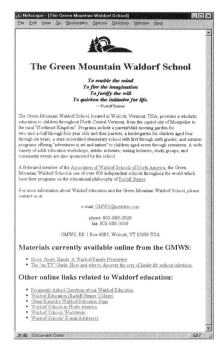

Figure 21.2.

Simple black-and-white graphics and a straightforward table of contents make this index page fast to view and easy to use.

Organizing a Larger Site

As the table of contents in Figure 21.2 grows, it will become more difficult for people to find the pages of interest to them in the list. One way to help people find their way around would be to place a more detailed summary of the most recent or most important information at the top of the list, as the long index in Figures 21.3 and 21.4 does.

Figure 21.3 also demonstrates another way to help people navigate through a large site without becoming lost and confused. Five graphical "buttons" allow readers to jump to the pages that contain the most important and popular information.

In this case, "READ ME" provides an overview of what the site is all about; "TALK TO ME" lets people comment or offer suggestions; "FREE STUFF" offers free software related to the site; and "ORDER FORM" lets people buy commercial products discussed on the site. These are rather archetypical pages that every good-sized site should contain in some form or another, though you may choose different names for them.

TIME SAVER

Here's another way to make long outlines like the one in Figures 21.3 and 21.4 easier to navigate: Put a short "index of the index" at the top of the page, with links leading down to the major sections of the page. (See Chapter 8, "Intra-Page and E-mail Links," for examples of intra-page links.)

For convenience, the buttons are repeated at both the top and bottom of the home page (see Figures 21.3 and 21.4).

The navigation buttons are also repeated at the bottom of every page in the site, as the sample page in Figure 21.5 shows. You should always provide some kind of "next step" at the end of your pages, and never make readers rely on the "Back" button to navigate through your site.

Note that a small banner is included at the top of the page in Figure 21.5 (and all other pages on this site). You should always provide either a banner, a unique icon, or another unmistakable visual clue that each page is part of the same site as the one the page reader just came from. Otherwise, they have no way of knowing whether they have suddenly jumped to a different site in Tasmania. Consistent backgrounds and color schemes are another visual cue that can keep people oriented as to where in the World Wide Web they are.

Note also that ultra-fancy eye-popping graphics and hokey visual clichés weren't necessary to make the site in Figures 21.3 through 21.5 easy to navigate. I'll probably jazz up this site visually in the future (it is a newsletter about computer graphics, after all), but you don't need to be a graphics designer to make a Web site that's visually appealing and conveniently organized.

21

Figure 21.3.

Navigation buttons and details about the most recent information help people find their way around a complex site.

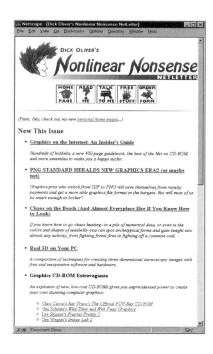

Figure 21.4.

This is the bottom half of the page in Figure 21.3. Lengthy pages can still be very readable if they are well-organized.

Figure 21.5.

The same banner and navigation buttons appear on every page listed in Figures 21.3 and 21.4.

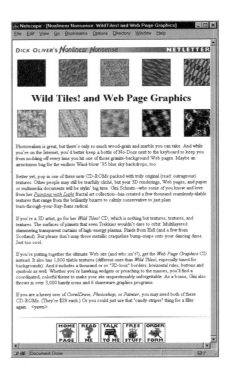

Organizing Your Files and Folders

Theoretically, you can put all your Web pages in one big fat directory folder. But if your site has (or will ever have) more than ten pages, lumping them all together in one folder will make it next to impossible to maintain either your site or your sanity while working on it.

If your site is updated on a fairly regular schedule, you can create a new directory folder for each new "issue." That's how I organized the files for the newsletters shown earlier in this chapter. However, most sites are updated either haphazardly or constantly, so you'll usually be better off grouping files by the main subject areas of your site.

For example, a food company's site might include a page about each product, pages with suggested recipes for using the products, and corporate information, such as a mission statement and a list of board members. You might put the Web pages for each category in separate folders, named products, recipes, and corpinfo. To link from a page in the recipes folder to a page named pres.htm in the corpinfo folder, you would use the following HTML:

```
<A HREF="../corpinfo/pres.htm">Our President</A> loves this recipe.
```

21

(Use of double dots (. .) to go up a level in the directory structure was introduced in Chapter 3, "Linking to Other Web Pages.")

If you have more than ten recipe pages, you might want to introduce subdirectory folders within `recipes`. You can use `..` and `/` as many times as necessary to link between the directories and subdirectories on your site. For example, to go from a page in the `products/cowchips` folder to a page named `cowcrunch` in the `recipes/desserts` folder, you would use the following link to go "up" twice, then back "down" into two levels of directory folders:

```
Try <A HREF="../../recipes/desserts">CowCrunch</A> for dessert.
```

TIME SAVER

> Maintaining your pages will be easier if your directory structure matches the main categories or navigation "buttons" shown on your Web pages.

Designing a Coherent "Look" for Your Site

Many of the techniques, presented in Part III, can also help the site's organization to improve the looks of your site when used consistently throughout all of your pages. To see how you can make aesthetics and organization work hand-in-hand, let's look at how an existing site was recently redesigned for both better appearance and clearer organization.

The home page in Figure 21.6 is quite typical of what are called "second generation" Web pages. It uses graphics and image maps to go beyond what "first generation" HTML was capable of. The site itself is also neatly organized into four categories of pages, accessible through the four regions of the image map or through the text links below them. The text on the page provides the essential information that someone would need to figure out what the site is about and whether or not they might be interested in looking further.

Figure 21.7 shows one of the pages you would get if you clicked on the image map in Figure 21.6. The banner at the top provides a strong visual relationship to the original page, and an icon at the bottom makes it easy to navigate back to the home page for further exploration.

If you produced pages similar to the ones in Figures 21.6 and 21.7 as your first site, you'd probably be proud, and rightly so. But you can use the techniques you've learned in this book to do even better.

21

Figure 21.6.

This site has nice graphics and good organization, but you can do even better.

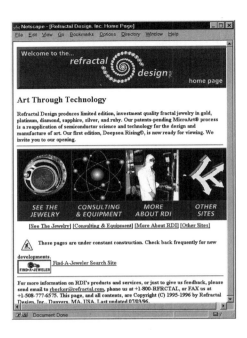

Figure 21.7.

If you click on "CON-SULTING & EQUIP-MENT" in Figure 21.6, you get this page.

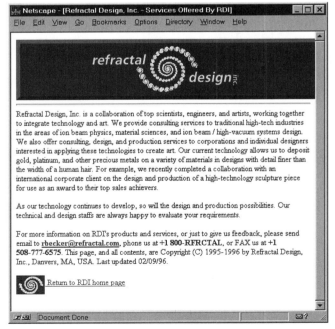

Figure 21.8 is a more recent look at the same company's home page. It differs from Figure 21.6 in several important ways, most of which you can apply to your own pages as well:

☐ The new background and graphical titles provide a more appropriate mood, and provide even more of a visual identity throughout the site than the blue banner graphic did.

☐ All text and foreground graphics on the new home page load in less than eight seconds using a 28.8Kbps modem (the background takes an extra four seconds to appear). The old home page takes over 25 seconds to finish loading, due to the large image map.

☐ Use of a table provides people with more information about where they will go if they click on the three main links. Quite a bit of text that was "buried" in other pages before is now visible on the first screen that people see.

☐ The prominent "OTHER SITES" link was removed. It is seldom a good business strategy to immediately refer visitors out the door.

☐ The under construction sign was removed. People expect sites to be updated, but if your site is missing enough key information to need an under construction sign, it probably isn't ready to be put on the Internet yet.

☐ The most compelling information that potential customers should see (the list of magazine articles and reviews) was moved to the home page. A table border separates it from the other text.

Figure 21.8.

A souped-up version of Figure 21.6 looks sharper, loads faster, and presents more key information immedi-ately.

Figure 21.9.

Though this page has about the same text content as Figure 21.7, it has a stronger look and more navigation aids.

All these changes to the home page help bring more of the company's message to the intended audience more quickly and clearly. Yet some more subtle changes also make it considerably faster and easier to navigate around all the pages of the site.

The same graphics that appear on the home page are used as topic headers on each subsequent page. This has the double benefit of providing an immediate sense of where you are within the site, and making the pages load almost instantly. (Web browsers will "remember" the graphics so they won't have to download them for the second page.)

Those same graphics are also placed at the bottom of each page as "navigation buttons." Re-using navigation graphics as headers is a great trick that can be incorporated into almost any Web site. The words "Refractal Design" are also a clickable link to the home page, though as a general rule, you shouldn't count on readers to find links that don't look like links.

Another subtle navigation aid: The company name at the bottom of every page (and in several other places throughout the site) is a link to a corporate identity page that explains the whos, whats, and whys of the company. Placing this obligatory information in the page footer and body text reduces the apparent complexity of the site by allowing for fewer main categories on the home page.

Perhaps the most important change in the site is the choice of organizational headings. Remember that the main categories you use to divide your pages are essentially answers to the question, "What is this site about?" In this case, "Jewelry, Infinity, and Technology" is likely to be a better answer than "Seeing Jewelry, Consulting and Equipment, Other Sites, and More." Think carefully about the main divisions of your site and the icons or headings you choose to represent those divisions. Your site will be much more compelling if they embody the primary message you want to convey to your audience.

COFFEE BREAK

A great way to improve the organization and presentation of your site is to look at some sites that really "suck" and avoid the common (but disastrous) mistakes the authors of these sites made.

I highly recommend Vincent Flander's "Web Pages that Suck" site for all aspiring Web page authors.

`http://www.webpagesthatsuck.com/`

On a more positive note, you'll find a list of Web sites that don't suck, in my honest and humble opinion, at the ever-improving *24-Hour HTML Café*.

`http://www.mcp.com/sams/books/235-8/cafe21.htm`

Summary

This chapter has given you examples and explanations to help you organize your Web pages into a coherent site that is informative, attractive, and easy to navigate. If you have only a few pages of primarily textual information, a simple outline or table of contents organizational scheme is likely to serve you well. For more complex and graphical sites, a strong visual identity, reuse of key images, and well-chosen headings and icons can make an enormous difference in the impact of your pages.

Q&A

Q Wouldn't it be better to organize my Web pages in a specific 1, 2, 3 order, like a book or brochure?

A Many authors try to arrange their Web site as a "story" or an ordered graphical presentation, but this approach is seldom effective because it goes against the nature of the Web. People are used to having control of their Internet experience and making their own choices about what to view. Unless your "story" is extremely compelling, don't count on people staying with it past page one. They are much more likely to click one of three or four options than to click "the only option."

Q I've seen pages that ask viewers to change the width of their browser window or adjust other settings before proceeding beyond the home page. Why?

A The idea is that the Web page author can offer a better presentation if they have some control over the size of reader's windows or fonts. Of course, nobody even bothers to change their settings, so these sites always look weird or unreadable. You'll be much better off using the tips you learn in this book to make your site readable and attractive at any window size and a wide variety of browser settings.

Q How many major categories or "navigation buttons" should my site have?

A Generally, no more than seven, since psychological tests have shown many times that people have difficulty keeping track of more than seven choices at a time. If your site has more than seven pages, use subcategories—preferably with each set of subcategories on its own page.

Q I was thinking of having a cool image map that portrays the pages of my site as the parts of a dog's body or the continents of the world or something. Good idea?

A Organizing your site around a big metaphorical image can work, if you can keep the size of the image small enough so that modem users don't grow old and die before they get to see it load. Repeating a piece of the big image on each page helps, so people know which metaphor they're supposed to be playing along with. Personally, I like a nice tacky bit of kitsch once in a while. But if that's not the tone you're after, try to steer clear of the "see?-my-site-is-really-an-X" thing.

Quiz

Questions

1. What are three ways to make a long list of links easier to read and navigate?
2. About how many pages should you keep in a single directory folder?
3. What are four ways to help people stay aware that all your pages form a single "site"?
4. What two types of information should always be included in the first home page that people encounter at your site?

21

Answers

1. (a) Put the most important links at the top, and add more detailed explanations of each link.

   (b) Use a "button bar" or image map to highlight key links.

   (c) Break up the list with sub-headings, and add links to those sub-headings from the top of the list.

2. Theoretically, you can put as many as you want. But any more than ten gets quite difficult to manage and keep track of.

3. (a) Using consistent background, colors, fonts, and styles.

   (b) Repeat the same link words or graphics on the top of the page the link leads to.

   (c) Repeat the same small header, buttons, or other element on every page of the site.

4. (a) Enough identifying information so that they can immediately tell the name of the site and what the site is about.

   (b) Whatever the most important message you want to convey to your intended audience is, stated directly and concisely.

Activities

☐ As an exercise in possibilities, surf on over to "The 10 Types of Web Page Design" at http://gate.cks.com/~patrick/types.html and see whether you can organize (or at least imagine) your site as it would look as each of these types.

☐ Grab a pencil (the oldfangled kind) and sketch out your Web site as a bunch of little rectangles with arrows between them. Then sketch a rough overview of what each page will look like by putting squiggles where the text goes and doodles where the images go. Each arrow should start at a doodle-icon that corresponds to the navigation button for the page the arrow leads to. This can give you a good intuitive grasp of which pages on your site will be easy to get to, and how the layout of adjacent pages will work together—all before you invest time in writing the actual HTML to connect the pages together.

21

Hour **22**

HTML Tags for Site Management

This is one of the shortest chapters in the book, but it may be the most important one for many Web page creators. The HTML tags and techniques you'll discover in this chapter won't make any visible difference in your Web pages today, but they can save you many hours (and dollars) when you revise your pages later.

Because Web sites can be (and usually should be) updated frequently, creating pages that can be easily maintained is essential. This chapter shows you how to add comments and other documentation to your pages so that you—or anyone else on your staff—can understand and modify your pages.

This chapter also shows you how to make one page automatically load another, and how to forward visitors to pages that have moved.

Including Comments in a Page

Whenever you type an HTML page, keep in mind that you or someone else will almost certainly need to make changes to it someday. Simple text pages are easy to read and revise, but complex Web pages with graphics, tables, and other layout tricks can be quite difficult to decipher.

For example, it isn't at all obvious from looking at the HTML in Figure 22.1 what the resulting page would actually look like. Even if you looked at the graphics files, it would take some serious brain work to figure out how they are being arranged on the page.

Figure 22.1.

*This will produce
a nice-looking page,
but the HTML itself
is a mess.*

```
<HTML><HEAD><TITLE>Dick Oliver's Home Page</TITLE></HEAD>
<BODY BACKGROUND="strip.gif" TEXT="white" LINK="red"
VLINK="red" ALINK="white"><IMG SRC="dickani.gif">
    . . . <IMG SRC="dickog.gif"><BR>  .<P>
So what can you do when you're too dumb to become a
physicist or mathematician, and not quite crazy enough
to qualify for free food at the asylum?
Write books, I figure. And software. And what the heck
maybe some newsletters and Web pages, too. But enough
about me already. On to these far more interesting topics:<BR>
<DIV ALIGN="center"><TABLE><TR><TD><IMG SRC="see.gif"></TD>
<TD><FONT COLOR="cyan"><I>See...</I></FONT><BR>
<A HREF="family.htm"><FONT COLOR="cyan">My family</FONT></A>
<BR><A HREF="house.htm"><FONT COLOR="cyan">My house</FONT></A>
<BR><A HREF="hotlist.htm"><FONT COLOR="cyan">My hotlist</FONT>
</A></TD><TD><IMG SRC="hear.gif"></TD><TD>
<FONT COLOR="yellow"><I>Hear...</I></FONT><BR>
<A HREF="hello.wav"><FONT COLOR="yellow">My voice</FONT></A>
<BR><A HREF="brillig.RA"><FONT COLOR="yellow">My favorite poem
</FONT></A><BR><A HREF="erica.RA"><FONT COLOR="yellow">
My daughter</FONT></A></TD><TD><IMG SRC="get.gif"></TD><TD>
<FONT COLOR="red"><I>Get...</I></FONT><BR><A HREF="news.htm">
My newsletter</A><BR><A HREF="books.htm">My books</A><BR>
<A HREF="inquirer.htm">My foolishness</A></TD></TR></TABLE><P>
Happy? Disgusted? Lonely? Enlightened? Just plain stupid?<BR>
Why not send some e-mail to
<A HREF="mailto:DICKO@netletter.com"><FONT COLOR="#00FF00">
DickO@netletter.com</FONT></A> to tell me about it?<P>
</DIV></BODY></HTML>
```

The HTML in Figure 22.2 will make exactly the same Web page as that in Figure 22.1—but it sure is easier to tell how in Figure 22.2! Actually formatting the text of your HTML is one way to make your pages easier to read and revise, and Figure 22.2 is much better than Figure 22.1 in this regard.

Even more importantly, Figure 22.2 uses the <COMMENT> tag to add plain-English explanations of the unusual tricks and potentially confusing tags. These are likely to be very helpful to anyone who might need to make changes to this page in the future, even if that person is the page's original author.

Anything you type in an HTML file between the <COMMENT> and </COMMENT> tags will not appear on the actual Web page. Only when someone selects View | Source or edits the HTML file with a text editor will he see your comments. Both Figures 22.1 and 22.2 will look like Figure 22.3 when viewed in a Web browser.

JUST A MINUTE

Notice that in Figure 22.2, every <COMMENT> tag is followed by <!-, and every closing </COMMENT> tag is preceded by ->. This is because previous versions of HTML used <!- and -> as comment tags, and older browsers won't recognize <COMMENT>.

If you follow my example, starting all your comments with <COMMENT><!- and ending them with -></COMMENT>, you can be sure that your comments will be hidden by both past and future Web browsers.

To Do:

It will be well worth your time now to go through all the Web pages you've created so far and add any comments that you or others might find helpful when revising them in the future.

- [ ] Put a comment explaining any fancy formatting or layout techniques before the tags that make it happen.
- [ ] Use a comment just before an <IMG> tag to briefly describe any important graphic whose function isn't obvious from the ALT message.
- [ ] Always use a comment (or several comments) to summarize how the cells of a <TABLE> are supposed to fit together visually.
- [ ] If you use hexadecimal color codes (such as <FONT COLOR="#8040B0">), insert a comment indicating what the color actually is ("blueish-purple").
- [ ] Indenting your comments (as I did in Figure 22.2) helps them to stand out and makes both the comments and the HTML easier to read. Don't forget to use indentation in the HTML itself to make it more readable, too.

Figure 22.2.

*Both this HTML and
the HTML in Figure
22.1 produce the same
results. But this page
is much easier to
maintain.*

```
<HTML><HEAD><TITLE>Dick Oliver's Home Page</TITLE></HEAD>
<COMMENT><!--  Background is white on top
                  and black on bottom
--></COMMENT>
<BODY BACKGROUND="strip.gif"
      TEXT="white" LINK="red" VLINK="red" ALINK="white">
<IMG SRC="dickani.gif" ALT="Dick Oliver">
<COMMENT><!--  The periods will be invisible, since they
                  are white on a white background.
--></COMMENT>
. . . .
<IMG SRC="dickog.gif" ALT="Welcome to the Land of DickO">
<BR>   <P>
<COMMENT><!--  Now we should be over the black part of
                  the background, so white text will show up.
--></COMMENT>
So what can you do when you're too dumb to become a
physicist or mathematician, and not quite crazy enough
to qualify for free food at the asylum?
Write books, I figure. And software. And what the heck
maybe some newsletters and Web pages, too. But enough
about me already. On to these far more interesting topics:<BR>
<COMMENT><!--  A 6-column, 1-row table with eye, ear, and
                  hand next to the links to see, hear, and get.
--></COMMENT>
<DIV ALIGN="center">
<TABLE><TR>
<TD><IMG SRC="see.gif"></TD>
<TD>
  <COMMENT><!--  Microsoft Internet Explorer 3 won't show
                    the font color set below. (It will show red
                    for all links.) Only Netscape 3 will.
  --></COMMENT>
  <FONT COLOR="cyan"><I>See...</I></FONT><BR>
  <A HREF="family.htm">
    <FONT COLOR="cyan">My family</FONT></A><BR>
  <A HREF="house.htm">
    <FONT COLOR="cyan">My house</FONT></A><BR>
  <A HREF="hotlist.htm">
    <FONT COLOR="cyan">My hotlist</FONT></A>
</TD>
<TD><IMG SRC="hear.gif"></TD>
<TD>
  <FONT COLOR="yellow"><I>Hear...</I></FONT><BR>
  <A HREF="hello.wav">
    <FONT COLOR="yellow">My voice</FONT></A><BR>
  <A HREF="brillig.RA">
    <FONT COLOR="yellow">My favorite poem</FONT></A><BR>
  <A HREF="erica.RA">
    <FONT COLOR="yellow">My daughter</FONT></A>
</TD>
<TD><IMG SRC="get.gif"></TD>
<TD>
  <FONT COLOR="red"><I>Get...</I></FONT><BR>
  <COMMENT><!--  The VLINK color is red, so no need
                    for FONT COLOR here.
  --></COMMENT>
  <A HREF="news.htm">My newsletter</A><BR>
  <A HREF="books.htm">My books</A><BR>
  <A HREF="inquirer.htm">My foolishness</A>
</TD>
</TR></TABLE>
<P>
Happy? Disgusted? Lonely? Enlightened? Just plain stupid?<BR>
Why not send some e-mail to
<A HREF="mailto:DICKO@netletter.com">
<FONT COLOR="#00FF00">DickO@netletter.com</FONT></A>
 to tell me about it?
<P></DIV> <COMMENT><!-- End of centered region --></COMMENT>
</BODY></HTML>
```

22

Figure 22.3.

The comments in Figure 22.2 don't show up on the actual Web page. The page in Figure 22.1 also looks just like this.

Documenting the Full Address of a Page

Suppose you create a Web page advertising your business, and a customer likes your page so much that she saves it on her hard drive. A couple of days later, she wants to show a friend your cool site, but... guess what? She forgot to bookmark it, and of course the page doesn't contain a link to itself. She clicks on the links to your order form, but they are only filename links (like <A HREF="orderform.htm">) so they don't work from her hard drive unless the order form is on her hard drive, too. So you lose two eager customers.

One way to avoid this heartbreaking scenario is to always use complete addresses starting with http:// in all links. However, this makes your pages difficult to test and maintain.

You could also include a link to the full address of your home page on every page, including the home page itself. Yet there's a more elegant way to make a page remember where it came from.

The <BASE> tag lets you include the address of a page within the <HEAD> section of that page, like this:

```
<HTML>
<HEAD>
 <BASE HREF="http://www.myplace.com/mypage.htm">
 <TITLE>My Page</TITLE>
</HEAD>
<BODY> ...the actual page goes here... </BODY>
</HTML>
```

For the HTML authors whose job is to maintain this page, the <BASE> tag provides convenient documentation of where this page should be put.

Even more importantly, all links within the page behave as if the page was at the <BASE> address, *even if it isn't*. For example, if you had the page in Figure 22.4 on your hard drive and you opened it with a Web browser, all images on the page would be loaded from the online site at http://netletter.com/look/ rather than from the hard drive. The links would also lead to pages in the look directory at http://netletter.com, instead of pages on the hard drive.

(By the way, pay no attention to the <META> tag in Figure 22.4 right now. The next section in this chapter will explain what this tag does.)

Figure 22.4.

No matter where this page is located, all images and links to act as if the page were at the address in the <BASE> tag.

```
<HTML>
<HEAD>
<BASE HREF="http://netletter.com/look/prelude.htm">
<META HTTP-EQUIV="Refresh"
       CONTENT="3; URL=http://netletter.com/look/look.htm">
<TITLE>LOOK LOOK</TITLE>
</HEAD>
<BODY BACKGROUND="eyetile1.jpg">
<DIV ALIGN="center"><A HREF="look.htm">
<IMG SRC="lookclr.gif" LOWSRC="lookclr2.gif" BORDER=0>
<IMG SRC="lookclr2.gif" LOWSRC="lookclr.gif" BORDER=0>
</A></DIV>
</BODY></HTML>
```

TIME SAVER

Don't put <BASE> tags in your pages until you're ready to upload them to the Web server. That way you can test them with all the images and link pages on your hard drive, then add the <BASE> tag at the last minute, to enjoy the benefits it offers once your pages are online.

Loading Another Page Automatically

When you are managing a Web site, it may become necessary to move some pages from one address to another. You might decide, for example, to change the service provider or domain name of your whole site. Or you might just reorganize things and switch some pages to a different directory.

What happens, then, when someone comes to the address of their favorite Web page on your site after you've moved it? If you don't want them to be stranded with a Not Found error message, you should put a page at the old address which says "This page has moved to..." with the new address (and a link to it).

Chances are, you've encountered similar messages on the Internet from time to time yourself. Some of them probably employed the neat trick you're about to learn; they automatically transferred you to the new address after a few seconds, even if you didn't click on a link.

In fact, you can make any page automatically load any other page after an amount of time you choose. The secret to this trick is the <META> tag, which goes in the <HEAD> section of a page and looks like this:

```
<META HTTP-EQUIV="Refresh"
 CONTENT="5; nextpage.htm">
```

Put the number of seconds to wait before loading the next page where I put 5 in the line above, and put the address of the next page to load instead of nextpage.htm.

For example, the page in Figure 22.4 looks like Figure 22.5. After three seconds, the <META> tag causes the page at http://netletter.com/look/look.htm to appear, as shown in Figure 22.6. In this case, I used the <META> tag for a special effect, making the background eye seem to open wide after three seconds. (For the impatient, I also included a link to the look.htm page, which someone could click on before the three seconds are up.)

JUST A MINUTE

Note that some very old Web browsers don't recognize <META>, so you should always put a normal link on the page leading to the same address as the <META> tag.

Figure 22.5.

The <BASE> and <A> tags in Figure 22.4 link the image on this page to the address shown at the bottom of the window.

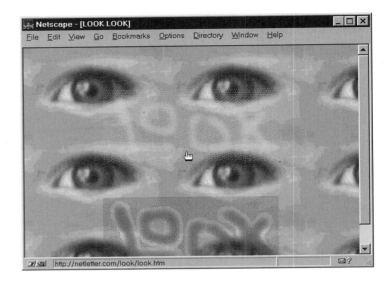

Figure 22.6.

The <META> tag in Figure 22.4 causes the page in Figure 22.5 to automatically load this page after three seconds.

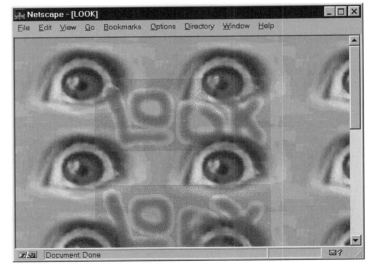

22

COFFEE BREAK

22

For a look at the Look pages in Figures 22.5 and 22.6, as well as a couple of other intriguing uses of automatic page loading, stop by the *24-Hour HTML Café* at

`http://www.mcp.com/sams/books/235-8/cafe22.htm`

You may also notice that I added a <BASE> address to the `cafe22.htm` document. Try saving it to your hard drive, and then open the copy you saved. You'll notice that it still loads all images correctly from the Web site (as long as you're connected to the Internet when you open it).

Advanced Header Tags

The <META> tag can actually be used for a wide variety of purposes besides automatically loading a new page. You can use it to specify any information you like about the document, such as the author or a page ID number. How and why you do this is beyond the scope of this introductory book, and very few Web page authors ever use the <META> tag for anything other than automatically loading a new page.

There are also a few other advanced tags that you may occasionally see in the <HEAD> section of Web pages. They are listed in Table 22.1 so that you'll have some general idea what they're for, just in case you ever encounter them. However, most of them are never used by most Web page authors today, so you don't need to worry about learning them now.

Table 22.1. Advanced HTML tags.

Tag	Function
<ISINDEX>	Indicates that this document is a gateway script that allows searches.
<LINK>	Indicates a link from this entire document to another (as opposed to <A>, which can create multiple links in the document.)
<NEXTID>	Indicates the "next" document to this one (as might be defined by a tool to manage HTML documents in series). <NEXTID> is considered obsolete.
<STYLE>	A very new tag used to define "style sheet" specifications for a document. Refer to Chapter 6, "Font Control and Special Characters," for more information on style sheets.
<SCRIPT>	A relatively new tag used to insert programming scripts directly into a Web page. Refer to Chapter 20, "Scripting, Applets, and ActiveX," for more information.

Summary

This chapter discussed the importance of making your HTML easy to maintain, and introduced the <COMMENT> tag to help you toward that end. It also showed you how to make a page remember its own address, and how to make a page load another page automatically. Finally, a few tags that you don't need to know were mentioned just in case you see them in someone else's documents and wonder what they are.

Table 22.2 lists the tags and attributes covered in this chapter (except for those listed earlier in Table 22.1).

Table 22.2. HTML tags and attributes covered in Chapter 22.

Tag	Attribute	Function
<!— ... —>		The old way to create a comment to be seen only by Web page authors. (The text in the comment won't be displayed by Web browsers.)
<COMMENT>...</COMMENT>		The new official way of specifying comments.
<BASE>		Indicates the full URL of the current document. This optional tag is used within <HEAD>.
	HREF="..."	The full URL of this document.
<META>		Indicates meta-information about this document (information about the document itself). Most commonly used to make a page automatically load another page, or reload itself. Used in the document <HEAD>.
	HTTP-EQUIV="..."	Gives a command to the Web browser or server. For example, HTTP-EQUIV="Refresh" will cause a new page to load automatically.
	NAME="..."	Can be used to specify which type of information about the document is

22

Tag	Attribute	Function
		in the CONTENT attribute. For example, NAME="Author" means the author's name or ID is in CONTENT.
	CONTENT="..."	The actual message or value for the information specified in HTTP-EQUIV or NAME. For example, if HTTP-EQUIV="Refresh" then CONTENT should be the number of seconds to wait, followed by a semi-colon and the address of the page to load.

Q&A

Q Won't lots of comments and spaces make my pages load slower when someone views them?

A All modems compress text when transmitting it, so adding spaces to format your HTML doesn't usually change the transfer time at all. You'd have to type hundreds of words of comments to cause even one extra second of delay when loading a page. It's the graphics that slow pages down, so squeeze your images as tightly as you can (refer to Chapter 11, "Making Pages Display Quickly"), but use text comments freely.

Q If the <BASE> tag is so great, why don't most pages on the Web use it?

A Many Web page authors don't even know about the <BASE> tag. Many who do know about it don't like the hassle of changing it when they want to test a page (including images and links) on their hard drive. I've tried to give you enough information in this chapter to choose for yourself whether the <BASE> tag is worthwhile for you.

Q Can I use the <META> tag to make a page automatically update itself every few seconds or minutes?

A Yes, but there's no point in doing that unless you have some sort of program or script set up to provide new information on the page. Some ways to do that are discussed in Chapter 20.

Quiz

Questions

1. If you wanted to say, "Don't change this image of me. It's my only chance at immortality," to future editors of a Web page, but you didn't want people who view the page to see that message, how would you do it?

2. What are three ways to make sure that people who save one of your pages on their hard drives can find your site online from it, even if they forget to add it to their Bookmarks or Favorites lists.

3. Suppose you recently moved a page from `http://mysite.com/oldplace/thepage.htm` to `http://mysite.com/newplace/thepage.htm`, but you're not quite sure if you're going to keep it there yet. How would you automatically send people who try the old address to the new address, without any message telling them there was a change?

Answers

1. Put the following just before the `<IMG>` tag:

```
<COMMENT><!- Don't change this image of me.
It's my only chance at immortality. -></COMMENT>
```

2. (a) Include a link to the site, using the full Internet address, on every page. Example:

```
The address of this page is:
<A HREF="http://mysite.com/home.htm">
http://mysite.com/home.htm</A>
```

   (b) Use full Internet addresses in all links between your pages. Example:

```
This is my home page. From here you can
<A HREF="http://mysite.com/personal.htm">
find out about my exciting personal life</A>, or
<A HREF="http://mysite.com/work.htm">
find out about my boring work life</A>.
```

   (c) Use the `<BASE>` tag to specify the full Internet address of a page. Example:

```
<HEAD><BASE HREF="http://mysite.com/home.htm">
<TITLE>My Home Page</TITLE></HEAD>
```

3. Put the following page at `http://mysite.com/oldplace/thepage.htm`:

```
<HTML><HEAD><META HTTP-EQUIV="Refresh" CONTENT="0; http://mysite.com/
newplace/thepage.htm"></HEAD>
</HTML>
```

22

To accommodate people using older browsers that don't support <META>, it would be a good idea to also include the following just before the </HTML> tag:

```
<BODY><A HREF="http://mysite.com/newplace/thepage.htm">Click here to get
the page you're after.</A></BODY>
```

Activities

☐ Can you think of some fun and/or useful ways to employ automatically changing pages (with the <META HTTP-EQUIV="Refresh"> tag)? I bet you can.

Hour 23

Web Site Authoring Tools

At the beginning of this book, I encouraged you to start creating HTML pages with the text editor or word processor that you are most familiar with. Now that you've got HTML under your belt, however, you should consider switching to one of the many software packages especially designed for creating Web pages. This chapter helps you choose the software that is best for you, and introduces some of the best and most popular HTML authoring tools.

There are essentially four types of HTML authoring tools:

☐ HTML text editors work a lot like the text editor or word processor you're used to, but speed up your work with custom button bars and menu commands for handling HTML.

☐ Graphical Web page editors let you build Web pages as you view them, complete with graphics and formatting, usually without showing the actual HTML tags at all.

☐ HTML add-ons to other software add special button bars or an "export Web page" command to your favorite word processor, page layout program, or office productivity suite.

☐ Web site construction and management tools provide organization and planning tools for handling large numbers of Web pages, with an integrated editor for building individual pages or groups of similar pages.

Which software you should use depends on the size you expect your Web site to be, and the number of people who are working with you to create it. It also depends somewhat on your personal tastes and skills. This chapter gives you the information you need to make an informed decision on which software is worth evaluating for yourself.

Text Editors Versus Graphical Editors

"What-you-see-is-what-you-get" (WYSIWYG) Web page editors like Netscape Composer (formerly known as Navigator Gold) incorporate a Web browser that attempts to show the Web page with graphics and special formatting as you build it. (See Figure 23.1.) The attraction of this sort of editor is that you theoretically don't have to even learn HTML to create Web pages.

Figure 23.1.

Netscape Composer is a Web browser with a built-in Web page editor (or vice versa, depending on how you look at it).

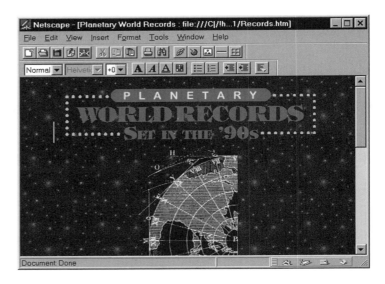

Most Web page authors, however, prefer using a text editor that shows the actual HTML commands. Any word processor or text editor will do, though specialized HTML editors,

23

such as the HTMLed program in Figure 23.2, offer convenient buttons and menu commands that can save you a lot of typing. Some HTML editors also automatically highlight HTML tags, which makes them easier to read.

Figure 23.2.
With HTMLed, you edit the HTML source code for a Web page directly.

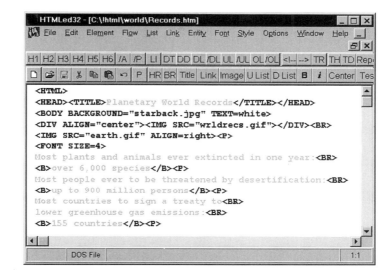

23

Why would you want to type HTML commands yourself instead of letting a graphical editor like Netscape Navigator Gold write them for you? There are at least five good reasons:

- [ ] You have more creative flexibility when you type the HTML yourself. Though graphical editors are becoming more powerful with each new version, none of them currently let you use all the HTML commands and techniques you'll learn in this book.

- [ ] Typing the commands yourself is often faster and easier than navigating through complex menus and dialog boxes, especially when you use an HTML editor like HTMLed.

- [ ] Hand-written HTML is much easier to read and maintain than the messy code created by most automated graphical editors. Learning HTML also gives you the ability to read and modify any Web page, no matter what tools were used to create it.

- [ ] You often don't get quite what you see with WYSIWYG editors. Even the Netscape Composer doesn't display pages exactly as they appear in Netscape Navigator! Writing HTML yourself also makes it easy to include special formatting that will only appear in certain circumstances.

☐ You don't need to learn a complex new software program. HTML itself is quite simple, and it often takes longer to figure out how to use the "helpful" graphical editor than to learn to help yourself.

Graphical WYSIWYG editors are best when you only need very simple pages—or if you are a very slow typist! The next generation of graphical editors, however, promises to offer more complete support for all HTML options and more efficient user-interfaces. You may want to have a look at new graphical editors as they come out, but meanwhile I recommend that all serious Web page authors stick to "the real thing"—straight, unadulterated HTML text.

To Do:

You'll find objective and thorough reviews of all the major Web page editors at The Ultimate Collection of Winsock Software (TUCOWS) at:

```
http://tucows.mcp.com/
```

☐ Before you decide which editor is best for you, pay a visit to this site to see what's new and which editors are currently rated best.

☐ Consider not only the ratings of an editor, but also the size and complexity of the Web site you plan to build.

☐ Once you narrow the choices down to one or two editors that seem best for you, you can download evaluation copies directly from TUCOWS.

HTML Support Within Applications

If you already use a word processor or page layout program, you may not have to switch software to get the convenient HTML shortcuts that a specialized HTML editor provides. The latest versions of almost all business software include support for HTML, and even older word processors can be enhanced with add-ons for building Web pages.

All the applications in the Microsoft Office 97 suite, for example, include the ability to open, edit, and save HTML pages. Microsoft also offers a free add-on for Word 7.0 (and other Microsoft Office 95 programs) called Internet Assistant. You can download this add-on at:

```
http://www.microsoft.com./msword/internet/ia/
```

As Figure 23.3 illustrates, Internet Assistant allows you to create HTML headings, lists, and other Web page formatting commands by selecting from pull-down lists. You can also make hypertext links directly within Word, as shown in Figure 23.4.

23

Figure 23.3.

Internet Assistant adds drop-down lists for most HTML tags to Microsoft Word.

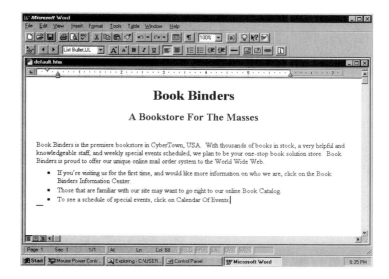

Figure 23.4.

Internet Assistant also lets you create hypertext links within Microsoft Word.

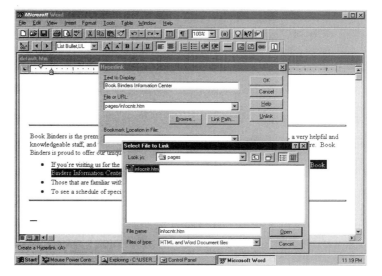

Internet Assistant for Word 7.0 (and Office 7.0) includes a built-in Web browser, as shown in Figure 23.5. Though this browser does a good job of showing basic HTML text and images, it doesn't support many of the advanced features of standalone Web browsers. For this reason, other applications and add-ons prefer to rely on Netscape Navigator or Microsoft Internet Explorer for viewing Web pages.

Figure 23.5.

Word with Internet Assistant, like many Web-enabled applications, includes a built-in Web browser.

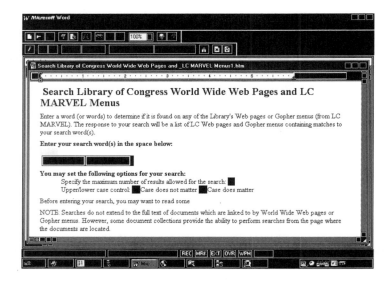

Though specialized Web editing programs are still the most popular choice among Web page authors, the trend of the future is definitely toward HTML-enabled applications. Expect upcoming versions of your favorite software to meet or exceed the Web page editing capabilities of today's standalone HTML editors.

TIME SAVER

> HTML-enabled applications and add-ons are especially useful for converting existing documents into HTML. In many cases, you can simply open a document and choose an "export as HTML" option to add HTML paragraph breaks, text formatting, and sometimes even image tags. This can be dramatically faster than adding all those tags by hand.

Web Site Management and Authoring Tools

All of the options discussed so far in this chapter are intended to help you build Web sites one page at a time. But planning, implementing, and managing a large Web site today can involve far more than writing HTML. For help with higher-level tasks like organizing your pages, automatic link verification and testing, multi-author version tracking, and multimedia Web publishing, you'll need to turn to more complex software tools.

23

To help you understand what these tools can do for you, let's take a look at two of the most popular site management and authoring packages, Adobe PageMill and Microsoft FrontPage.

JUST A MINUTE

I chose PageMill and FrontPage as examples in this chapter because they are two of the most popular and capable tools currently available, and they are simple enough for beginners to use. Don't take that as a recommendation against competing programs that may be as good or better for your needs.

There are also more advanced products available such as Macromedia Backstage and NetObjects Fusion. These are billed as the "ultimate" complete site production solution, but are far too complex to cover in this book.

Other products, such as HomePage and PageMill's "big brother" SiteMill, offer many of the same features as FrontPage, plus bells and whistles of their own. More promising Web site authoring packages are appearing on the market almost daily, so look around on the Internet and evaluate the latest before you invest in one.

The line between an "editor" and a "site management tool" can't be sharply drawn, and Adobe PageMill is a good example of a software package that straddles the line. Its primary function is similar to Netscape Composer: a graphical Web browser that lets you build and edit pages as you view them (see Figure 23.6).

Figure 23.6.

At first glance, PageMill is just a graphical HTML editor like Netscape Composer.

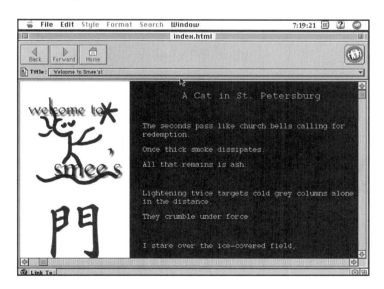

PageMill offers a number of features that help you quickly edit multiple similar pages and get an overall picture of how a page fits into your site. These include the Pasteboard, color palette, and Inspector windows shown in Figure 23.7, among other features.

Figure 23.7.

PageMill offers a number of bells and whistles that go beyond what you'd expect from a simple page editor.

To really get a handle on major site development, however, you need to move up to a product such as Adobe SiteMill or Microsoft FrontPage. By providing a visual overview of your entire site, these programs can help you understand and control how the Web components are associated and linked. Icons are generally used to show relationships between pages and to indicate if there is a problem, such as a broken link.

The Explorer module of FrontPage (see Figure 23.8), for example, is closely integrated with FrontPage Editor. You can do things like moving files between directories while automatically modifying all links for all pages affected by the move.

Microsoft FrontPage also includes Web wizards and Web templates, which guide you through the creation of a complete Web site based on a pre-designed "standard" format. You get to pick which parts of the design you want to include in your Web site, and provide the actual graphics and text to implement the pages. Figure 23.9 shows one of the dialog boxes you would encounter when using the Web wizard called Corporate Presence.

23

Figure 23.8.

Microsoft FrontPage Explorer gives you a birds-eye view of your entire Web site.

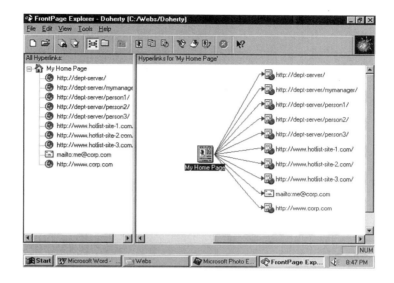

Figure 23.9.

Microsoft FrontPage's Corporate Presence Web Wizard lets you specify the main components of your Web site all at once.

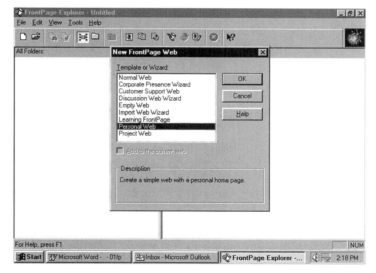

Though its emphasis is on helping you produce a professional-quality site quickly, FrontPage offers some more advanced features, such as integrating databases and multimedia into your pages. FrontPage also provides some fairly simple tools to aid you in administering your own Web server.

If cutting-edge features are your top priority, you should probably look beyond tools like FrontPage toward more powerful (and expensive) packages, such as Macromedia Backstage or NetObjects Fusion.

It would take us far beyond the scope of this book to delve into these advanced packages, but they essentially enable you to make your site look different for every visitor. Macromedia Backstage gives you powerful tools for accessing databases, managing online discussion groups, and building interactive animation, sound, and video into your pages. NetObjects Fusion includes many similar features, but places more emphasis on advanced page layout and interactive site management tools.

If you'd like to see some of what's possible with these cutting-edge tools, check out the Macromedia site at:

http://www.macromedia.com/

and the NetObjects site at:

http://www.netobjects.com/

JUST A MINUTE

The kind of dynamic, interactive, individualized Web sites that high-end tools can create are an exciting glimpse into the future of the Web. However, even with the fanciest tools, you'll still need to make a significant investment of both time and money—maybe even involving a development team rather than an individual author.

Since you've just learned HTML, you may not be quite ready for the Web site of the future. The chapters in Part V, "Interactive Web Pages," can show you how to use good old HTML tags to add some interactivity to your site.

COFFEE BREAK

I didn't use any advanced tools to develop the *24-Hour HTML Café* site, so you won't find a cafe23.htm version of that site for this chapter. However, you might like to compare the completed *24-Hour HTML Café* (http://www.mcp.com./sams/books/235-8/cafe.htm) to sites built with the big tools. You might find out that the "plain-old HTML" covered in this book can do everything you need and more.

23

Summary

This chapter introduced the four basic types of HTML editing and site management tools. With Netscape Navigator Gold, HTMLed, Microsoft Internet Assistant, Adobe PageMill, and Microsoft FrontPage as examples, you learned what each kind of tool can do to speed up your Web page development.

Q&A

23

Q If interactive, dynamic sites are the wave of the future, am I wasting my time learning plain old HTML?

A Absolutely not. Even the most advanced interactive sites use HTML to glue everything together. The hype on some Web page development software packages may claim "no HTML experience required," but ask any Web site developer using those tools and you'll hear a different story. A solid working knowledge of HTML will continue to be a strong advantage and practical pre-requisite for developing Web sites far into the future.

Q Technology is changing so fast. How can I find out about the latest tools?

A The Web itself is by far your best research tool if you're shopping for Web development tools. For example, try the Yahoo! list of World Wide Web software companies at:

```
http://www.yahoo.com/Business_and_Economy/
Companies/Computers/Software/Internet/World_Wide_Web/
```

or the official World Wide Web consortium list of HTML tools at:

```
http://www.w3.org/pub/WWW/Tools/
```

Quiz

Questions

1. Do WYSIWYG HTML editors actually produce pages that look exactly the same in a Web browser as they do in an editor?
2. What is the biggest advantage of text-based HTML editors, as compared to graphical editors?

3. What is the biggest advantage of graphical editors over text-based editors?

4. Do advanced site development tools actually do anything that you can't achieve with HTML?

Answers

1. No. At least none of the current versions have delivered on this promise yet (especially since HTML can look quite different in various browsers anyway).

2. Text-based editors give you more complete control over the HTML that goes into the document.

3. Graphical editors make it easier to tell approximately what pages will look like, even if you're not versed in HTML.

4. Yes. No matter how well you fine-tune your HTML, you simply can't implement some advanced interactive features without programmed "objects" or special server enhancements.

Activities

☐ There are demonstration copies of many HTML editors and site development tools available from their respective company's Web sites. Download and try out a few editors, and pick the one that best suits your own tastes and habits.

Hour 24

Preparing for the Future of HTML

Almost everything you have learned in this book is likely to work flawlessly with HTML-compatible software for many years to come. There are tens of millions of pages of information written in standard HTML, and even as that standard evolves, tomorrow's Web browsers and business software will retain the capability to view today's Web pages.

Some of the most exciting applications of HTML, however, are still rapidly developing. This chapter introduces the latest HTML extensions and helps you understand what these new capabilities will enable you to do.

You won't see any screen shots in this chapter, because future Web browsers obviously don't exist yet. What you read here is, however, based on "inside information" and prerelease copies of Microsoft Internet Explorer 4.0 and Netscape Navigator 4.0.

To Do:

When this chapter was written, "now" meant early 1997. Because you are living in "the future," you can check to make sure my crystal ball wasn't too cloudy.

☐ Your best source for the latest HTML standards (and proposed future standards) is the World Wide Web Consortium site:

```
http://www.w3.com
```

☐ To see how the standards are actually implemented in the latest Web browsers, and to see what nonstandard HTML extensions may be available, visit the Microsoft and Netscape Web sites:

```
http://www.microsoft.com
http://home.netscape.com
```

You can also get copies of the latest Web browser updates from these two Web sites.

HTML as the User Interface of the Future

The computer was once considered a device for accounting and number crunching. Then it evolved into a device for crunching all types of information, from words and numbers to graphics and sounds. Today and tomorrow, the computer is above all a communications device; its primary use is the transmission of information between people.

As the role of the computer evolves, HTML is becoming more and more central to nearly everything we do with computers. HTML is *the* global standard for connecting text, graphics, and other types of information together in a predictable and presentable way.

The "Web browser" as a distinct program is rapidly disappearing. Microsoft Internet Explorer 4.0, for instance, does much more than retrieve pages from the World Wide Web. It lets you use HTML pages as the interface for organizing and navigating through the information on your own computer, including directory folders and the Windows desktop itself. In conjunction with HTML-enabled software like Office 97, HTML becomes the common standard interface for word processing, spreadsheets, and databases as well.

The new Netscape Communicator 4.0 is also much more than a Web browser. It uses HTML to integrate all types of media into e-mail, discussion groups, schedule management, business documents, and collaborative project management.

24

Meanwhile, HTML support is being included in every major software release so that every program on your computer will soon be able to import and export information in the form of HTML pages. In a nutshell, HTML is the "glue" that holds together all the diverse types of information on our computers and ensures that it can be presented in a standard way that will look the same to everyone in the world.

The New HTML

The bad news is that HTML as it exists today is poorly suited for the enormous role that history has handed it to take on. Because it was designed for the much more modest job of linking together documents on yesterday's Internet, it doesn't let you do many of the things that a "universal information glue" obviously ought to do.

The good news is that the next version of HTML will include a number of essential capabilities specifically designed for the many roles that HTML now plays. The new HTML will let you

24

- ☐ Keep "style sheet" information, such as fonts, colors, background graphics, and detailed typographical specifications, separate from the contents of individual documents.

- ☐ Allow fonts to be attached to documents so that everyone will always see the document in the correct font.

- ☐ Position text, graphics, and any other visible element precisely where you want them to go with x,y pixel coordinates.

- ☐ Place multiple layers of information on top of each other, with the front elements automatically covering those further back.

- ☐ Include almost any conceivable type of information or program in a document with one standard <OBJECT> tag. This will include images, image maps, multimedia, applets, ActiveX controls, three-dimensional virtual reality scenes, and anything else that comes along.

Enhancements to JavaScript, Java, and ActiveX (refer to Chapter 20, "Scripting, Applets, and ActiveX") will allow programmers to control all of the previously mentioned features for dynamic interaction. For example, a JavaScript might adjust the fonts and positions of graphics to fit the size of an individual user's viewing window. The latest round of HTML viewing software also includes more robust security and better support for streaming multimedia.

In addition to the new HTML features listed here, the proposed platform for Internet content selection (PICS) standard provides a highly flexible way for the content of any page to be rated according to any criteria that a rating authority or individual user might select. Restricting access to adult-oriented or confidential information is one of many applications.

JUST A MINUTE

You can read more about style sheets and new advances in font technology under "The Future of Web Fonts" section in Chapter 6, "Font Control and Special Characters."

More information on streaming multimedia, interactive programming, and uses for the new <OBJECT> tag can be found in Chapter 19, "Embedding Multimedia in Web Pages," and Chapter 20.

The Digital Media Revolution

The most important changes in the next few years may not be in HTML itself, but in the audience you can reach with your HTML pages. Many Web site developers hope that Internet-based content will have enough appeal to become the mass-market successor to television and radio. Less optimistic observers note that the Web has a long way to go before it can even deliver television-quality video to most users.

I won't pretend to have a magic mirror that lets me see how and when HTML becomes a mass-market phenomenon. But one thing is certain: all communication industries, from television to telephony, are moving rapidly toward exclusively digital technology. As they do so, the lines between communication networks are blurring. New Internet protocols promise to optimize multimedia transmissions at the same time that new protocols allow wireless "broadcasters" to support two-way interactive transmissions. The same small satellite dish can give you both Internet access and high-definition TV.

Add to this trend the fact that HTML is the only widely supported worldwide standard for combining text content with virtually any other form of digital media. Whatever surprising turns the future of digital communication takes, it's difficult to imagine that HTML won't be sitting in the driver's seat.

What You Can Do Today to Be Ready for Tomorrow

If you've made your way through most of the chapters of this book, you already have one of the most important ingredients for future success in the online world: a solid working knowledge of HTML.

Here are some of the other factors you should consider when planning and building your Web site today, so that it will also serve you well tomorrow.

24

☐ The multimedia and interactive portions of your site are likely to need more revisions to keep up with current technology than the text and graphics portions. When possible, keep the more "cutting-edge" parts of your site separate, and take especially good care to document them well with the <COMMENT> tag. (See Chapter 22, "HTML Tags for Site Management.")

☐ Though new technologies like Java and Shockwave may be the wave of the future, avoid them today, except when you absolutely need the unique features they provide. Even when everyone is using the new 33Kbps and 56Kbps modems, many people will still move on to a different site before they'll wait for an applet or interactive movie to download, initialize, and start working. (See Chapter 19 and Chapter 20.)

☐ Because style sheets will soon give you complete control over the choice and measurements of type on your Web pages, it would be a good idea to study basic typography now, if you aren't familiar with it. Understanding and working with things like leading, kerning, em spaces, and drop caps has long been essential for producing truly professional-quality paper pages. It will soon be essential for producing outstanding Web pages, too.

☐ One of the most popular and important features that will be added to many Web sites in the near future is interactive discussions and work groups. If you only have time to evaluate one new technology, that might be the one to pick. The new Netscape Communicator 4.0 package has especially strong support for group collaboration and communication.

☐ When you design and lay out your pages, keep in mind that you will soon be able to position graphics more precisely than you can today. So for now, put them approximately where you want them to go and document in the comments where you would place them if you could specify a more exact position.

☐ You will soon be able to layer images and text on top of each other and choose fonts for text more reliably. That means that many things that you need large images for today you will be able to do much more efficiently with several small image elements and custom fonts tomorrow. Always keep copies of each individual image element that goes into a larger graphic, without any text. This will let you easily optimize the graphics later without recreating everything from scratch. (See Chapter 10, "Creating Web Page Images," and Chapter 14, "Page Design and Layout.")

☐ When you design your pages, don't assume that everyone who sees them will be using a computer. Televisions, video-telephones, game consoles, and many other devices may have access to them as well. Some of these devices have very low resolution screens (with as few as 320×200 pixels). Though it's difficult to design a Web page to look good at that resolution, you'll reach the widest possible audience if you do.

☐ Whenever you run into something that you'd like to do on a Web page, but can't with HTML as it stands today, include a comment in the page so you can add that feature when it becomes possible in the future.

COFFEE BREAK

The completed *24-Hour HTML Café* site is located at:

`http://www.mcp.com/sams/books/235-8/`

In addition to providing an easy way to review all the sample pages and HTML techniques covered in this book, it offers many links to other great HTML resources and a few tricks and tips that this book didn't have room for.

As a way of refreshing your knowledge of all that you've learned in this book, you might walk through the development of the *24-Hour HTML Café* site again. The pages named `cafe1.htm` through `cafe22.htm` show that development process, step by step.

Summary

This chapter has provided a bird's-eye view of the future of HTML. It discussed the new roles that HTML will play in global communications as well as the specific extensions of the HTML standard that are now planned. Finally, it offered some advice for planning and constructing Web pages today that will continue to serve you well into the future.

Q&A

Q So what is the difference between "digital communication" and other communication, anyway? Does "digital" mean it uses HTML?

A When information is transferred as distinct bits of information, which are essentially numbers, it's called *digital*. It's much easier to store, retrieve, and process information without losing or changing it when it is transferred digitally. Any information from a computer (including HTML) is by its nature digital, and in the not-too-distant future, telephone, television, radio, and even motion picture production will be digital.

24

Q **I've heard about this new kind of disk called DVD. Is it suitable for Web pages?**

A Yes. The new digital versatile disk (DVD) standard will provide a minimum of 4,700 megabytes (4.7 gigabytes) of storage, and can transfer data to a computer at least twice as fast as today's 6× CD-ROM drives. That will make DVD an excellent way to deliver multimedia Web pages.

Q **How soon can I start designing Internet Web pages that aren't limited by what I can transfer over a 28.8Kbps modem?**

A That depends on who you want to read your pages. There will be millions of 28.8Kbps modems (and the marginally faster 33.6Kbps and 56Kbps modems) in use for many years to come. But more and more people will have 128Kbps ISDN lines, 400Kbps satellite dishes, and 1Mbps (1,000Kbps) or faster cable, "copper-optic," and wireless connections, too. Before long, the number of 1.4Mbps users will just about match the number of 14.4Kbps users. That difference of 100× in speed will lead more and more Web page publishers to offer separate "high speed" and "low speed" sites.

Q **Man, I'm ashamed of you for not mentioning VRML in a chapter about the future of the Internet! What gives?**

A Hey everyone, did I mention that interactive, immersive three-dimensional worlds will be the future of the Internet? Virtual Reality Modeling Language (VRML) 2.0 is the current standard for making it happen, and it's compatible with your Web browser today. Unfortunately, VRML isn't quite ready for mass consumption and it's well beyond the scope of this book. But if you don't think it's going to change the world, think again. Go to http://www.vrml.org to read all about it.

Quiz

Questions

1. List the five big changes to HTML that will be supported by both Microsoft Internet Explorer 4.0 and Netscape Navigator 4.0.
2. What is PICS?
3. What types of information will you be able to include on a Web page in the future?

Answers

1. (a) Style Sheets
   (b) Automatically downloading fonts
   (c) Exact positioning for graphics, text, and interactive elements
   (d) Multiple overlapping layers
   (e) Use of the <OBJECT> tag to insert any non-textual information on a page

2. The *platform for Internet content selection*, a proposed standard system for rating Web pages by any criteria that a rating authority or individual publisher chooses.

3. The same types you can today: just about all of them! (It'll just be easier to arrange and control them in the future.)

Activities

☐ Once you have your Web site online, I strongly recommend that you take some time to review each chapter of this book to pick up the parts of HTML that you may have missed the first time around. Exploring the "Coffee Break" and "Activities" sections that you might have skipped will help build your HTML skills as well.

☐ This book provides a solid foundation in all the HTML tags commonly used by Web page authors today. Once you are familiar with those, any information you find on the Internet about advanced uses of HTML will become much more comprehensible and useful. An excellent place to start learning more about new HTML advances and techniques is the Internet/HTML topic at Yahoo! (http://yahoo.com).

24

PART

VII

Appendixes

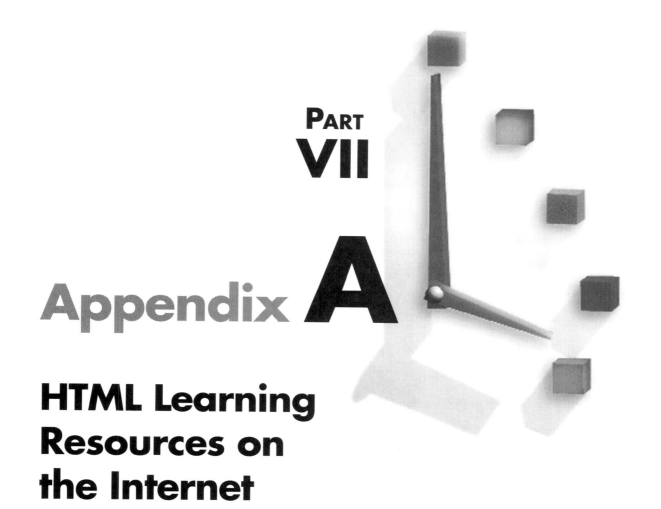

Appendix **A**

**HTML Learning
Resources on
the Internet**

General HTML Information

The *24-Hour HTML Café* (The online companion to this book)

`http://www.mcp.com/sams/books/235-8/`

Microsoft Internet

`http://www.microsoft.com/internet`

Netscape Communications

`http://home.netscape.com`

The Developer's JumpStation

`http://oneworld.wa.com/htmldev/devpage/dev-page.html`

The HTML Writer's Guild

`http://www.hwg.org/`

The Web Developer's Virtual Library

`http://WWW.Stars.com/`

Netscape's HTML Assistance Pages

`http://home.netscape.com/assist/net_sites/index.html`

The World Wide Web FAQ

`http://www.boutell.com/faq/`

Tim Berners-Lee's Style Guide

`http://www.w3.org/hypertext/WWW/Provider/Style/Overview.html`

Web Pages that Suck

`http://www.webpagesthatsuck.com/`

The HTML Guru

`http://members.aol.com/htmlguru/index.html`

Carlos' Forms Tutorial

`http://robot0.ge.uiuc.edu/~carlosp/cs317/cft.html`

A

Recommended Software

Paint Shop Pro (A highly recommended Windows graphics editor)

`http://www.jasc.com`

GIFTool (UNIX)

`http://www.homepages.com/tools/`

Perl Library to Manage CGI and Forms

`http://www.bio.cam.ac.uk/cgi-lib/`

Mapedit (A tool for Windows and X11 for creating image map map files)

`http://www.boutell.com/mapedit/`

HotSpots (A Windows image map tool)

`http://www.cris.com/~automata/index.html`

Software Archives

Shareware.com (Best source for almost any type of free or inexpensive software for all types of computers)

`http://www.shareware.com`

The Ultimate Collection of Winsock Software

`http://www.tucows.com/`

Dave Central Software Archive

`http://www.davecentral.com/`

Cool Helpers Page

`http://www.teleport.com/~alano/coolhelp.html`

WinSite Windows Software Archive

`http://www.winsite.com/`

Graphics

Graphics Wonderland

`http://www.geocities.com/SiliconValley/Heights/1272/index.html`

Kira's Icon Library

`http://fohnix.metronet.com/~kira/icongifs/`

Anthony's Icon Library

`http://www.cit.gu.edu.au/~anthony/icons/index.html`

Barry's Clip Art Server

`http://www.barrysclipart.com`

256 Color Square

`http://www59.metronet.com/colors/`

Color Triplet Chart

`http://www.phoenix.net/~jacobson/rgb.html`

Imaging Machine

`http://www.vrl.com/Imaging/`

Frequently Asked Questions About JPEG

`http://www.cis.ohio-state.edu/hypertext/faq/usenet/jpeg-faq/faq.html`

Frequently Asked Questions from comp.graphics

`http://www.primenet.com/~grieggs/cg_faq.html`

Dick Oliver's Nonlinear Nonsense Netletter

`http://netletter.com/`

A

Multimedia and Virtual Reality

RealAudio

`http://www.realaudio.com`

Streamworks

`http://www.xingtech.com`

QuickTime

`http://quicktime.apple.com`

VDOLive

`http://www.vdolive.com`

Macromedia's Shockwave

`http://www.macromedia.com/`

NCompass Plug-in for Netscape Navigator

`http://www.ncompasslabs.com/`

Multimedia Authoring Languages

`http://www.mcli.dist.maricopa.edu/authoring/lang.html`

The VRML Repository

`http://www.sdsc.edu/vrml/`

JavaSoft

`http://www.javasoft.com/`

Gamelan (Java resource registry)

`http://www.gamelan.com/`

TechWeb's ActiveXpress

`http://www.techweb.com/activexpress/`

Standards and Specifications

The Home of the WWW Consortium

http://www.w3.org/

Secure HTTP Information

http://www.eit.com/projects/s-http/

Secure Sockets Layer (SSL) Information

http://www.netscape.com/info/security-doc.html

Current List of Official MIME Types

ftp://ftp.isi.edu/in-notes/iana/assignments/media-types/media-types

HTML Validators

HTML Validation Service

http://www.webtechs.com/html-val-svc/

Htmlchek

http://uts.cc.utexas.edu/~churchh/htmlchek.html

Lvrfy (Link checker)

http://www.cs.dartmouth.edu/~crow/lvrfy.html

Weblint

http://www.unipress.com/cgi-bin/WWWeblint

A

Directories with HTML Information

Yahoo! World Wide Web

`http://www.yahoo.com/Computers/Internet/World_Wide_Web/`

HotWired's WebMonkey

`http://www.webmonkey.com/`

Cool Site of the Day

`http://cool.infi.net/`

HTML and WWW Tools Index

`http://www.w3.org/hypertext/WWW/Tools/`

Internet Resources Meta-Index

`http://www.ncsa.uiuc.edu/SDG/Software/Mosaic/MetaIndex.html`

Web Service Providers List

`http://union.ncsa.uiuc.edu/HyperNews/get/www/leasing.html`

Lycos Web Publishing Index

`http://a2z.lycos.com/Internet/Web_Publishing_and_HTML/`

InfoSeek HTML Index

`http://www.infoseek.com/Internet/HTML`

TechWeb's HTML Authoring Tools

`http://www.techweb.com/tools/html/`

Appendix B

HTML Quick Reference

This appendix is a reference to the HTML tags you can use in your documents. Unless otherwise noted, all of the tags listed here are supported by both Microsoft Explorer 3.0 and Netscape Navigator 3.0. Note that some other browsers do not support all the tags listed.

The proposed HTML style sheet specification is also not covered here. Refer to the Netscape (http://home.netscape.com/) or Microsoft (http://www.microsoft.com/) Web sites for details on this and other late-breaking changes to the HTML standard.

HTML Tags

These tags are used to create a basic HTML page with text, headings, and lists. An (MS) beside the attribute indicates that it is only supported by Microsoft Internet Explorer.

Comments

`<! — ... —>`	Creates a comment. Can also be used to hide JavaScript from browsers that do not support it.
`<COMMENT>...</COMMENT>`	The new official way of specifying comments.

Structure Tags

Tag	Attribute	Function
`<HTML>...</HTML>`		Encloses the entire HTML document.
`<HEAD>...</HEAD>`		Encloses the head of the HTML document.
`<BODY>...</BODY>`		Encloses the body (text and tags) of the HTML document.
	`BACKGROUND="..."`	The name or URL of the image to tile on the page background.
	`BGCOLOR="..."`	The color of the page background.
	`TEXT="..."`	The color of the page's text.
	`LINK="..."`	The color of unfollowed links.
	`ALINK="..."`	The color of activated links.
	`VLINK="..."`	The color of followed links.
	`BGPROPERTIES="..."` (MS)	Properties of background image. Currently allows only the value FIXED, which prevents the background image from scrolling.
	`TOPMARGIN="..."` (MS)	Top margin of the page, in pixels.
	`BOTTOMMARGIN="..."` (MS)	Bottom margin of the page, in pixels.
`<BASE>`		Indicates the full URL of the current document. This optional tag is used within `<HEAD>`.
	`HREF="..."`	The full URL of this document.

B

Tag	Attribute	Function
`<ISINDEX>`		Indicates that this document is a gateway script that allows searches.
	`PROMPT="..."`	The prompt for the search field.
	`ACTION="..."`	Gateway program to which the search string should be passed.
`<LINK>`		Indicates a link between this document and some other document. Generally used only by HTML-generating tools. `<LINK>` represents a link from this entire document to another, as opposed to `<A>`, which can create multiple links in the document. Not commonly used.
	`HREF="..."`	The URL of the document to call when the link is activated.
	`NAME="..."`	If the document is to be considered an anchor, the name of that anchor.
	`REL="..."`	The relationship between the linked-to document and the current document; for example, `"TOC"` or `"Glossary"`.
	`REV="..."`	A reverse relationship between the current document and the linked-to document.
	`URN="..."`	A Uniform Resource Number (URN), a unique identifier different from the URL in `HREF`.
	`TITLE="..."`	The title of the linked-to document.
	`METHODS="..."`	The method with which the document is to be retrieved; for example, FTP, Gopher, and so on.

continues

Tag	Attribute	Function
`<META>`		Indicates meta-information about this document (information about the document itself); for example, keywords for search engines, special HTTP headers to be used for retrieving this document, expiration dates, and so on. Meta-information is usually in the form of a key/value pair. Used in the document `<HEAD>`.
	`HTTP-EQUIV="..."`	Creates a new HTTP header field with the same name as the attribute's value; for example, `HTTP-EQUIV="Expires"`. The value of that header is specified by the `CONTENT` attribute.
	`NAME="..."`	If meta-data is usually in the form of key/value pairs, `NAME` indicates the key; for example, `Author` or `ID`.
	`CONTENT="..."`	The content of the key/value pair (or of the HTTP header indicated by `HTTP-EQUIV`).
`<NEXTID>`		Indicates the "next" document to this one (as might be defined by a tool to manage HTML documents in series). `<NEXTID>` is considered obsolete.

Headings and Title

Tag	Attribute	Function
`<H1>...</H1>`		A first-level heading.
`<H2>...</H2>`		A second-level heading.
`<H3>...</H3>`		A third-level heading.
`<H4>...</H4>`		A fourth-level heading.
`<H5>...</H5>`		A fifth-level heading.
`<H6>...</H6>`		A sixth-level heading.
`<TITLE>...</TITLE>`		Indicates the title of the document. Used within `<HEAD>`.

All heading tags accept the following attribute:

	`ALIGN="..."`	Possible values are `CENTER`, `LEFT`, and `RIGHT`.

B

Paragraphs and Regions

Tag	Attribute	Function
<P>...</P>		A plain paragraph. The closing tag (</P>) is optional.
	ALIGN="..."	Align text to CENTER, LEFT, or RIGHT.
<DIV>...</DIV>		A region of text to be formatted.
	ALIGN="..."	Align text to CENTER, LEFT, or RIGHT.

Links

Tag	Attribute	Function
<A>...</A>		With the HREF attribute, creates a link to another document or anchor; with the NAME attribute, creates an anchor that can be linked to.
	HREF="..."	The URL of the document to be called when the link is activated.
	NAME="..."	The name of the anchor.
	REL="..."	The relationship between the linked-to document and the current document; for example, "TOC" or "Glossary". REL="…" is not commonly used.
	REV="..."	A reverse relationship between the current document and the linked-to document (not commonly used).
	URN="..."	A Uniform Resource Number (URN), a unique identifier different from the URL in HREF (not commonly used).
	TITLE="..."	The title of the linked-to document (not commonly used).
	METHODS="..."	The method with which the document is to be retrieved; for example, FTP, Gopher, and so on (not commonly used).
	TARGET="..."	The name of a frame that the linked document should appear in.

B

Lists

Tag	Attribute	Function
`<OL>...</OL>`		An ordered (numbered) list.
	`TYPE="..."`	The type of numerals to label the list. Possible values are A, a, I, i, and 1.
	`START="..."`	The value with which to start this list.
`<UL>...</UL>`		An unordered (bulleted) list.
	`TYPE="..."`	The bullet dingbat to use to mark list items. Possible values are DISC, CIRCLE (or ROUND), and SQUARE.
`<MENU>...</MENU>`		A menu list of items.
`<DIR>...</DIR>`		A directory listing; items are generally smaller than 20 characters.
`<LI>`		A list item for use with `<OL>`, `<UL>`, `<MENU>`, or `<DIR>`.
	`TYPE="..."`	The type of bullet or number to label this item with. Possible values are DISC, CIRCLE (or ROUND) SQUARE, A, a, I, i, and 1.
	`VALUE="..."`	The numeric value this list item should have (affects this item and all below it in `<OL>` lists).
`<DL>...</DL>`		A definition or glossary list.
	`COMPACT`	The COMPACT attribute specifies a formatting that takes less whitespace to present.
`<DT>`		A definition term, as part of a definition list.
`<DD>`		The corresponding definition to a definition term, as part of a definition list.

Character Formatting

Tag	Attribute	Function
`<EM>...</EM>`		Emphasis (usually italic).
`<STRONG>...</STRONG>`		Stronger emphasis (usually bold).
`<CODE>...</CODE>`		Code sample (usually Courier).
`<KBD>...</KBD>`		Text to be typed (usually Courier).
`<VAR>...</VAR>`		A variable or placeholder for some other value.
`<SAMP>...</SAMP>`		Sample text (not commonly used).
`<DFN>...</DFN>`		A definition of a term.
`<CITE>...</CITE>`		A citation.
`<B>...</B>`		Boldface text.
`<I>...</I>`		Italic text.
`<TT>...</TT>`		Typewriter (monospaced) font.
`<PRE>...</PRE>`		Preformatted text (exact line endings and spacing will be preserved—usually rendered in a monospaced font).
`<BIG>...</BIG>`		Text is slightly larger than normal.
`<SMALL>...</SMALL>`		Text is slightly smaller than normal.
`<SUB>...</SUB>`		Subscript.
`<SUP>...</SUP>`		Superscript.
`<STRIKE>...</STRIKE>`		Puts a strikethrough line in text.

Other Elements

Tag	Attribute	Function
`<HR>`		A horizontal rule line.
	`SIZE="..."`	The thickness of the rule, in pixels.
	`WIDTH="..."`	The width of the rule, in pixels or as a percentage of the document width.
	`ALIGN="..."`	How the rule line will be aligned on the page. Possible values are LEFT, RIGHT, and CENTER.
	`NOSHADE`	Causes the rule line to be drawn as a solid line instead of a transparent bevel.
	`COLOR="..."` (MS)	Color of the horizontal rule.

continues

Tag	Attribute	Function
` `		A line break.
	`CLEAR="..."`	Causes the text to stop flowing around any images. Possible values are RIGHT, LEFT, and ALL.
`<NOBR>...</NOBR>`		Causes the enclosed text not to wrap at the edge of the page.
`<WBR>`		Wraps the text at this point only if necessary.
`<BLOCKQUOTE>... </BLOCKQUOTE>`		Used for long quotes or citations.
`<ADDRESS>...</ADDRESS>`		Used for signatures or general information about a document's author.
`<CENTER>...</CENTER>`		Centers text or images.
`<BLINK>...</BLINK>`		Causes the enclosed text to blink in an irritating manner.
`<FONT>...</FONT>`		Changes the size of the font for the enclosed text.
	`SIZE="..."`	The size of the font, from 1 to 7. Default is 3. Can also be specified as a value relative to the current size; for example, +2.
	`COLOR="..."`	Changes the color of the text.
	`FACE="..."`	Name of font to use if it can be found on the user's system. Multiple font names can be separated by commas, and the first font on the list that can be found will be used.
`<BASEFONT>`		Sets the default size of the font for the current page.
	`SIZE="..."`	The default size of the font, from 1 to 7. Default is 3.

B

Images, Sounds, and Embedded Media

Tag	Attribute	Function
<IMG>		Inserts an inline image into the document.
	ISMAP	This image is a clickable image map.
	SRC="..."	The URL of the image.
	ALT="..."	A text string that will be displayed in browsers that cannot support images.
	ALIGN="..."	Determines the alignment of the given image. If LEFT or RIGHT, the image is aligned to the left or right column, and all following text flows beside that image. All other values such as TOP, MIDDLE, and BOTTOM, or the Netscape-only TEXTTOP, ABSMIDDLE, BASELINE, and ABSBOTTOM determine the vertical alignment of this image with other items in the same line.
	VSPACE="..."	The space between the image and the text above or below it.
	HSPACE="..."	The space between the image and the text to its left or right.
	WIDTH="..."	The width, in pixels, of the image. If WIDTH is not the actual width, the image is scaled to fit.
	HEIGHT="..."	The height, in pixels, of the image. If HEIGHT is not the actual height, the image is scaled to fit.
	BORDER="..."	Draws a border of the specified value in pixels to be drawn around the image. In the case of images that are also links, BORDER changes the size of the default link border.
	LOWSRC="..."	The path or URL of an image that will be loaded first, before the image specified in SRC. The value of LOWSRC is usually a smaller or lower resolution version of the actual image.

continues

Tag	Attribute	Function
	USEMAP="..."	The name of an image map specification for client-side image mapping. Used with `<MAP>` and `<AREA>`.
	DYNSRC="..." (MS)	The address of a video clip or VRML world (dynamic source).
	CONTROLS (MS)	Used with DYNSRC to display a set of playback controls for inline video.
	LOOP="..." (MS)	The number of times a video clip will loop. (-1, or INFINITE, means to loop indefinitely.)
	START="..." (MS)	When a DYNSRC video clip should start playing. Valid options are FILEOPEN (play when page is displayed) or MOUSEOVER (play when mouse cursor passes over the video clip.
`<BGSOUND>` (MS)		Plays a sound file as soon as the page is displayed.
	SRC="..."	The URL of the WAV, AU, or MIDI sound file to embed.
	LOOP="..." (MS)	The number of times a video clip will loop. (-1, or INFINITE, means to loop indefinitely.)
`<SCRIPT>`		An interpreted script program.
	LANGUAGE="..."	Currently only JAVASCRIPT is supported by Netscape. Both JAVASCRIPT and VBSCRIPT are supported by Microsoft.
	SRC="..."	Specifies the URL of a file that includes the script program.
`<OBJECT>`		Inserts an image, video, Java applet, or ActiveX control into a document.

JUST A MINUTE

Usage of the `<OBJECT>` tag is not yet finalized. Check http://www.w3.org/ for the latest attributes supported by the HTML 3.2 standard.

B

Tag	Attribute	Function
<APPLET>		Inserts a self-running Java applet.
	CLASS="..."	The name of the applet.
	SRC="..."	The URL of the directory where the compiled applet can be found (should end in a slash / as in http://mysite/myapplets/). Do not include the actual applet name, which is specified with the CLASS attribute.
	ALIGN="..."	Indicates how the applet should be aligned with any text that follows it. Current values are TOP, MIDDLE, and BOTTOM.
	WIDTH="..."	The width of the applet output area, in pixels.
	HEIGHT="..."	The height of the applet output area, in pixels.
<PARAM>		Program-specific parameters. (Always occurs within <APPLET> or <OBJECT> tags.)
	NAME="..."	The type of information being given to the applet or ActiveX control.
	VALUE="..."	The actual information to be given to the applet or ActiveX control.
	REF="..."	Indicates that this <PARAM> tag includes the address or location of the object.
<EMBED> (Netscape only!)		Embeds a file to be read or displayed by a plug-in application.

JUST A MINUTE

In addition to the following standard attributes, you can specify applet-specific attributes to be interpreted by the plug-in which displays the embedded object.

continues

B

Tag	Attribute	Function
	SRC="..."	The URL of the file to embed.
	WIDTH="..."	The width of the embedded object in pixels.
	HEIGHT="..."	The height of the embedded object in pixels.
	ALIGN="..."	Determines the alignment of the media window. Values are the same as for the <IMG> tag.
	VSPACE="..."	The space between the media and the text above or below it.
	HSPACE="..."	The space between the media and the text to its left or right.
	BORDER="..."	Draws a border of the specified size in pixels to be drawn around the media.
<NOEMBED>...</NOEMBED>		Alternate text or images to be shown to users who do not have a plug-in installed.
<MAP>...</MAP>		A client-side image map, referenced by <IMG USEMAP="...">. Includes one or more <AREA> tags.
<AREA>		Defines a clickable link within a client-side image map.
	SHAPE="..."	The shape of the clickable area. Currently, only RECT is supported.
	COORDS="..."	The left, top, right, and bottom coordinates of the clickable region within an image.
	HREF="..."	The URL that should be loaded when the area is clicked.
	NOHREF	Indicates that no action should be taken when this area of the image is clicked.

B

Forms

Tag	Attribute	Function
`<FORM>...</FORM>`		Indicates an input form.
	`ACTION="..."`	The URL of the script to process this form input.
	`METHOD="..."`	How the form input will be sent to the gateway on the server side. Possible values are GET and POST.
	`ENCTYPE="..."`	Normally has the value application/x-www-form-urlencoded. For file uploads, use multipart/form-data.
	`NAME="..."`	A name by which JavaScript scripts can refer to the form.
`<INPUT>`		An input element for a form.
	`TYPE="..."`	The type for this input widget. Possible values are CHECKBOX, HIDDEN, RADIO, RESET, SUBMIT, TEXT, SEND FILE, or IMAGE.
	`NAME="..."`	The name of this item, as passed to the gateway script as part of a name/value pair.
	`VALUE="..."`	For a text or hidden widget, the default value; for a check box or radio button, the value to be submitted with the form; for Reset or Submit buttons, the label for the button itself.
	`SRC="..."`	The source file for an image.
	`CHECKED`	For check boxes and radio buttons, indicates that the widget is checked.
	`SIZE="..."`	The size, in characters, of a text widget.
	`MAXLENGTH="..."`	The maximum number of characters that can be entered into a text widget.
	`ALIGN="..."`	For images in forms, determines how the text and image will align (same as with the <IMG> tag).

B

continues

Tag	Attribute	Function
`<TEXTAREA>...</TEXTAREA>`		Indicates a multi-line text entry form element. Default text can be included.
	`NAME="..."`	The name to be passed to the gateway script as part of the name/value pair.
	`ROWS="..."`	The number of rows this text area displays.
	`COLS="..."`	The number of columns (characters) this text area displays.
	`WRAP="..."`	Controls text wrapping. Possible values are `OFF`, `VIRTUAL`, and `PHYSICAL`.
`<SELECT>...</SELECT>`		Creates a menu or scrolling list of possible items.
	`NAME="..."`	The name that is passed to the gateway script as part of the name/value pair.
	`SIZE="..."`	The number of elements to display. If `SIZE` is indicated, the selection becomes a scrolling list. If no `SIZE` is given, the selection is a pop-up menu.
	`MULTIPLE`	Allows multiple selections from the list.
`<OPTION>`		Indicates a possible item within a `<SELECT>` element.
	`SELECTED`	With this attribute included, the `<OPTION>` will be selected by default in the list.
	`VALUE="..."`	The value to submit if this `<OPTION>` is selected when the form is submitted.

Tables

Tag	Attribute	Function
`<TABLE>...</TABLE>`		Creates a table that can contain a caption (`<CAPTION>`) and any number of rows (`<TR>`).
	`BORDER="..."`	Indicates whether the table should be drawn with or without a border. In Netscape, `BORDER` can also have a value indicating the width of the border.
	`CELLSPACING="..."`	The amount of space between the cells in the table.
	`CELLPADDING="..."`	The amount of space between the edges of the cell and its contents.
	`WIDTH="..."`	The width of the table on the page, in either exact pixel values or as a percentage of page width.
	`ALIGN="..."` (MS)	Alignment (works like `IMG ALIGN`). Values are `LEFT` or `RIGHT`.
	`BGCOLOR="..."`	Background color of all cells in the table that do not contain their own `BACKGROUND` or `BGCOLOR` attribute.
	`BACKGROUND="..."` (MS)	Background image to tile within all cells in the table that do not contain their own `BACKGROUND` or `BGCOLOR` attribute.
	`BORDERCOLOR="..."` (MS)	Border color (used with `BORDER="..."`).

continues

Tag	Attribute	Function
	`BORDERCOLORLIGHT="..."` (MS)	Color for light part of 3D-look borders (used with `BORDER="..."`).
	`BORDERCOLORDARK="..."` (MS)	Color for dark part of 3D-look borders (used with `BORDER="..."`).
	`VALIGN="..."` (MS)	Alignment of text within the table. Values are TOP and BOTTOM.
	`FRAME="..."` (MS)	Controls which external borders will appear around a table. Values are void (no frames), above (top border only), below (bottom border only), hsides (top and bottom), lhs (left hand side), rhs (right hand side), vsides (left and right sides), and box (all sides).
	`RULES="..."` (MS)	Controls which internal borders appear in the table. Values are none, basic (rules between THEAD, TBODY, and TFOOT only), rows (horizontal borders only), cols (vertical borders only), and all.
`<CAPTION>...</CAPTION>`		The caption for the table.
	`ALIGN="..."`	The position of the caption. Possible values are TOP and BOTTOM.
`<TR>...</TR>`		Defines a table row, containing headings and data (`<TR>` and `<TH>` tags).
	`ALIGN="..."`	The horizontal alignment of the contents of the cells within this row. Possible values are LEFT, RIGHT, and CENTER.

B

Tag	Attribute	Function
	`VALIGN="..."`	The vertical alignment of the contents of the cells within this row. Possible values are TOP, MIDDLE, BOTTOM, and BASELINE.
	`BGCOLOR="..."`	Background color of all cells in the row that do not contain their own BACKGROUND or BGCOLOR attributes.
	`BACKGROUND="..."(MS)`	Background image to tile within all cells in the row that do not contain their own BACKGROUND or BGCOLOR attributes.
	`BORDERCOLOR="..."(MS)`	Border color (used with BORDER="...").
	`BORDERCOLORLIGHT="..."(MS)`	Color for light part of 3D-look borders (used with BORDER="...").
	`BORDERCOLORDARK="..."(MS)`	Color for dark part of 3D-look borders (used with BORDER="...").
`<TH>...</TH>`		Defines a table heading cell.
	`ALIGN="..."`	The horizontal alignment of the contents of the cell. Possible values are LEFT, RIGHT, and CENTER.
	`VALIGN="..."`	The vertical alignment of the contents of the cell. Possible values are TOP, MIDDLE, BOTTOM, and BASELINE.
	`ROWSPAN="..."`	The number of rows this cell will span.
	`COLSPAN="..."`	The number of columns this cell will span.
	`NOWRAP`	Does not automatically wrap the contents of this cell.
	`WIDTH="..."`	The width of this column of cells, in exact pixel values or as a percentage of the table width.
	`BGCOLOR="..."`	Background color of the cell.
	`BACKGROUND="..." (MS)`	Background image to tile within the cell.

continues

Tag	Attribute	Function
	BORDERCOLOR="..." (MS)	Border color (used with BORDER="...").
	BORDERCOLORLIGHT="..." (MS)	Color for light part of 3D-look borders (used with BORDER="...").
	BORDERCOLORDARK="..." (MS)	Color for dark part of 3D-look borders (used with BORDER="...").
<TD>...</TD>		Defines a table data cell.
	ALIGN="..."	The horizontal alignment of the contents of the cell. Possible values are LEFT, RIGHT, and CENTER.
	VALIGN="..."	The vertical alignment of the contents of the cell. Possible values are TOP, MIDDLE, BOTTOM, and BASELINE.
	ROWSPAN="..."	The number of rows this cell will span.
	COLSPAN="..."	The number of columns this cell will span.
	NOWRAP	Does not automatically wrap the contents of this cell.
	WIDTH="..."	The width of this column of cells, in exact pixel values or as a percentage of the table width.
	BGCOLOR="..."	Background color of the cell.
	BACKGROUND="..." (MS)	Background image to tile within the cell.
	BORDERCOLOR="..." (MS)	Border color (used with BORDER="...").
	BORDERCOLORLIGHT="..." (MS)	Color for light part of 3D-look borders (used with BORDER="...").
	BORDERCOLORDARK="..." (MS)	Color for dark part of 3D-look borders (used with BORDER="...").

B

Frames

Tag	Attribute	Function
<FRAMESET>...</FRAMESET>		Divides the main window into a set of frames that can each display a separate document.
	ROWS="..."	Splits the window or frameset vertically into a number of rows specified by a number (such as 7), a percentage of the total window width (such as 25%), or as an asterisk (*) indicating that a frame should take up all the remaining space or divide the space evenly between frames (if multiple * frames are specified).
	COLS="..."	Works similar to ROWS, except that the window or frameset is split horizontally into columns.
	BORDER="..."	Size of frame border in pixels (0 turns off borders). This tag is Netscape-specific—Microsoft IE uses FRAMEBORDER and FRAMESPACING instead.
	FRAMEBORDER="..." (MS)	Specifies whether to display a border for a frame. Options are YES and NO.
	FRAMESPACING="..." (MS)	Space between frames, in pixels.
<FRAME>		Defines a single frame within a <FRAMESET>.
	SRC="..."	The URL of the document to be displayed in this frame.
	NAME="..."	A name to be used for targeting this frame with the TARGET attribute in <A HREF> links.
	MARGINWIDTH="..."	The amount of space to leave to the left and right side of a document within a frame, in pixels.

continues

Tag	Attribute	Function
	`MARGINHEIGHT="..."`	The amount of space to leave above and below a document within a frame, in pixels.
	`SCROLLING="..."`	Determines whether a frame has scrollbars. Possible values are `YES`, `NO`, and `AUTO`.
	`NORESIZE`	Prevents the user from resizing this frame (and possibly adjacent frames) with the mouse.
`<NOFRAME>...</NOFRAME>`		Provides an alternative document body in `<FRAMESET>` documents for browsers that do not support frames (usually encloses `<BODY>...</BODY>`).

Character Entities

Table B.1 contains the possible numeric and character entities for the ISO-Latin-1 (ISO8859-1) character set. Where possible, the character is shown.

JUST A MINUTE

> Not all browsers can display all characters, and some browsers might even display characters different from those that appear in the table. Newer browsers seem to have a better track record for handling character entities, but be sure to test your HTML files extensively with multiple browsers if you intend to use these entities.

Table B.1. ISO-Latin-1 character set.

Character	Numeric Entity	Character Entity (if any)	Description
	`&#00;–&#08;`		Unused
	`&#09;`		Horizontal tab
	`&#10;`		Line feed
	`&#11;–&#31;`		Unused
	`&#32;`		Space

B

Character	Numeric Entity	Character Entity (if any)	Description
!	&#33;		Exclamation mark
"	&#34;	&quot;	Quotation mark
#	&#35;		Number sign
$	&#36;		Dollar sign
%	&#37;		Percent sign
&	&#38;	&amp;	Ampersand
'	&#39;		Apostrophe
(	&#40;		Left parenthesis
)	&#41;		Right parenthesis
*	&#42;		Asterisk
+	&#43;		Plus sign
,	&#44;		Comma
-	&#45;		Hyphen
.	&#46;		Period (fullstop)
/	&#47;		Solidus (slash)
0–9	0–9		Digits 0–9
:	&#58;		Colon
;	&#59;		Semicolon
<	&#60;	&lt;	Less than
=	&#61;		Equal sign
>	&#62;	&gt;	Greater than
?	&#63;		Question mark
@	&#64;		Commercial "at"
A–Z	A–Z		Letters A–Z
[	&#91;		Left square bracket
\	&#92;		Reverse solidus (backslash)
]	&#93;		Right square bracket
^	&#94;		Caret
—	&#95;		Horizontal bar
`	&#96;		Grave accent

continues

Table B.1. continued

Character	Numeric Entity	Character Entity (if any)	Description
a–z	a–z		Letters a–z
{	&#123;		Left curly brace
|	&#124		Vertical bar
}	&#125;		Right curly brace
~	&#126;		Tilde
	&#127;–		Unused
¡	&#161;	&iexcl;	Inverted exclamation
¢	&#162;	&cent;	Cent sign
£	&#163;	&pound;	Pound sterling
¤	&#164;	&curren;	General currency sign
¥	&#165;	&yen;	Yen sign
¦	&#166;	¦ or brkbar;	Broken vertical bar
§	&#167;	&sect;	Section sign
¨	&#168;	&uml;	Umlaut (dieresis)
©	&#169;	© (Netscape only)	Copyright
a	&#170;	&ordf;	Feminine ordinal
‹	&#171;	&laquo;	Left angle quote, guillemot left
¬	&#172;	&not;	Not sign
-	&#173;	&shy;	Soft hyphen
®	&#174;	® (Netscape only)	Registered trademark
¯	&#175;	&hibar;	Macron accent
°	&#176;	&deg;	Degree sign
±	&#177;	&plusmn;	Plus or minus
2	&#178;	&sup2;	Superscript two
3	&#179;	&sup3;	Superscript three
′	&#180;	&acute;	Acute accent
μ	&#181;	&micro;	Micro sign

Character	Numeric Entity	Character Entity (if any)	Description
¶	&#182;	&para;	Paragraph sign
·	&#183;	&middot;	Middle dot
¸	&#184;	&cedil;	Cedilla
¹	&#185;	&sup1;	Superscript one
º	&#186;	&ordm;	Masculine ordinal
›	&#187;	&raquo;	Right angle quote, guillemot right
¼	&#188;	&frac14;	Fraction one-fourth
½	&#189;	&frac12;	Fraction one-half
¾	&#190;	&frac34;	Fraction three-fourths
¿	&#191;	&iquest	Inverted question mark
À	&#192;	&Agrave;	Capital A, grave accent
Á	&#193;	&Aacute;	Capital A, acute accent
Â	&#194;	&Acirc;	Capital A, circumflex accent
Ã	&#195;	&Atilde;	Capital A, tilde
Ä	&#196;	&Auml;	Capital A, dieresis or umlaut mark
Å	&#197;	&Aring;	Capital A, ring
Æ	&#198;	&AElig;	Capital AE diphthong (ligature)
Ç	&#199;	&Ccedil;	Capital C, cedilla
È	&#200;	&Egrave;	Capital E, grave accent
É	&#201;	&Eacute;	Capital E, acute accent
Ê	&#202;	&Ecirc;	Capital E, circumflex accent

continues

Table B.1. continued

Character	Numeric Entity	Character Entity (if any)	Description
Ë	&#203;	&Euml;	Capital E, dieresis or umlaut mark
Ì	&#204;	&Igrave;	Capital I, grave accent
Í	&#205;	&Iacute;	Capital I, acute accent
Î	&#206;	&Icirc;	Capital I, circumflex accent
Ï	&#207;	&Iuml;	Capital I, dieresis or umlaut mark
Ð	&#208;	&ETH;	Capital Eth, Icelandic
Ñ	&#209;	&Ntilde;	Capital N, tilde
Ò	&#210;	&Ograve;	Capital O, grave accent
Ó	&#211;	&Oacute;	Capital O, acute accent
Ô	&#212;	&Ocirc;	Capital O, circumflex accent
Õ	&#213;	&Otilde;	Capital O, tilde
Ö	&#214;	&Ouml;	Capital O, dieresis or umlaut mark
×	&#215;		Multiply sign
Ø	&#216;	&Oslash;	Capital O, slash
Ù	&#217;	&Ugrave;	Capital U, grave accent
Ú	&#218;	&Uacute;	Capital U, acute accent
Û	&#219;	&Ucirc;	Capital U, circumflex accent
Ü	&#220;	&Uuml;	Capital U, dieresis or umlaut mark
Ý	&#221;	&Yacute;	Capital Y, acute accent

B

Character	Numeric Entity	Character Entity (if any)	Description
Þ	&#222;	&THORN;	Capital THORN, Icelandic
ß	&#223;	&szlig;	Small sharp s, German (sz ligature)
à	&#224;	&agrave;	Small a, grave accent
á	&#225;	&aacute;	Small a, acute accent
â	&#226;	&acirc;	Small a, circumflex accent
ã	&#227;	&atilde;	Small a, tilde
ä	&#228;	&aauml;	Small a, dieresis or umlaut mark
å	&#229;	&aring;	Small a, ring
æ	&#230;	&aelig;	Small ae diphthong (ligature)
ç	&#231;	&ccedil;	Small c, cedilla
è	&#232;	&egrave;	Small e, grave accent
é	&#233;	&eacute;	Small e, acute accent
ê	&#234;	&ecirc;	Small e, circumflex accent
ë	&#235;	&euml;	Small e, dieresis or umlaut mark
ì	&#236;	&igrave;	Small i, grave accent
í	&#237;	&iacute;	Small i, acute accent
î	&#238;	&icirc;	Small i, circumflex accent
ï	&#239;	&iuml;	Small i, dieresis or umlaut mark

continues

Table B.1. continued

Character	Numeric Entity	Character Entity (if any)	Description
ð	&#240;	&eth;	Small eth, Icelandic
ñ	&#241;	&ntilde;	Small n, tilde
ò	&#242;	&ograve;	Small o, grave accent
ó	&#243;	&oacute;	Small o, acute accent
ô	&#244;	&ocirc;	Small o, circumflex accent
õ	&#245;	&otilde;	Small o, tilde
ö	&#246;	&ouml;	Small o, dieresis or umlaut mark
÷	&#247;		Division sign
ø	&#248;	&oslash;	Small o, slash
ù	&#249;	&ugrave;	Small u, grave accent
ú	&#250;	&uacute;	Small u, acute accent
û	&#251;	&ucirc;	Small u, circumflex accent
ü	&#252;	&uuml;	Small u, dieresis or umlaut mark
ý	&#253;	&yacute;	Small y, acute accent
þ	&#254;	&thorn;	Small thorn, Icelandic
ÿ	&#255;	&yuml;	Small y, dieresis or umlaut mark

Glossary

ActiveX   A relatively new technology that makes it easy to embed animated objects, data, and computer code on Web pages. With ActiveX controls, a Web browser that supports ActiveX can play just about any item you might encounter on a Web page.

anchor   A named point on a Web page. (The same HTML tag is used to create Hypertext links and anchors, which explains why the tag is named <A>).

Animated GIF   An animated graphic exploiting looping and timing features in the GIF89a format.

ASCII file   A text file that conforms to the American Standard Code for Information Interchange.

attributes   Special code words used inside an HTML tag to control exactly what the tag does.

bandwidth   The maximum information-carrying capacity of an electronic connection or network.

binary file   An executable file or a file that is not in ASCII text format.

browse   To wander around a portion of the Internet looking for items of interest. Also known as *surfing* or *cruising.*

browser   A software program for viewing HTML pages.

cache   A temporary storage area that a Web browser uses to store pages that it has recently opened. The cache enables the browser to quickly load these pages if you decide to return to them.

cascading style sheets   Invented by Håkon Lie, CSS is a new addition to HTML 3.0 that allows page designers to have greater control over the rendering of a document. Browsers that support style sheets will allow font and color attributes to be specified. CSS1 is the first phase of cascading style sheets.

client-side image maps   A new HTML method for linking an image to more than one address. The advantage of this approach is that the browser can display the destination URL of a region when the mouse passes over it, and some network traffic is saved because the browser can directly request the new document when a click is made.

comment   Text in an HTML document (or computer program) that will be seen only by the people who edit the *source* for that page. Comments are normally invisible when a page is viewed with a Web browser.

Common Gateway Interface (CGI)   An interface for external programs to talk to a Web server. Programs that are written to use CGI are called CGI programs or CGI scripts, and are commonly used for processing HTML forms.

compression The process of making a computer file smaller so that it can be copied more quickly between computers.

cyberspace A broad expression used to describe the activity, communication, and culture happening on the Internet and other computer networks.

definition list An indented list without a number or symbol in front of each item. (See also *ordered list* and *unordered list*.)

digital Electronic circuits generally considered to use an on or off sequence of values to convey information.

digitized Converted to a digital format suitable for storage.

direct connection A permanent, 24-hour link between a computer and the Internet. A computer with a direct connection can use the Internet at any time.

directory service An Internet service that maintains a database on individuals, including e-mail, fax, and telephone numbers, that is searchable by the public.

domain The address of a computer on the Internet. A user's Internet address is made up of a username and a domain name.

domain name system (DNS) An Internet addressing system that uses a group of names that are listed with dots (.) between them, working from the most specific to the most general group. In the United States, the top (most general) domains are network categories such as edu (education), com (commercial), and gov (government). In other countries, a two-letter abbreviation for the country is used, such as ca (Canada) and au (Australia).

download To retrieve a file or files from a remote machine to your local machine.

e-mail (electronic mail) A system that enables a person to compose a message on a computer and transmit that message through a computer network, such as the Internet, to another computer user.

e-mail address The word-based Internet address of a user, typically made up of a username, an at (@) sign, and a domain name (that is, *user@domain*). E-mail addresses are translated from the numeric IP addresses by the domain name system (DNS).

encryption The process of encoding information so that it is secure from other Internet users.

FAQ Short for *frequently asked questions*, a computer file containing the answers to frequently asked questions about a particular Internet resource.

Favorites menu In Internet Explorer, a menu that contains a list of your favorite Web pages and Internet resources. You can add items to this menu at any time. Favorites are equivalent to bookmarks in Netscape Navigator.

firewall   A security device placed on a LAN to protect it from Internet intruders. This can be a special kind of hardware router, a piece of software, or both.

form   A page that includes areas to be filled out by the reader. HTML forms allow information to be sent back to the company or individual who made (or maintains) the page.

frame   A rectangular region within the browser window that displays a Web page alongside other pages in other frames.

freeware   Software available to anyone, free of charge, unlike shareware, which requires payment.

FTP (File Transfer Protocol)   The basic method for copying a file from one computer to another through the Internet.

graphics   Digitized pictures and computer-generated images.

graphical editor   A program that allows you to edit an approximation of what a Web page would look like when viewed with a Web browser. Graphical editors usually hide the actual HTML tags they are creating from view.

Helper Application   An application that is configured to launch and view files that are unreadable to a Web browser.

HTML (Hypertext Markup Language)   The document formatting language used to create pages on the World Wide Web.

HTTP (Hypertext Transfer Protocol)   The standard method for exchanging information between HTTP servers and clients on the Web. The HTTP specification lays out the rules of how Web servers and browsers must work together.

hypertext   Text that allows readers to jump spontaneously among onscreen documents and other resources by selecting highlighted keywords that appear on each screen. Hypertext appears most often on the World Wide Web.

image compression   The mathematical manipulation that images are put through to squeeze out repetitive patterns. It makes them load and display much faster.

image map   An image on a Web page that leads to two or more different links, depending on which part of the image someone clicks. Modern Web browsers use *client-side image maps,* but you can also create *server-side image maps* for compatibility with old browsers.

interlaced GIF   An image file that will appear blocky at first, then more and more detailed as it continues downloading. (Similar to a *progressive JPEG* file.)

Internet   A large, loosely organized integrated network connecting universities, research institutions, government, businesses, and other organizations so that they can exchange messages and share information.

Internet Explorer   An advanced Web browser created by Microsoft Corporation. Internet Explorer is powerful and easy to use.

Internet service provider (ISP)   The company that provides you or your company with access to the Internet. ISPs usually have several servers and a high-speed link to the Internet backbone.

intranet   A private network with access restricted to one organization, but which uses the same standards and protocols as the global public *Internet*.

ISDN (Integrated Digital Services Network)   Essentially operates as a digital phone line. ISDN delivers many benefits over standard analog phone lines, including multiple simultaneous calls and higher-quality data transmissions. ISDN data rates are 56Kbps to 128Kbps.

Java   The Web-oriented language developed by Sun Microsystems.

Kbps (kilobits per second)   A rate of transfer of information across a connection such as the Internet.

LAN (local area network)   A computer network limited to a small area.

link   An icon, a picture, or a highlighted string of text that connects the current Web page to other Web pages, Internet sites, graphics, movies, or sounds. On the Web, you skip from page to page by clicking on links.

Mbps (megabits per second)   A rate of transfer of information across a connection such as the Internet. (Equal to 1,000Kbps.)

modem (modulator/demodulator)   A device to convert the digital signals of a computer to an analog format for transmission across telephone lines.

multimedia   A description for systems capable of displaying or playing text, pictures, sound, video, and animation.

navigation   Movement within a computer environment (for example, navigation of a Web site).

Netscape   Short for Netscape Communications Corporation, a software company that developed and markets a popular World Wide Web browser called Navigator. Some people casually refer to Navigator as Netscape.

network   A set of computers interconnected so that they can communicate and share information. Most major networks are connected to the global network-of-networks, called the Internet.

ordered list   An indented list that has numbers or letters in front of each item. (See also *unordered list* and *definition list*.)

password   A secret code, known only to the user, that allows that user to access a computer that is protected by a security system.

pixel   An individual dot of color in a computer graphics image.

POTS   Plain old telephone service.

PPP (Point-to-Point Protocol)   A communications protocol that enables a dial-up Internet connection.

progressive JPEG   An image file that appears blurry at first, then gradually comes into focus. (Similar to an *interlaced GIF* file.)

protocol   Specific rules and conventions defining how data may be exchanged between any two devices.

provider   A general reference to an Internet access provider, a company that has its own dedicated access to the Internet and can therefore sell dial-up IP accounts to Internet users.

public domain   Material that is freely usable by anyone, but still could be copyrighted.

relative address   An address describing the path from one Web page to another, instead of a full (or *absolute*) URL address.

resolution   The number of individual dots, or *pixels*, that make up an image.

resource   A generic term to describe the varied information and activities available to Internet users.

search engine   A program that provides a way to search for specific information.

server   A networked computer that "serves" a particular type of information to users. See also *Web server*.

server-side image maps   A technique for implementing Web page images that lead to more than one link, so that the server computer determines which link to go to. This method is now less commonly used than *client-side image maps*.

shareware   Software programs that users are permitted to acquire and evaluate for free. Shareware is different from freeware in that, if a person likes the shareware program and plans to use it on a regular basis, he is expected to send a fee to the programmer.

Shockwave   An interactive multimedia system for the Web that views applications developed by Macromedia Director.

source   The actual text and commands stored in an HTML file, including tags, comments, and scripts that may not be visible when the page is viewed with a Web browser.

surfing   Another term for browsing.

T-1 line   A digital circuit capable of transferring data at 1.544Mbps.

T-3 line   A digital circuit equivalent to 28 T-1 lines.

table   Text and/or images arranged into orderly rows and columns. HTML provides several tags specifically for creating tables.

tag   A coded HTML command used to indicate how part of a Web page should be displayed.

TCP/IP (Transmission Control Protocol/Internet Protocol)   The agreed-on set of computer communications rules and standards that allows communications between different types of computers and networks that are connected to the Internet.

text editor   Any program that allows you to edit text with your computer.

unordered list   An indented list with a special bullet symbol in front of each item. (See also *ordered list* and *definition list*.)

URL (uniform resource locator)   Also commonly called a location or address. This is an addressing system that locates documents on the Internet.

username   Used with a password to gain access to a computer. A dial-up IP user typically has a username and password for dialing the access provider's Internet server.

VBScript   A script language developed by Microsoft. A technical competitor to Java and JavaScript applications.

VRML (Virtual Reality Modeling Language)   A three-dimensional navigation specification used to create three-dimensional worlds.

Web server   A computer on the Internet that hosts data that can be accessed by Web browsers using the HTTP protocol.

World Wide Web (WWW or the Web)   A set of Internet computers and services that provide an easy-to-use system for finding information and moving among resources. WWW services feature hypertext, hypermedia, and multimedia information, which can be explored through browsers such as Netscape or Internet Explorer.

INDEX

J-K-L

JASC, Inc. Web site, 116
Java, 272-273
JavaScript, 269-271
JavaSoft Web site, 339
JPEG
　compression, controlling, 121
　progressive, 125-127
JPEG FAQ Web site, 338

<KBD> tag (HTML), 349
Kira's icon library Web
　site, 338

labeling images, 104-105
<LI> tag (HTML), 80, 348
line breaks, 18-20
LINK attribute (<BODY>
　tag), 158
<LINK> tag (HTML),
　307, 345
linking frames, 220-221
　special names, 221
linking multimedia
　<A> tag, 251-252
　<EMBED> tag, 255-259
　<IMG> tag, 252-255
　<NOEMBED> tag, 259-260
　<OBJECT> tag, 261
links, 27
　colors, 34, 158-159
　intra-page, 90-92
　named anchors, 92-93
　same Web site, 30-32
　see also anchors; hypertext;
　　image maps; URLs
lists, 79-83
　nesting, 81-83
　types, 80
LOOP attribute (<IMG>
　tag), 252
looping (animation), 152
LOWSRC attribute
　(<IMG> tag), 134
Lvrfy Web site, 340
Lycos Web Publishing Index
　Web site, 341

M

Macromedia
　Backstage, 322
　Web site, 322, 264, 339
management (Web sites),
　318-322
<MAP> tag (HTML), 186, 354
Mapedit Web site, 337
MARGINHEIGHT attribute
　(<FRAME> tag), 221
MARGINWIDTH attribute
　(<FRAME> tag), 221
MAXLENGTH attribute
　(<INPUT> tag), 237
memory, cache, 370
<MENU> tag (HTML), 348
<META> tag (HTML),
　305-307, 346
METHOD attribute
　(<FORM> tag), 233
Microsoft
　FrontPage, 319-322
　IE3
　　Save Picture As
　　　option, 116
　　Show Pictures option, 105
　　Source command (View
　　　menu), 8
　IE4, 326
　Internet Assistants, 316-318
　Web sites, 4, 326
　　Internet, 336
　　Internet Assistants, 316
　　TrueType fonts, 68
MIME types list Web site, 340
MPEG, 264
multimedia
　background sounds, 255
　linking
　　<A> tag, 251-252
　　<EMBED> tag, 255-259
　　<IMG> tag, 252-255
　　<NOEMBED> tag,
　　　259-260
　　<OBJECT> tag, 261
　plug-ins, 268-269
　programming, 267-276
　　ActiveX, 274-276
　　Java, 272-273

　　JavaScript, 269-271
　　streaming, 263-264
　　video formats, 264
Multimedia Authoring
　Languages Web site, 339

N

NAME attribute
　<A> tag, 34, 90-92
　<FRAME> tag, 220
named anchors, 90-93
NCompass Labs Web site,
　275, 339
nesting
　frames, 223-224
　lists, 81-83
　tables, 204-206
NetObjects Fusion, 322
Netscape
　Communicator 4.0, 326
　Navigator
　　Auto Load Images
　　　option, 104
　　Document Source
　　　command (View
　　　menu), 8
　　Save Picture As
　　　option, 116
　Web sites, 4, 326
　　communications, 336
　　HTML Assistance, 336
　　plug-ins, 256
networks, 373
<NEXTID> tag (HTML),
　307, 346
<NOBR> tag (HTML), 350
<NOEMBED> tag (HTML),
　259-260, 354
<NOFRAME> tag (HTML),
　224-225, 362
NORESIZE attribute
　(<FRAME> tag), 221-222

O-P

<OBJECT> tag (HTML), 261,
　275-276, 327, 352
　CLASSID attribute, 275
<OL> tag (HTML), 80, 348

MACMILLAN COMPUTER PUBLISHING USA

A VIACOM COMPANY

 **Support:**

If you need assistance with the information in this book or with a CD/Disk
accompanying the book, please access the Knowledge Base on our Web
site at **http://www.superlibrary.com/general/support**. Our most
Frequently Asked Questions are answered there. If you do not find the
answer to your questions on our Web site, you may contact Macmillan
Technical Support **(317) 581-3833** or e-mail us at **support@mcp.com**.

Teach Yourself Microsoft Office 97 in 24 Hours

— *Greg Perry*

An estimated 22 million people use Microsoft Office, and with the new features of Office 97, much of that market will want the upgrade. To address that market, Sams has published a mass-market version of its best-selling *Teach Yourself* series. *Teach Yourself Microsoft Office 97 in 24 Hours* shows readers how to use the most widely requested features of Office. This entry-level title includes many illustrations, screen shots, and a step-by-step plan for learning Office 97. Teaches how to use each Office product and how to use the products together. Readers learn how to create documents in Word that include hypertext links to files created with one of the other Office products. Covers Office 97.

Price: $19.99 USA/$28.95 CDN　　　*User Level: New - Casual - Accomplished*
ISBN: 0-672-31009-0　　450 pp.　　Integrated Software/Suites

Teach Yourself Access 97 in 24 Hours

— *Timm Buchanan & David Nielsen*

As organizations and end users continue to upgrade to NT Workstation and Windows 95, a surge in 32-bit productivity applications, including Microsoft Office 97, is expected. Using an easy-to-follow approach, this book teaches the fundamentals of a key component in the Microsoft Office 97 package: Access 97. Readers will learn how to use and manipulate existing databases, create databases with Wizards, and build databases from scratch in 24 one-hour lessons. Covers Microsoft Access 97.

Price: $19.99　USA/$28.95 CDN　　　*User Level: New - Casual*
ISBN: 0-672-31027-9　　400 pp.　　Databases

Teach Yourself Access 97 in 14 Days, Fourth Edition

— *Paul Cassel*

Through the examples, workshop sessions, and Q&A sections in this book, users will master the most important features of Access. In just two weeks they'll be able to develop their own databases and create stunning forms and reports. Updated for Access 97. Covers Wizards, tables, data types, validation, forms, queries, artificial fields, macros, and more. Readers learn how to program with Access Basic and Access lingo. Covers Access.

Price: $29.99 USA/$42.95 CDN　　　*User Level: New - Casual*
ISBN: 0-672-30969-6　　700 pp.　　Databases

Access 97 Unleashed, Second Edition

— *Dwayne Gifford, et al.*

Access, one of Microsoft's database managers for Windows, has become one of the most accepted standards of database management for personal computers. The *Unleashed* format for this book allows current and new users to quickly and easily find the information they need on the new features. It also serves as a complete reference for database programmers new to Access. Readers learn advanced techniques for working with tables, queries, forms, and data. Shows how to program Access and how to integrate the database with the Internet. CD-ROM includes Access utilities and applications and an electronic Access Reference Library. Covers Access.

$49.99 USA/$70.95 CDN　　　*User Level: Accomplished - Expert*
ISBN: 0-672-30983-1　　1,100 pp.　　Databases

Microsoft Office 97 Unleashed, Second Edition

— Paul McFedries, et al

Microsoft has brought the Web to its Office suite of products. Hyperlinking, Office Assistants, and Active Document Support let users publish documents to the Web or an intranet site. It also completely integrates with Microsoft FrontPage, making it possible to point and click a Web page into existence. This book details each of the Office products—Excel, Access, PowerPoint, Word, and Outlook—and shows the estimated 22 million registered users how to create presentations and Web documents. Shows how to extend Office to work on a network. Describes the various Office Solution Kits and how to use them. CD-ROM includes powerful utilities and two best-selling books in HTML format.

Price: $39.99 USA/$56.95 CDN   *User Level: Accomplished - Expert*
ISBN: 0-672-31010-4   *1,200 pp.*   *Integrated Software/Suites*

Alison Balter's Mastering Access 97 Development, Second Premier Edition

— Alison Balter

One of the premier corporate database applications, Access is a powerful application that can be programmed and customized. This book shows users how to develop both simple and complex applications for Access 97. Demonstrates how to create tables, forms, queries, reports, and objects. Teaches how to program Access applications for a client/server environment. CD-ROM includes source code, reusable functions, forms, and reports. Covers Access 97.

Price: $49.99 USA/ $70.95 CDN   *User Level: Accomplished - Expert*
ISBN: 0-672-30999-8   *1,100 pp.*   *Databases*

The World Wide Web 1997 Unleashed

— John December

This book has unleashed the latest Web topics previously known only to the field experts. It is designed to be the only book readers will need from their initial logon to the Web to creating their own Web pages. Takes the reader on an updated tour of the Web—highlighting sites and outlining browsing techniques. Includes Sams.net *Web 1,000 Directory*—the "yellow pages" of the Internet. CD-ROM contains everything from starter software to advanced Web site development tools. Covers the World Wide Web.

Price: $49.99 USA/$70.95 CDN   *User Level: All User Levels*
ISBN: 1-57521-184-X   *1,300 pp.*   *Internet—General/WWW Applications*

Teach Yourself Web Publishing with Microsoft Office 97 in a Week

— Michael Larson

As the number-one selling office suite in the business world, with more than 22 million users, Microsoft Office is taking the market by storm. Using a clear, step-by-step approach and practical examples, users will learn how to effectively use components of Microsoft Office to publish attractive, well-designed documents for the World Wide Web or an intranet. Focuses on the Web publishing features of the latest versions of Microsoft Word, Excel, Access, and PowerPoint. Explains the basics of Internet/intranet technology, the Microsoft Internet Explorer browser, and HTML. CD-ROM is loaded with Microsoft Internet Explorer 3.0 and an extensive selection of additional graphics, templates, scripts, ActiveX controls, and multimedia clips to enhance Web pages. Covers Microsoft Office 97.

Price: $39.99 USA/$56.95 CDN   *User Level: New - Casual - Accomplished*
ISBN: 1-57521-232-3   *500 pp.*   *Integrated Software/Suites*

Add to Your Sams.net Library Today
with the Best Books for Internet Technologies

ISBN	Quantity	Description of Item	Unit Cost	Total Cost
0-672-31009-0		Teach Yourself Microsoft Office 97 in 24 Hours	$19.99	
0-672-31027-9		Teach Yourself Access 97 in 24 Hours	$19.99	
0-672-30969-6		Teach Yourself Access 97 in 14 Days, Fourth Edition	$29.99	
0-672-30983-1		Access 97 Unleashed, Second Edition (Book/CD-ROM)	$49.99	
0-672-31010-4		Microsoft Office 97 Unleashed, Second Edition (Book/CD-ROM)	$39.99	
0-672-30999-8		Alison Balter's Mastering Access 97 Development, Second Premier Edition (Book/CD-ROM)	$49.99	
1-57521-184-X		The World Wide Web 1997 Unleashed (Book/CD-ROM)	$49.99	
1-57521-232-3		Teach Yourself Web Publishing with Microsoft Office 97 in a Week (Book/CD-ROM)	$39.99	
		Shipping and Handling: See information below.		
		TOTAL		

Shipping and Handling: $4.00 for the first book, and $1.75 for each additional book. If you need to have it NOW, we can ship product to you in 24 hours for an additional charge of approximately $18.00, and you will receive your item overnight or in two days. Overseas shipping and handling adds $2.00. Prices subject to change. Call between 9:00 a.m. and 5:00 p.m. EST for availability and pricing information on latest editions.

201 W. 103rd Street, Indianapolis, Indiana 46290

1-800-428-5331 — Orders   1-800-835-3202 — FAX   1-800-858-7674 — Customer Service

Book ISBN 1-57521-235-8